M000266225

DARING STEPS

DARING STEPS

Traversing the Path of the Buddha

Ringu Tulku Rinpoché

edited and translated by
Rosemarie Fuchs

SNOW LION PUBLICATIONS
ITHACA, NEW YORK

Snow Lion Publications
P. O. Box 6483
Ithaca, NY 14851 USA
(607) 273-8519
www.snowlionpub.com
Copyright © 2005, 2010 Ringu Tulku
Illustrations copyright © 2010 Salga

All rights reserved. No part of this book may be reproduced
without prior written permission from the publisher.

Printed in U.S.A. on acid-free recycled paper.

ISBN-13 978-1-55939-354-6

Text designed and typeset by Gopa & Ted2, Inc.

*The Library of Congress cataloged the previous edition
of this book as follows:*

Ringu Tulku.
   Daring steps toward fearlessness : the three vehicles of Buddhism /
Ringu Tulku Rinpoche ; edited and translated by Rosemarie Fuchs.
      p. cm.
   ISBN-13: 978-1-55939-225-9 (alk. paper)
   ISBN-10: 1-55939-225-8 (alk. paper)
 1. Buddhist sects. 2. Buddhism.—Doctrines. I. Fuchs, Rosemarie,
1950- II. Title.
BQ7060.R57 2005
294.3'4—dc22

2005012503

CONTENTS

Editor's Introduction

THE BOOK PRESENTED HERE is quite unique in that it provides an insight into the entirety of the Buddha's teachings, doing so in a manner equally suited to those with an initial interest in Buddhism and to those who already follow its path. It strongly emphasizes the fact that all the instructions of the Buddha form an integral system that allows for the different mentalities and capacities of human beings, and that will gradually lead any individual to complete enlightenment, as long as the teachings are respected as a whole and practiced in this light. Nowadays in the West there are quite a few Buddhists who, considering themselves followers of the Vajrayana, believe that they can neglect the other vehicles, especially the teachings pertaining to the Shravakayana system. Here Ringu Tulku Rinpoché shows that this is a fundamental misunderstanding, that one will not reach anywhere while maintaining this mistaken view.

The Buddha taught his direct vision of the truth in gradual stages, allowing his students to be in tune with their respective capacities of insight and to refine them slowly from one stage to the next. In reality, apart from the Four Noble Truths and the Noble Eightfold Path, the first set of teachings, there is nothing else in the whole of Buddhism. Gradually, though, these are expanded and enriched by the teachings on the bodhisattva path. Those teachings simply make clear that a human being is not alone in this world: there are countless sentient beings, and not only humans, who equally suffer and need to be released from pain. Thus the initial vision and conduct as suggested by the first vehicle are just broadened and deepened to embrace every other sentient being as well. We are thus shown the way to strive for the enlightenment of all by developing genuine love and compassion. This is the Mahayana level of teaching. Finally, when the disciple shows appropriate understanding and devotion and the teacher is qualified, there are very effective means to gain true vision of reality extremely quickly. As the culmination of these means, it can be transmitted and received directly from mind to mind. This is based upon the fact that enlightenment is not taught as something very far away that needs to be gained from somewhere. The Vajrayana teachings point out that enlightenment is ingrained in all sentient beings in terms of their true nature, but that it is obscured by removable stains. The presence or absence of these stains marks the only difference between a buddha and a being bound to the cycle of existence. The defilements that hinder realization are removable, since they do not truly exist. As is clearly shown in the course of the preceding vehicles, the impediments to enlightenment are not permanent, having come about through causes and conditions.

Therefore, neglecting the other teachings and attempting to "practice only the Vajrayana," one might not be following the teachings of the Buddha at all. This is a great danger, especially in our day, as this approach is quite widespread and even suggested by some who are looked upon as Buddhist teachers. As with any spiritual teaching, the instruction of the Buddha can be shaped into any form, whether that form is true to the Buddha's intent or not.

In this book the author has taken great care to base his discussions on authentic scriptural sources. The book begins with the teachings of the Shravakayana, and relies on the words of the Buddha himself when expounding the Four Noble Truths. Next the book turns to the Mahayana, explaining these teachings through *The Thirty-seven Practices of a Bodhisattva* by Ngulchü Thogmé, a highly acclaimed scholar as well as a genuine saintly bodhisattva who truly practiced what he taught. His text is an abbreviation of the *Bodhicharyavatara* by Shantideva and conveys its content in an easily comprehensible form, fit for those who do not have the time and fortune to study all the words of the Buddha on the bodhisattva path in their entirety and vastness.

To elucidate the main principles of Vajrayana, Ringu Tulku Rinpoché has used a text not previously available in a Western language. It is called *Babble of a Fool: A Note on the Creation and Completion Stages*, and was composed by Dzogchenpa Shönnu Yeshé Dorjé, who is also known as Do Khyentse or "Crazy Khyentse." As the text will show, he was an eminent Nyingma master to whom a follower of the Karma Kagyü tradition would pay equal respect. The fact that the author has chosen this text is a fine example of how enlightenment does not depend upon different schools, thus reminding us that whenever sectarianism prevails, spirituality will be diminished.

In the final section of this book, Ringu Tulku Rinpoché explains the teachings on Mahamudra, and there resorts to his personal background as a member of the Karma Kagyü lineage. As is the tradition when giving an initial introduction to Mahamudra, he bases his instructions on the *Dorjé Chang Tungma*, a short lineage prayer by Bengar Jampal Zangpo, which contains the essence of the Mahamudra teachings in a very concise form.

At this level, devotion and respect become very essential and personal, so that the lineage may unfold its prevailing influence. Without a living lineage there cannot be any Buddhism. In the same way practice is very individual and might include all or some of the aspects of the Buddha's teaching in one go. As long as it is genuine, it will be beneficial. As the author points out, practice is not a fixed entity. It includes anything that helps us to improve our attitude and to gain authentic experiential understanding of the true nature of everything. We ourselves are our practice and the only measure is our own spiritual development.

A few remarks about the presentation of this book might be useful. It is based on oral teachings which Ringu Tulku Rinpoché gave in 1996 at Thegsum Tashi Chöling, Hamburg, and in 1995 at Kagyü Benchen Ling, Todtmoos-Au. Since Mahamudra teachings, as the author points out, are mainly given in the setting of a very personal encounter of master and disciple and usually take place in terms of question and answer, the original dialogue that took place at the time has been maintained in this section. The Vajrayana part contains quite a number of terms that some readers may not yet know and may want to have explained further. Here it has to be noted that large parts of the Vajrayana teachings cannot be explained in public, as they are strictly a matter of the personal relationship between teacher and disciple. This is especially true of practice instructions. Nevertheless, it is to be hoped that any reader will derive some benefit from this chapter. The text used to explain tantric teaching and practice was composed by a truly accomplished master and describes, as Ringu Tulku Rinpoché points out, the ideal practice of the creation and completion stages of meditation. It may be a matter of many years or even a lifetime until the ability is reached to perform this practice as it should be. Since this is the first translation of Dzogchenpa Shönnu Yeshé Dorjé's short commentary on creation and completion into a Western language, the text is presented in full, although the reader may feel that some parts of it are not explained sufficiently. This is done out of respect for the author and because the text gives practical advice for beginners as well. Apart from that, it contains a perspective on where the endeavor should meet fruition. Traditionally this is meant to give a first impression and should be regarded as an encouragement to seek further appropriate instruction, if wanted. Completion stage practice is not explained in great detail in the section on Tantra. It is explained in the section on Mahamudra from the point of view of the Karma Kagyü tradition, Mahamudra being the essence of any completion stage practice.

Ringu Tulku Rinpoché was born in 1952 in Lintsang, an area in the province of Kham, East Tibet. He is an eminent Buddhist teacher whose scholarship, fluent command of English, and responsive teaching style have become greatly appreciated among followers of Buddhism throughout the world. He was recognized as the reincarnation of the abbot of Rigul Monastery in Tibet and was the first Kagyü lama to obtain the Acharya degree at the Central Institute of Higher Tibetan Studies in Varanasi, India. The title of Khenpo was awarded to him by His Holiness the Sixteenth Gyalwa Karmapa. In addition, he received the Lopön Chenpo (Ph.D.) title from the International Nyingma Society.

His root gurus are His Holiness the Sixteenth Gyalwa Karmapa and His Eminence Dilgo Khyentse Rinpoché, and he has studied and practiced under the guidance of many distinguished masters from all traditions of Tibetan Buddhism.

Ringu Tulku Rinpoché was a professor of Tibetology in India for seventeen years. He lived in Sikkim and during this time created teaching materials and books. Especially notable among his writings is a work on Jamgön Kongtrül Lodrö Thayé and the Rimé movement, the unbiased approach, in Tibet.

Taking into account the content of this book, it seems appropriate to introduce it by means of one of Ringu Tulku Rinpoché's favorite prayers from the *Bodhicharyavatara*:

> As long as space exists
> and as long as beings endure,
> may I too remain
> to dispel the misery of the world.

Hamburg
Rosemarie Fuchs

Author's Acknowledgments

IN THE FALL OF 1996 I was asked to teach on the Three Vehicles of Buddhism, including teachings on Mahamudra, by the Buddhist center Thegsum Tashi Chöling, Hamburg, and this book is the result of those teachings, and of teachings given the year before at Kagyü Benchen Ling, Todtmoos-Au. Rosemarie Fuchs transcribed them, translated the Tibetan scriptural sources they are based upon into English, and edited the manuscript over and over again for several years. The credit for this book fully goes to her. I have no words to thank her for her tireless work and for her dedication. My heartfelt thanks go to Holly Gayley and Ann Helms for revising the manuscript. Further, I am very grateful to Kim Speller, who read the manuscript, made very valuable suggestions, and also offered to publish it. Ana-Rosalia Findeisen read the proof and was a great source of encouragement. Many other people helped in various ways and, although I cannot mention all their names here, I would like to express my deep gratitude to them all.

My special thanks go to Chris Hatchell and Steven Rhodes for their wonderful editing and to Snow Lion Publications for taking up the publication of this book in such a short time.

Above all, I must express my deeply felt gratitude to all my teachers. If there is anything worthwhile in this book, it comes entirely from those great masters who embody the teachings.

Ringu Tulku
Gangtok

The Buddha

INTRODUCTION

THE SOLE PURPOSE of all Buddhist teachings is to develop our minds and hearts in terms of inner growth. Buddhism is nothing but a way or method to work on our inner or spiritual development. Through its teachings we try to change and transform the way we are, as well as the way we see ourselves and everything around us.

This attempt is made because it is clearly evident that we all experience certain problems and confusions. Each of us is subject to emotional conflicts and various kinds of suffering. Therefore, we try to address these problems, which are mostly very basic and common to all human beings. In doing so we find that some problems cannot be changed. This is true, for instance, of the fact of change itself. Change takes place all the time but usually we cannot face it or accept it. Due to this incapacity we are afraid and fear the realities of life, such as death, sickness, and so forth.

So the question arises of how we should deal with these. How do we find a solution to our basic problems? We must change those we can change, but there are many that we cannot make go away. Trying to change them "out there" is impossible. Such attempts are in vain and lead only to further suffering. This is the situation in which Buddhism or any other kind of spiritual teaching and practice is needed. The purpose of spiritual teaching and practice is to enable us to solve the problems that we have to face, not from the outside but from within. In this way we can change our attitude, our way of feeling and experiencing, our manner of saying and doing things. Through this process of inner change, our confusion will gradually diminish and allow for an increase of clarity. This in turn will bring about a true transformation.

For this reason we should try to develop inner strength. This will enable us to change and transform ourselves, and thereby gain the ability to solve those basic human problems that cannot be changed externally. This does not mean that we should not change any of our outer circumstances. One might think that there is no need to do anything about social and ecological issues, for instance, since all problems can be solved through a process of inner transformation. This would be a total misunderstanding. Of course we should do what we can to improve whatever is improvable. A house with no heating system is very cold and uncomfortable in the winter. There is nothing wrong with installing heating, provided the necessary means are at hand. But a heating system does not solve all our problems. We can find ourselves amidst all the luxury we could possibly dream of, and still be very unhappy. Equally, we can be in a very bad situation and still not feel too desperate about it. The difference lies in the degree of our inner development, in the way we see and experience our world.

So the aim is to transform ourselves in such a way that we will be able to be happy when we have everything we need, and equally when it is otherwise. The way to develop inwardly is to gain independence by understanding that both happiness and unhappiness do not depend too much on outer conditions. It is our own development that determines whether or not we are able to be happy. With inner strength we can feel quite well, even while our situation is not too bright.

Inner strength means to understand and accept the realities of life. The great Tibetan yogi Milarepa said, "I was so afraid of death that I ran away into the mountains, where I meditated so much on impermanence and death that finally I attained deathlessness." He opened his eyes. He came to know and understand that death is inevitable and therefore tried to deal with it and worked hard.

In the Buddhist teachings the necessity of acceptance is often mentioned, but sometimes this is misinterpreted to mean a kind of passivity. With this attitude one might say, "If someone gives me a slap in the face, he can give me another. Whatever happens I'll just accept it." This is not quite what is meant, and our acceptance should be more active. If we try to deny death, for instance, and avoid thinking and talking about it, this is not acceptance in the Buddhist sense. Milarepa knew that no one can escape from death, that it will surely come, as an unalterable fact. He saw the problem clearly, in an unconfused way. Consequently, he did not try to avoid it, but exerted every effort to work on it. Once we see our problem clearly with open eyes, we will be able to overcome it. When Milarepa said that he meditated on the inevitability of death to the extent that he attained deathlessness, it meant that he had no more fear of dying. This is the true transformation we need to achieve. It does not mean that he did not die. He did. Yet, since he understood death completely, in its true perspective, it did not haunt him anymore. Once we are able to deal with our problems and work upon them in this way, even the inevitability of our own death, which is usually regarded as something extremely negative and frightful, will no longer constitute a problem. Whereas, as long as we are incapable of the type of fearlessness that Milarepa attained, our problems will remain severe.

So this is the purpose of Dharma, the teaching of the Buddha. Why did the Buddha feel compelled to leave his palace and seek the Dharma? Because he found that the fundamental problems each human being has to face cannot be avoided. We cannot escape from dying, falling ill, aging, getting what we do not want, not getting what we do want, and so on. Seeing this, he tried to find a solution. In this context, we can only work on ourselves. We work on our own hearts and minds. Our mind is the practice. We ourselves are the practice.

The teachings of the Buddha are the expression of his own experience, which he conveyed in accordance with the different and specific requirements of individual people. Human beings differ so much in terms of their levels of spiritual development, their capacities, mentalities, and attitudes, that one way of teaching could never suffice for everybody. For this reason the Buddha gave many teachings and provided a multitude of different approaches. He started with the Four Noble Truths and the Noble Eightfold Path, and then proceeded to a more advanced level of philosophy and meditation. This again was presented even more deeply and directly in a third cycle of teachings.

In this way, the Buddha's teachings were written down in different sutras and tantras, each dealing with a specific subject matter on a specific level. The Buddha himself did not categorize his teachings, but to facilitate study and understanding they have been put into categories. These have emerged as three sets of teachings known as Shravakayana, Mahayana, and Vajrayana. Nowadays in the West, the Shravakayana is commonly called "the Hinayana." This term is not quite appropriate, though, as it literally means "small or lesser vehicle" and thus bears a falsely belittling connotation. From the Buddhist point of view these three *yanas* or vehicles are not separate from each other. They constitute, in their entirety, the one and complete teaching given by the Buddha. This complete teaching was originally written down in Sanskrit and later translated into Tibetan. In Tibet it is preserved in either one hundred and one or one hundred and three volumes, according to different systems of presentation. These volumes are of different sizes, ranging from six hundred to more than twelve hundred pages, and are collectively known in Tibetan as the *Kangyur*. Together they comprise the entire teaching of the Buddha and present it in terms of three *yanas*, or vehicles. Their followers today are called Theravadin, Mahayana, and Vajrayana Buddhists, respectively.

Of these, Theravadins rely mainly or even solely on the Shravakayana sutras as their basis of understanding and practice. There is a slight distinction between the terms "Shravakayana" and "Theravada," with the name "Theravada" originating in the following way. After the Buddha's *parinirvana*, or visible presence passing from this world, it was part of a monk's discipline to recite the Vinaya, the set of rules observed by an ordained person, every fortnight. A certain division developed among the monks regarding this tradition. The elder ones wanted to do the recitation in Pali, a more colloquial form of Sanskrit, while the younger and more erudite monks preferred to recite in Sanskrit. The term *thera* denotes a senior monk and thus the name "Theravada" came about in reference to these senior monks. From India, Theravada Buddhism went mainly south and is now to be found in Sri Lanka, Thailand, Burma, and so forth. Mahayana Buddhism, based upon the Mahayana sutras, spread to China, Korea, Japan, and Vietnam. Vajrayana Buddhism developed mainly in Tibet and Mongolia, and to a lesser extent in Japan, China, and Korea.

Vajrayana Buddhism aims at presenting the entirety of the Buddha's teaching. The teachings of the Shravakayana and Mahayana are not considered as being separate from it. All three vehicles form an integral system of instruction, and their categorization is just for the sake of easier understanding. The Shravakayana contains the most fundamental teachings. Without this basis it is not possible to understand the Mahayana or Vajrayana. The relationship of the three *yanas* can be illustrated in terms of three concentric circles. The outer circle is the Vajrayana. It embraces and encompasses the other two. The next is the Mahayana, which embraces the Shravakayana at the center. Alternatively, their relationship can be illustrated in terms of the levels of a mountain. In this metaphor, the Shravakayana forms the base, the Mahayana the bulk, and the Vajrayana the peak. Whatever is taught in the Shravakayana system is not rejected by the Mahayana or Vajrayana teachings. It is just further clarified and revealed to open the way for our understanding to develop into ever deepening levels, until true depth is attained.

The teachings of the three *yanas* should not be discussed and presented on just an academic or intellectual level. To do so would be quite easy. It is considerably more difficult to explain them in a way that evokes a personal experience and understanding, and enables us to put them into practice. This challenge should be accepted though. If I were to explain the three *yanas* academically, conveying just another province of knowledge, it would not be very difficult. At the same time it would be quite dry, and useless as well. There would be an intellectual understanding in our heads and we would come away having memorized yet another piece of information. Instead of that, we have to learn how to put the teachings we receive into practical use, how to make them into our path and integrate them into our daily lives. Especially in the West, we come into contact with so many teachings from all kinds of levels, with so much Maha Ati, Mahamudra, Tantra, and so forth. The information is so overabundant that it can easily turn into a stew. All the ingredients are mixed up to such an extent that they cannot be told apart anymore. As a dish this might be delicious, but as far as understanding is concerned, such a glut of information can be slightly confusing, and can also be more than is really needed.

What is required, therefore, is a clear view and perception of how these three levels of teaching build upon one another and where each instruction falls into place. This needs to be understood experientially. An intellectual understanding is not enough. The real and actual practice of Dharma does not take place in the brain. Practice means just working on ourselves. I am often asked whether it is possible to practice different aspects simultaneously, such as combining Zen and Mahamudra practices or the *sadhana* of Avalokiteshvara and calm abiding. I respond with another question: What is practice? It is not Avalokiteshvara and so forth. It is yourself. You are your practice, so you must use whatever is helpful. If the practice of Zen helps to improve yourself, use this method. We should use anything that contributes to our improvement. If we take ourselves as the practice and work on ourselves, nothing is contradictory. There is no conflict between anything. If we can build an understanding in this way, it will be well grounded. Often our understanding is very fragmented, and for this reason we are not on solid ground. Most of the time we gain information from here and there, both in study and practice, and then try to rely on this wobbly surface.

In this situation it is very important to start at the beginning. Personally speaking, the more teachings I received, the more they caused me to go back. When I received Maha Ati and Mahamudra instructions, I thought, "This is wonderful, but I cannot do it without having taken the preceding step." So I retraced my steps evermore back to the actual starting point. At first we will be looking for a swift way out and be attracted by teachings that say, "If you practice this in the morning, you will be enlightened in the evening, and if you practice this in the evening, you will be enlightened in the morning." When statements like that are misunderstood, they can arouse false expectations. We will hope for a quick result and an easy way to achieve it.

This happened even to Milarepa. At first, he had been an extremely powerful black magician who was able to launch hailstorms and so forth. Then finally he repented of his evil deeds and wanted to practice the Dharma. The first teacher he turned to had mastered a very high and effective instruction. Being slightly proud of that, he said to Milarepa, "You are very fortunate. My teaching is such that whoever practices it in the morning will be enlightened in the evening and vice versa." This flattered Milarepa, and he thought to himself, "I am really a very special person. First I was a black magician and with just a little effort attained great powers. Now the practice of the Dharma is even easier. I am a genius!" After having bestowed the necessary instructions, the teacher advised him to practice. A week later, he went to Milarepa's retreat and inquired as to his results. Milarepa replied, "Since your instructions will yield such quick results, I have not yet started to practice. I had a rest first." Then the teacher realized that he had been too rash and said, "Being so fond of my teaching I have been bragging too much. These instructions are not suitable for you. You must go and find Marpa." Hearing this name, Milarepa was instantaneously filled with great faith and followed the advice. Then, following that, Marpa gave him real trouble before even accepting him as a disciple. It can happen, therefore, that someone practices in the morning and is enlightened in the evening, but it needs some doing. It needs starting at the beginning.

This applies to most of us. If we do not start at the beginning, we may gain a certain amount of understanding, but we will not have laid the foundations. That problem is especially true for a teacher. It is comparatively easy to talk about "higher things." With a little quotation here and a little quotation there it is not difficult to produce an academic paper. But this approach does not work as far as the basics are concerned. In order to talk about these, we have to come down to our everyday lives. We have to deal with the assumptions we build up all the time and upon which we then operate and function. As long as we cannot see whether these are right or wrong, there is no working basis. Clearing away all our false assumptions is the most difficult part of the whole task. Writing a book for children, for instance, is particularly difficult, especially when it is meant for very small ones, whereas writing for older children is comparatively easier. In the same way, it takes much more effort and skill to impart a valid understanding of the most basic teachings of the Buddha, while his higher teachings are somewhat easier to convey.

Then again, anything that is worthwhile is not easy. For instance, when it is said that it is possible to reach enlightenment in one lifetime, this has to be understood in the right way. Of course it is possible, but only if a genuine understanding is gained and then applied accordingly. It depends on the degree to which we understand everything that needs to be practiced, and then on the degree to which we actually practice it. As for the term "enlightenment" itself, there is also sometimes a slight misunderstanding. When we hear about reaching enlightenment, there is the tendency to think, "Now I am not enlightened, but in the future I will reach this goal." According to the Vajrayana, though, enlightenment is nothing other than the realization that we are already enlightened. It is probably for this reason that the Vajrayana teachings seem so easy. What they express is the fact that reaching enlightenment is not something that can be compared to climbing a mountain, to struggling hard and then finally reaching the top. Enlightenment is not obtained from somewhere else. Once we know how to look and see everything clearly as it is, without any delusion, this is enlightenment. For this reason, the concept, "I have to reach enlightenment in one lifetime," this kind of struggling and fighting attitude, can almost become a hindrance. Through our practice of Dharma we should become increasingly more relaxed, up to the point where we almost do not want to reach enlightenment anymore. So when it happens, we might say, "What I thought was so big is just that simple." Thus an attitude based upon struggle is difficult.

The methods of the Vajrayana are not accessible through understanding alone. They offer simple techniques, and then the experience has to come from ourselves, once the techniques are understood correctly. In this way these methods are very effective and strong. At the same time, they are not so easy to apply, because we normally do not trust these methods. Our assumptions and concepts that form our intellectual understanding do not allow us to follow them. These techniques need to be to carried out in an experiential way; they simply need to be applied and thereby turned into our own experience. Not being used to such an approach, we will not find them easy. Furthermore, once we are able to apply these methods, we will have to work hard.

Milarepa's best disciple was Gampopa. After he had received all the necessary instructions and gained genuine experience of them, Milarepa told him to go to a mountain called "Gampodar" near the Nepalese border, where he would find his disciples. When Gampopa was ready to leave, Milarepa accompanied him part of the way, until they had reached a small stream. Here Milarepa said, "Now you go, my son." Then he hesitated and said, "I have not given you my most secret instruction, though, but maybe I should not do so either." Gampopa prostrated himself many times, offered a mandala, and entreated him to bestow this teaching. Milarepa would not be moved, and so finally Gampopa went on his way. After he had crossed the water and reached the far bank, Milarepa called him back and said, "After all, you are my best disciple. If I do not give this teaching to you, to whom else should I give it?" Gampopa was filled with joy and prostrated himself over and over again, expecting a very sublime and outstanding instruction. Then, Milarepa turned around and, lifting his clothes, showed Gampopa his backside. It was covered with innumerable scars from meditating sitting on rocks for so long. He said, "Look, my son. This is my final and most secret instruction!"

It is therefore vital to start at the beginning to provide a sound working basis.

PART ONE

SHRAVAKAYANA

INTRODUCTION

To begin with it is very important to understand that the three sets of teachings called Shravakayana, Mahayana, and Vajrayana are not to be considered as separate entities. They are one and the same subject presented on different levels. Whatever is introduced at the beginning is then explained further and thereby widened and deepened into another level. A good example for this process is the term "bodhisattva." This term is also used in the Shravakayana sutras to describe the Buddha before he had reached his ultimate realization. But though the term is mentioned in the Shravakayana context, it is not explained further until the Mahayana level of teachings. There, it is explained in great detail what is to be understood by the term "bodhisattva," what is the attitude of a bodhisattva, and what view, meditation, and action constitute a bodhisattva's way of being. This is the only difference between the Shravakayana and Mahayana systems. Nothing is taken away from the Shravakayana teachings; when they are supplemented by the instructions on the bodhisattva path, they become the Mahayana level of teaching.

The same process is true of the Vajrayana. To the Shravakayana and Mahayana teachings the Vajrayana adds the teaching that all sentient beings have buddha-nature, also called self-born wisdom, (truly) ordinary mind, basic goodness, or inherent purity. The Vajrayana clarifies that there is a nature within us that is already pure and complete, and that only needs to be realized. For this reason, it is said that we do not have to construct anything in order to reach enlightenment. Nothing needs to be added to what is already there. It is just a question of realization. The sole subject of the Vajrayana teachings is to show us how to awaken and realize this buddha-nature. There is nothing more than that.

Thus, the Shravakayana system represents the most fundamental teaching. Without it, there is no way to add anything. Without this basic ground, we would be hanging in the air.

THE FOUR NOBLE TRUTHS

The first instruction of the Buddha was the teaching on the Four Noble Truths. These cannot be said to be "just Shravakayana." They are everything. Apart from the Four Noble Truths, there is nothing else in Buddhism. So they are the most important thing. The Buddha taught the Four Noble Truths in accordance with the way a person would normally solve a problem. That is, when a problem arises, first we try to find out what that problem is, we try to see its nature and depth and how much of it is actually there. Once this is seen clearly, we can look further and find its causes. The first teaching of the Buddha is very down to earth. No matter what kind of problem we have, first we need to see it clearly. Then we have to recognize its causes, and after recognizing these we have to find a way to eliminate them in order to achieve the result, which is freedom from the problem. This is the most important part. In this context mere understanding is not enough. We have to learn how to make use of our understanding and apply it to our lives.

When the Buddha taught the Four Noble Truths he repeated them three times, expanding them successively. First he said, "There is suffering in this world. There are causes of this suffering. There is cessation of suffering, and there are ways to reach the cessation of suffering." Then he said, "There is suffering in this world, one has to understand it. There are causes of this suffering, and one has to eliminate them. There is cessation of suffering, and one has to attain it. There are ways to reach the cessation of suffering, and one has to work upon them." The third time he said, "There is suffering in this world, one has to understand it, but actually there is nothing to understand. There are causes of this suffering, and one has to eliminate them, but actually there is nothing to eliminate. There is cessation of suffering, and one has to attain it, but actually there is nothing to attain. There are ways to reach the cessation of suffering, and one has to work upon them, but actually there is nothing to work upon." This was the first teaching of the Buddha, which he gave at Sarnath to his first five disciples: Kaundinya, Bhaddiya, Vappa, Mahanama, and Asvajit.

The Truth of Suffering

So the first subject the Buddha taught was *duhkha*, as it is called in Sanskrit, which is sometimes translated as "suffering," and also as "dissatisfaction" or "misery." I do not know which translation is best. What it means is that we have to understand whatever problem is there. We have to see it clearly and we have to accept it, not in a passive way, but by opening our eyes and looking at it. Without doing so, there is not the slightest chance to find a way to overcome any problem.

The Buddha just looked at life, at samsaric or human existence, and then talked about the problems he saw. If there were no problems, there would be no need to worry. But because there are problems, we have to talk about them and point them out in order to find a solution. It is sometimes said that Buddhism is a very pessimistic religion, since it constantly talks about suffering. But Buddhism does not aim at creating suffering or a pessimistic attitude. It talks about suffering in order to engender an optimistic outlook. It conveys the message, "Yes, there is suffering, but it can be removed." In order to do so, we have to open our eyes. If we try to pretend that everything is all right, it will not be of much avail, especially when a problem arises that is so great that it cannot be denied.

Therefore, we must understand clearly whatever problem is there, so that we can also see its causes and create the necessary conditions to be able to actually work on it. If we looked into our lives and found that there was no problem whatsoever and that everything was perfectly all right, there would be no need for Dharma. But when we look in this way, we might find that there is some problem, that we are not completely satisfied and happy. We might feel that something is not quite right, that there are things irritating us, tormenting us, and making us unhappy. This feeling will alert us to the fact that there must be something that we can do about it as well. The very recognition of the problem raises the question, "Why do I not feel completely wonderful all the time? What is it that prevents me from being happy?"

Thus the Buddha's teaching on suffering is meant to be positive and constructive. It does not mean that we cannot enjoy anything. Rather, the message is that it is possible to enjoy ourselves completely, all the time, provided we have the necessary means. As soon as we are able to remove the causes of suffering, it will cease, and there will be the possibility of continuous and uninterrupted happiness.

The teaching on *duhkha* means that we first look at our lives and try to see what kind of life we have. Is it always peaceful and happy? Is it always like walking on roses? When we look into this question, we may find that there are things which are not so nice. We may fall ill, for instance, or we may get something we do not want, or lose something we love. Then we will feel sad, dissatisfied, frustrated, and very miserable. Once these feelings arise, we will wish them away and try to ignore them. But this will not work. We have to open our eyes to what we have.

The Buddha categorized suffering into three types. The first is called "the suffering of suffering." This refers to real pain, such as being deeply hurt or having had a truly terrible experience. It is the type of suffering everybody recognizes for what it is. Nobody needs an introduction. This kind of suffering everybody knows.

Yet, apart from this, there are less apparent types of suffering that we may not even recognize. These are called "the suffering of change" and "all-pervasive suffering." The first refers to a situation where we may not be experiencing the suffering of suffering. Nothing really painful is happening, we are quite happy and peaceful, and yet there is some kind of dissatisfaction. Why should this be? It is because we fear that our present fortunate situation might change. When we are asked, "How are you," we will not say, "I'm happy." We will say, "I'm quite all right," because we anticipate in terms of a dull understanding that something negative might happen soon. Thus the feeling of anxiety and uneasiness is ingrained even in our moments of happiness. This is the second kind of suffering.

On top of this, there is a third type of suffering, created by the fact that this changing nature is all-pervasive. Everything moves on, including ourselves, and we cannot hold on to anything. Although we long for complete security, we know that we can never get it. Our bodies are composite and impermanent, just as everything else. If I were to insure my life for a large sum of money, this would not prevent me from dying. The money would be there after my death and might be of use to other people, but it would not be useful to me. There is no real security. At the same time, every human being seeks security and longs for unchangingness. This longing proves impossible to fulfill. Everything changes all the time, and whenever change happens we experience a shock.

Once we know this, once we know the way things are and clearly see the condition of our lives, at least we will no longer be in the dark. But knowledge is not enough on its own. We have to recognize the causes and work on them. It is important to remember that the words of the Buddha are the expression of his experience. So the key is to evaluate his teachings as facts and use them in an experiential way. We cannot treat his words as if they were simply information, telling us that there are so and so many different types of suffering. We have to go beyond the words and see from our own experience whether or not there is suffering, what kind of suffering there is, what are its causes, and so forth. We have to open our eyes to our own lives. Looking directly and openly at life, we will gain an understanding of the way it functions and what it actually is. This is the true understanding we need to achieve.

Seeing life as it is will be of great benefit, even while we cannot yet see the causes of suffering. We will no longer be shocked by anything that comes to pass. We will be open to what is there and see it in perspective. It happens quite often that when people visit me, they are feeling low, and they tell me that everything in their lives is so bad. Sometimes I suggest that these people visit some Third World country. Such a comparison with other people's suffering can be helpful. Lacking a realistic perspective, we can make ourselves miserable without any need.

There is a story about a man, his wife, and their many children, all of whom were living together in a very small house, in extremely cramped conditions. This caused the man a lot of problems and increasingly he felt so oppressed that one day he went out to get some advice from a relative who was a local priest. After he had told him how he was nearly going mad with the house being so small and the children so obnoxious, his relative reflected for a while and then told him to buy a goat and take it back home. The man followed the advice, but a few days later he went back and lamented, "Oh, it is so much worse! On top of everything else, now the goat is running around in the house and making everything dirty." His relative advised him to buy a cock and take it home as well. The man did so, but it did not even take three days before he was back and said, almost choking with tears, "I cannot cope any longer. This is unbearable! Now the goat and the cock together mess up the whole house and make everything filthy." His relative thought for a moment and said, "Just go and sell the bird." After seven days, they met again and the relative asked how he felt. The reply was,

"Oh, my life is much better." The relative said, "All right, sell the goat as well."
When they met a week later, incidentally, the relative inquired about the
man's situation. He got the answer, "My life is just wonderful. Everything is
so peaceful!"

This shows how a problem can become comparatively small or big, when
seen in perspective. Thinking in this way will allow us to appreciate the full
extent of all the problems that might occur and to have an eye for the various difficulties of our fellow beings, which are often much more severe than
our own. Once we are able to see that, we can be more confident in dealing
with whatever is at hand, it will be seen in due proportion. As long as our
field of vision is narrowed down to just our own problem and our feelings
about it, we get easily upset. When we look at the palm of our hand from a
certain distance, it is neither too big nor too small. It is just a hand. Yet, if we
hold it in front of our eyes, it blots out everything and we cannot see anything else. In addition, what we do see is completely unclear since it is far too
near to our eyes. As long as we do not see clearly and in proper perspective,
even the smallest thing can be completely overwhelming.

When, on the contrary, we are able to see how things are and perceive their
inevitability, there will be a greater amount of clarity. We will be more broad-
minded and thus gain inner strength. That is the benefit of just knowing the
state of affairs. As soon as we see how things are, we know suffering, or in
other words, reality. When reality is seen more precisely and in greater
depth, the solution is almost at hand.

Once we know the suffering of suffering, we are able to go further: we can
see that it is caused by constant change, which in its turn cannot be avoided.
Change happens all the time. The reason is that nothing whatsoever has any
essence of its own. Everything comes into existence due to interdependence, to different influences affecting each other. Nothing stands still. Looking into this fact more deeply, we will eventually see the interdependent
nature of everything, the way everything is due to causes and effects. Then
we will perceive how things really are, their actual nature. Having gained
this capacity, we will see ourselves as being part of this ongoing process of
change.

When we discover that we ourselves are subject to this interrelatedness,
we will no longer feel separate and cut off from anything else. Usually we
endeavor to be separate from everybody and anything else. We constantly
try to be just ourselves, and the only measure for everything that happens is

whether it is good for us. This manner of being egoistic and making ourselves the center of our attention contradicts reality, and therefore leads to dire suffering.

Normally, we act and react in tems of "I" and "the rest of the world." Whatever another person does is seen and evaluated in relation to ourselves. This leads to a constant need to protect ourselves, and we then become so defensive that we completely close up and experience everything as an attack or as pain. Figuratively speaking, we become like a wound filled with puss, ever so sensitive to the slightest touch. Once we change this unrealistic way of experiencing, knowing the interrelatedness of ourselves and everything else, this sensitivity and isolation is broken. We open up, and become freer and more relaxed. This will happen just by knowing the realities of life, that interdependence is the true nature of things.

The Truth of the Causes of Suffering

Once we gain this realistic view of ourselves and everything around us, as it is shown by the Buddha's teaching on the Truth of Suffering, we cannot leave it at that. We have to go deeper and see the cause. This is the most important teaching of the Buddha, his most significant discovery. It is where his whole teaching comes from, and the focal point to which it is directed.

In Buddhism, it is said that the actual and final cause of all our sufferings and problems consists of two things: karma and the mental poisons or afflictions. This constitutes, in my view, the real discovery the Buddha made. No one had said this before. In order to fully understand that karma and the mental poisons are the true causes of suffering, we have to have a genuine experience of the Truth of the Path.

To begin with, we should look into what is meant by the term "karma." Nowadays, almost everybody talks about karma. Yet, it is not that easy to understand, and there are many misconceptions about it. Karma is cause and effect. When we talk about karma, we talk about the law of cause and effect. A similar cause yields a similar result. A sweet seed will result in a sweet fruit, and a bitter seed will result in a bitter fruit. This is the philosophy of karma.

To comprehend karma, we need to understand what is meant by the term "interdependence." This does not mean that just one single thing gives rise to another. Rather it means that there are many influences on each and every thing, and each single thing in its turn affects many others. Everything comes about due to a multitude of causes of various kinds. Even not obstructing something else is a kind of cause. A flower, for example, was caused by whatever was helpful to its growth, by everything that actively furthered its development, and also by everything that did not prevent or obstruct it. When encountering a flower, I am also in a way a cause of this flower, because I do not cut it down and prevent it from growing.

Furthermore, karma is not just limited to that of the individual. There is also the karma of a family, a community, a nation, the whole world, and so forth. As far as individual karma is concerned, we sometimes tend to think, "I have done something in the past, which now inevitably has to surface. Everything is predestined. Whatever my future may be, it is all written down. I cannot do anything about it." This is a misconception. Karma is not static. It is very changing and dynamic. It is true that what I am now is the result of my past actions. Whatever I did in my last life and in my lives before, whatever I have done in this life from its very beginning until the present, all of that has made what I am now. This is called the "skandhas of complete ripening." I am the result of all my actions.

This result has already happened, but the way it continues into the future is not predetermined. Whatever has left a strong impression in my mind will affect my stream of being and change the course of my life to a certain extent. I am like a river. If someone puts something very big into it or forcefully manipulates its banks, the course of a river will change. It can become a flood, or divide into two streams, or turn into a narrow canal. So, a certain limitation through what has already happened is there. But given this limitation, I can still go in any direction. What I do from now onward is in my own hands. Karma, therefore, does not mean that we cannot do anything. Karma is very dynamic. Every single moment a new karma is created. Thus everything changes all the time.

There are different types of karma, and thus a variety of impacts that our actions can have. Karma ripens in four ways. The strongest karma is a cause that yields an immediate result, a result experienced in this very life. The second is a cause yielding an effect experienced in the next life. The third will produce a result at an uncertain time. The fourth is indefinite in the sense that it may produce a fruit or it may not. Of these, the first is called "the karma we see and experience directly." This will take precedence over any less powerful karma such as that resulting from our last life or from the preceding ones. This means that if we make a strong decision, from now onward we can lessen or even neutralize the impact of the karma we have to deal with. Thus there is a chance to overcome it.

In short, karma means that any good and positive action will result in a corresponding fruit, in more pleasure and happiness; any negative and harmful deed will also result in its equivalent, in more suffering and pain. Neutral actions will yield an equally neutral fruit.

So how does karma function and what are its causes? In Buddhism, the mental poisons or afflictions are held to be the causes of karma; of these poisons, ignorance is the root. It is a state of mind that is extremely unclear and confused. It is delusion in the sense of not knowing how things truly are. This is considered to be the real basis of karma. Due to confusion and lack of clarity, we identify ourselves with something that is not the truth and does not correspond to the actual state of reality. Thus ignorance is basically a misconception.

What does it mean when it is said that karma arises from ignorance? It is very important to understand this, but at the same time, it is quite difficult to comprehend. Thus, it is better to explain it strictly according to the tradition. In the Buddhist sense, ignorance is equivalent to the identification of a self as being separate from everything else. It consists of the belief that there is an "I" that is not part of anything else. On this basis we think, "I am one and unique. Everything else is not me. It is something different." This is what is called *atman* in Sanskrit, meaning a self or ego in terms of an existing entity.

In Buddhist terminology the term "ego" means the following. When we look at ourselves, we find that we are not just a single entity. We are compounded: we consist of form, feeling, consciousness, and so forth. Nevertheless, we take all these different constituents as being just one thing. We conceive of them as an "I" and say, "This is me." Thereby, we make an identification and a projection.

From this identification stems the dualistic view, since once there is an "I," there are also "others." Up to here this is "me." The rest is "they." As soon as this split is made, it creates two opposite ways of reaction: "This is nice. I want it!" and "This is not nice. I do not want it!" There may be a neutral reaction as well, but this can be neglected as it does not constitute a major problem. The first two are far more serious.

On the one hand there are those things that seem to threaten and undermine us. Maybe they will harm us or take away our identity. They are a danger to our security. Due to this way of thinking, aversion comes up, which in turn gives rise to fear and anxiety. We are afraid that the threat associated with these things might prove true. So we reject them and try to run away from them or fight them off. Thus aggression arises.

Then, on the other hand, there are those things that are so nice. We think, "I want them. I want them so much. I must run after them! I have to get them! Once I have got them I cannot part with them!" Through this way of thinking, first attraction and desire occur, then clinging, and finally strong attachment arises.

In this way the mental poisons are aversion/attachment based upon ignorance, or not knowing how reality truly is. The functioning of karma is propelled by these. As long as we are subject to these three poisons, we are in samsara. Tibetans have a traditional painting called "the Wheel of Life," which depicts the samsaric cycle of existence. In the center of this wheel there are three animals: a pig, a snake, and a bird. They represent the three poisons. The pig stands for ignorance, although a pig is not necessarily more stupid than other animals. The comparison is based on the Indian concept of a pig being the most foolish of all animals, since it always sleeps in the dirtiest places and eats whatever comes to its mouth. Similarly, the snake is identified with anger because it will be aroused and leap up at the slightest touch. The bird represents desire and clinging. In Western publications it is frequently referred to as a cock, but this is not exactly accurate. This particular bird does not exist in Western countries, as far as I know. It is used as a symbol because it is very attached to its partner. These three animals represent the three main mental poisons, which are at the core of the Wheel of Life. Stirred by these, the whole cycle of existence evolves. Without them, there is no samsara.

Samsara, therefore, is not a place. It is a state of mind. Wherever these three mental poisons are active, samsara is present. It is a state of mind in which we are constantly running. Either we are running away from something, or we are running after something else. Being caught in this circle, there is no peace, no relaxation, and no rest. As long as our frame of mind is like that, we are in samsara and always running. Suffering is also to be understood in these terms. All our problems are rooted in either trying to get something, or in trying to avoid something else. In this constant endeavor we are never satisfied. To want something means not to have it. We are therefore in pursuit of something; we are searching and struggling for it. This is not an agreeable experience. Equally, running away from something means that we do not like it, that there is a strong apprehension and fear of it. This again is a painful experience. As long as we are in this state of mind, marked by aversion and attachment stemming from ignorance, we are in samsara and thus bound to suffering. We are in constant struggle, trying and fighting all the time.

Within this frame of mind we create karma in three different ways, through actions that are positive, negative, or neutral. When we feel kindness and love and with this attitude do good things, which are beneficial to both ourselves and others, this is positive action. When we commit harmful deeds out of equally harmful intentions, this is negative action. Finally, when our motivation is indifferent and our deeds are neither harmful nor beneficial, this is neutral action. The results we experience will accord with the quality of our actions.

Yet, no matter how good our actions may be, as long as we are caught in a state of mind dominated by aversion and attachment based upon ignorance, we remain within the samsaric world. We can reduce our suffering and augment our happiness but cannot dispel all the causes of suffering. The true cause of all our suffering is ignorance, which gives rise to aversion and attachment. These three are called "the mental poisons," and as long as we do not succeed in uprooting these, we will continue to suffer. We can run after all kinds of things, after wealth, fame, or pleasure. We can even run after enlightenment or spiritual attainment. Yet, this kind of spiritual activity will not make any real change, it is still the same mentality, the same attitude of being constantly in pursuit of or on the run from something.

Deep down inside, we all have a very basic feeling of insecurity. In a way we know that our identification with a self is not based on anything real, concrete, or substantial. There is not really anything to hold on to. For this reason, we feel insecure in a very deep-rooted way. Yet, despite our faint notion of its insubstantiality and intangibility, we try to hold on to this self. We do not want to know about or accept the truth. We want to make sure that there is something to identify with. There is the urge to define ourselves in terms of thinking, "I am here and the others are there." This is our main ignorance and it causes us to react within the pattern of aversion and attachment

The Buddha has said from his experience that once we succeed in eliminating our ignorance, we will actually break the functioning of karma. There will no longer be any basis for it. Without ignorance, there will be no attachment and no aversion, and thus there will be no ground on which to create any karma. This state of freedom from ignorance is called *nirvana*, and a person who has reached this state is called an *arhat*. The Tibetan word for arhat is *dra chom pa*, which means literally "the one who has defeated all enemies." The enemies to be defeated are our own mental poisons. Someone who has uprooted all mental poisons through eliminating ignorance has attained the state of nirvana. This is freedom from all suffering without exception. Since all confusion and misinterpretation have ceased, there is no more duality and thus no more suffering. This is expounded in the teaching on the Third Noble Truth, the Truth of Cessation.

The Truth of Cessation

Once we have developed a genuine understanding that ignorance is the cause of all suffering, we will eventually be able to overcome suffering and reach the point where all afflictions cease. This understanding, therefore, is vital. At the same time, it is not that easy to achieve. In order to gain this insight, we should not just accept what Buddhism says. If we find ourselves unable to believe in its validity, we have to admit that. Being born in a Buddhist society, I may have less difficulty accepting the teachings of the Buddha. To me their logic seems to come together so that I feel strongly that they are true. There are other ways and approaches though. Due to that, just a slight change in the manner of explanation can make all the difference. In the West, for instance, people tend to be oriented outwardly. Everything is seen as happening out there, so consequently cause and effect are also viewed in this light.

Recently somebody asked me, "How can we change society? How can we teach and help other people?" This shows a very good motivation. It has to be seen, though, that the emphasis is collective: "How can *we* change things and be helpful to others?" As opposed to that, the Buddhist approach is to ask, "What can *I* do?" The emphasis is on first solving our own problems, and gaining more knowledge and true understanding. These in turn will generate the capacity to help others to do the same. As long as we experience others as being the cause of our suffering, we will have a very hard time. Whereas, as soon as we are able to put the blame on ourselves by saying, "This is my problem and my confusion," there will be a greater amount of clarity. We are capable of turning our own problem into our own experience.

Working on ourselves in this way, we will eventually reach the cessation of suffering. There will be a gradual change in our usual manner of seeing things and reacting to them. We will understand that the strong impulse to always run away from or after something, which is initiated by aversion and attachment, is due to our own confusion. Once we see that our usual reactions are caused by a wrong way of seeing things, we will also understand how unnecessary it is to function in this pattern. When we deeply feel that there is not the slightest need for this struggle, when we have gained a genuine and profound experiential understanding of this, our confusion will be cleared up. Our misunderstanding will be eliminated, and we will see reality as it is. When this is seen, there will be peace, tranquility, and freedom.

This is the state of an arhat, which the Buddha described in terms of five qualities. Literally these qualities are called "elephant," "the task is done," "the burden is cast off," "one's own aim is achieved," and "free from pride." First, an arhat is said to be like an elephant who is not afraid of anything or anybody and does not need any protection when roaming the forests. Such a person is completely independent. Secondly, an arhat is comparable to someone who has achieved a great feat, who has been working hard for a very long time and suddenly finds that all his dreams have come true. There is a feeling of accomplishment and deep satisfaction. Thirdly, having reached the destination, the end of the journey, one has relieved oneself from the heavy burden that was carried for so long. In this way, fourth, one has accomplished one's own purpose and interest to its full extent. There is nothing more to achieve for oneself. Having done everything that is needed, one is completely free. There is the capacity and a natural and spontaneous willingness to work for the benefit of all other beings. Finally, fifth, the realization that is reached does not entail the notion, "Now I have done it!" It does not involve any pride. It simply means that things are seen as they really are. This is not experienced as being a big deal. It is rather comparable to awakening from sleep. While we are sleeping, we have all kinds of dreams. The moment we wake up, all these dreams are simply no longer there. We will not be particularly proud of having woken up.

This is how the Buddha described the attainment of the cessation of suffering. This attainment is brought about through realizing how needless it is to react through aversion and attachment. These impulses are due to confusion, our perverted way of perceiving reality in terms of "I" and "other than I." Once this confusion is seen, we have a clear view. Our mind is cleared. There is nothing to learn. Just by seeing our misconception, we eliminate it and thereby also eliminate our wrong way of saying and doing things. This is the state of an arhat.

There are different views on the meaning of the term "arhathood." The question often arises: What is the difference between a buddha and an arhat? I personally think that this does not matter too much for us at the moment. The realization is the same. The difference lies in the degree. A person who has gained the understanding described above is completely at peace and satisfied resting in this state of peace. From the Mahayana point of view, though, there are still very subtle habitual tendencies that are not yet removed. These are overcome on the path toward buddhahood. The realization of a buddha is clearer and more complete than that of an arhat. The difference lies in the depth and vastness of the realization. This can be illustrated by the example of looking at the sky. It looks different from within a small house or from a wide beach or a very high mountain. The sky is the same, but there is a great difference in the range of vision.

A lot more could be said in relation to this subject. This is just meant to give an impression. The important thing to understand in the context of the Four Noble Truths is that someone who has attained the cessation of suffering, or the state of nirvana, will no longer react within the pattern of aversion and attachment. The way such a person sees things will be nondualistic and therefore nonconceptual. This statement again can easily provoke all kinds of ideas as to its meaning. Most people will think that once this realization is reached, we will no longer bother about anything and react like a vegetable. Being nondualistic, we will no longer know who we are and who others are, as if we have become like a blank space. Though this notion will frequently arise, the truth is something quite different. At present, we see and react to everything in terms of contrasts and judgments such as, "This is good. This is bad. I like it. I don't like it. I want it. I don't want it. I fear it. I desire it." Everything is seen in this fragmented and totally distorted way. Whatever is perceived is immediately labeled as "good" or "bad," and so forth. These labels are then elaborated upon into "very good" or "very bad," and so on, and the pattern continues to infinity. We never see the thing as such. We only see what is in our mind and what has been built up by all kinds of concepts.

Take a flower for example. The very first instant our eyes come into contact with it, it is seen distinctly in all its parts, like in a photograph. But the moment the message is passed on to the mental consciousness, our mind sees only a fragment. We say, "This is a tulip. It is yellow. It is a yellow tulip." Once this has happened, our mind sees only that. The many parts of the flower are not seen but are confused and solidified into just one thing. We may even say, "This is a very beautiful yellow tulip." But still we do not see it in total. We do not see most of its features, such as its shape, its leaves, and so forth.

Our perception is based upon habit. We see only what we are used to see-ing, and we neglect the rest. New sense-experiences are matched with simi-lar ones from the past and then labeled as pleasant, unpleasant, and so forth. In this way our perception is very fragmented. We do not see what really is. If, on the contrary, we can see in a way that is unconfused, without aversion and attachment, we truly see what is there. Then there is no need for fear and attachment. We see who we are, how and what we are, precisely, without any mental construction. Nothing is added to what is actually there to be seen. There is direct, clear, and unpolluted experience. This is described as being nonconceptual, since nothing is added from our own part.

When we call something beautiful, that is our contribution. "Beauty lies in the eye of the beholder," as the saying goes. Therefore it is not necessary to have attachment. The same is true of its opposite. Aversion will not arise unless we think, "This is bad. I don't like it." Once this judgment is made, we will have a problem. If, for instance, we do not like some part of our job, usu-ally we will not leave it at that. We will build on this resentment and make it bigger, until one day we cannot stand our work at all. Then, we will desper-ately search for something different, for something that we like or are sup-posed to like. Once it is found, we will elaborate our feelings again, first into clinging, and finally into attachment.

When this dual reaction is gone, nothing is haunting or fearful anymore. We see clearly, and nothing seems imposing, since nothing is imposed from our part. When there is nothing we do not like, there is nothing to fear. Being free from fear, we are peaceful. There is no need to run away from anything and therefore no need to run after anything either. In this way, there is no burden. We can have inner peace, strength, and clarity, almost independent from circumstances and situations. This is complete freedom of mind with-out any circumstantial entanglement; the state is called "nirvana," which lit-erally means "gone beyond." Someone who has reached this state has gone beyond our usual way of being imprisoned in habitual patterns and dis-torted ways of seeing things.

The Truth of the Path

The teachings of the Four Noble Truths form a natural sequence. The understanding of the preceding one leads to an understanding of the next. Once we acknowledge that there is suffering and truly understand the problems at hand (1), we will see the necessity to discover their cause. This cause is not a minor thing, like the usual psychological disturbances we have, but is the one thing that is the actual and fundamental root of all suffering (2). When this cause is seen, we will understand that by working on this root we can clearly perceive how things really are and thereby overcome all our problems (3). With this insight the way is paved: we are ready for the Truth of the Path. In the context of the Four Noble Truths our understanding should not just be in terms of words. Otherwise, the statements of the first three Noble Truths can easily become mere slogans. Knowing suffering, the cause of suffering, and the cessation of suffering could be just empty talk. Therefore, we should not use these terms too much. We need words for whatever we want to express, but sometimes we get too familiar with words without understanding them deeply. This can almost become an obstacle. Words do not mean anything on their own. We need to understand the actual meaning behind them. As long as we do not manage to do that, it is very difficult to progress. This is especially true of the words that express the basic teachings of the Buddha.

Having gained a genuine understanding of their actual meaning, we will have a real chance to go forward. Otherwise we may lose our ground. Having no grip on the ground, we may be left floating and unable to relate to practice in a real and experiential way. The teachings conveyed by the first three Noble Truths are very fundamental and important. At the same time, they will be quite difficult to apply when accompanied by too many assumptions. The more we realize their actual meaning, the more our practice will be improved. We will increasingly understand what practice is and that it can really do something for ourselves and all others.

Once genuine understanding is gained, the question arises: How do we work on the causes of suffering? This has to be done slowly and gradually. It is not achieved by starting in the morning and becoming enlightened in the evening. Some individuals may be capable of such a feat, but most are not. On the other hand, each tiny improvement will be of great help and yield an enormous benefit.

The Buddha showed the gradual way toward the cessation of suffering by means of the Noble Eightfold Path. Again, this is a very basic teaching, yet it is not just a preliminary one. When examined deeply, it proves to cover the whole journey. Even the Mahamudra or Maha Ati systems do not present anything else. They just contain clearer and more direct means. The entire teaching of the Buddha is included in this path, which provides the basic guideline on how to work with and overcome the sources of suffering.

The branches of the Noble Eightfold Path are called right view, right thought, right speech, right action, right livelihood, right effort, right mindfulness, and right concentration. These can also be categorized into three, which are right view, right action, and right meditation. The view comprises right understanding and thought. The action includes right speech, livelihood, and effort; and the meditation is equivalent to right mindfulness and concentration.

Right View

Right view is the correct way of seeing things. This is considered to be the most important element of practice, since the basic problem to be solved comes from a wrong view, a perverted and distorted perception of reality. To get rid of our wrong views and attitudes is therefore the most fundamental issue in Buddhism. This does not mean that we should try to adopt a "Buddhist" way of seeing things. Rather, we should try to find out how things really are. Toward that end, an intellectual understanding is helpful, but is not sufficient by itself. What needs to be developed is the right view in terms of direct and genuine experience.

There is a difference between an understanding derived from a chain of reasoning and an actual experience or realization. By merely understanding it intellectually we are not able to annihilate any deep-rooted habit, let alone the fundamental root of suffering. Seeing reality directly as it is, without any doubt, is what completely shatters ignorance. So we need to arrive at this direct experiential vision. This is what is meant when the Buddha speaks of right understanding. A correct intellectual understanding, though, is a very important step toward this goal. In order to achieve the direct and clear view that is required, three aspects are needed: study, reflection, and meditation. Besides these, we also need the right circumstances. These are provided by right action and right livelihood. All of these are interrelated.

In this way the first branch of the Noble Eightfold Path is very important, since the right view is the real weapon against ignorance and confusion. The clear, direct, and unwavering experience of the truth is the only means to dispel all delusion. It is therefore the most essential and powerful practice. To arrive at this vision, we have to build our understanding gradually, starting with the Four Noble Truths. A correct knowledge of the Four Noble Truths is also right understanding. Knowing that things are constantly changing, that they are interrelated, and that nothing exists as a result of itself, we will eventually be able to see the nature of everything. So we should try to understand little by little, going deeper and deeper in this process. Once we are able to see that there is a cause to everything we experience, we will also see that there is an effect as well. Each cause, in turn, is the result of multiple causes. In this way, karma is just a sequence of causes and effects. This leads to an understanding of the impermanent nature of everything. If all things are both cause and effect, they keep changing. There is no real tangible substance to anything. Refining our understanding in this way, we will arrive at the genuine vision of the ultimate truth.

For my part, I try not to talk about this subject too much. There seems to be a reluctance to understand it correctly. A student once told me that she felt everything was empty and nonexistent, that there was no self. She said that she could not find anything concrete within her, that everything was flowing. At first I said this was very good, a certain experience of egolessness. Later I discovered that this was not quite what was happening. It was more like going crazy. When true egolessness is experienced, one is joyful and stable. All one's problems are solved. On the contrary, she became gloomier than she was before. She could not find any purpose in life. When the teaching on the absolute truth engenders such a feeling, something is wrong. Also, there are so many people who would say, "I do not like myself. I hate myself." To tell such a person, "You do not truly exist," would not be beneficial. Such persons have to be told beforehand, "You are very much there, you are very good, and first you must take care of yourself." If you say, "You are just an illusion," this will confirm the feeling that is already there, but in a totally distorted way. Human beings with this character trait first have to learn how to love, cherish, and appreciate themselves.

When the right view is described, it is usually called "the Middle Way." This term is used because our view should be free from any extreme. Knowing that everything arises in terms of cause and effect, we will not fall into the extreme of nihilism. There is not just nothing at all. On the other hand, cause and effect are not substantial either. They do not constitute a solid reality. As long as they are there, they are there. But as soon as they have changed, they have changed. Therefore, the right view is not eternalistic either. The truth lies in between.

This is not easy to grasp. Normally we understand in terms of this or that, black or white, yes or no. But the way things really are is not exactly a matter of these contrasts. It is slightly more complicated and beyond our usual yes-and-no approach. There is no word and no concept for it. As soon as we apply a word to it, it is solidified and thereby distorted. Right view is direct understanding without any words and concepts. That is what needs to be achieved. All the other branches of the Noble Eightfold Path are just different methods, which help us to develop the right view. Once it is there, our task is almost at its end.

If a word must be used to describe the right view, "interdependence" is a very good one. The term "emptiness" is often used but this can be a bit scary and is easily subject to misconception. Emptiness is nothing other than interdependence. It means that there is no independent substance to anything. Nothing exists as a result of itself; nothing is permanent or independent from everything else. Everything is conditioned and interrelated through being cause and effect. Once this interdependence is understood, we understand the empty nature of everything. In this way the right view is very basic and very advanced at the same time.

To generate this understanding, we should train ourselves through study, reflection, and meditation. These are the main methods to gain the right view. First, we gain information by listening to teachings or reading books and acquire an initial intellectual understanding. Then, the information is processed inwardly and we try to put it into place. We have heard about the Four Noble Truths, Mahamudra, bardo, wrathful deities, Madhyamaka, chö, and so forth. So where to put what? Where does it all fall into place. This process of gaining an all-encompassing view and putting everything where it belongs is the stage of reflection. Both study and reflection are intellectual. They do not really change our way of being. Meditation is needed to turn our intellectual understanding into an actual experience that allows us to be within it and bring it from the head to the heart. This is said to be the longest journey. With these three aspects we gradually develop the right view.

Right Thought

Here, it is most important to comprehend the predominant influence of thought. Whatever actions we do, right or wrong, are preceded and initiated by a thought. Many people will not agree with this and claim that their emotions, like anger for instance, come up before they can even think. Looking more closely, we will find this to be a misperception. For anger to arise, first there has to be the concept of something being unpleasant. This process will usually happen so fast that it goes unnoticed. It does not mean, though, that there is no initial thought giving rise to our anger. But since we are so used to it, that thought happens too quickly to be recognized. Everything that follows from this initial thought, all our positive and negative emotions, and even all the positive and negative deeds that we do, are habits we have acquired over time.

What kind of person we become is just a matter of habitual tendencies. The more we get into a particular habit, such as being prone to anger, jealousy, and so forth, the more we will turn into a person with this particular character. But for this same reason we are also able to change. Bad and good habits are equally changeable. The more we cultivate good habits, the more we will weaken the negative ones, and the other way around. This is the central point to be understood. In this context, Shantideva said, "If one is habituated, there is nothing that will not come easier." The more we familiarize ourselves with something, the more it will become our second nature. This is true of positive and negative tendencies alike.

So it is very important to understand that a thought is the master of every action we take. If we have thoughts characterized by kindness, compassion, love, or joy, our actions will have a corresponding quality. Our thoughts, in turn, are not arbitrary. They are habits that can be changed. This change has to be brought about actively. It will not happen by itself. For instance, if we would like to be a joyful person, we have to grow into this aptitude. We have to adopt the habit of being joyful. When we are very depressed and narrow, we cannot expect to become joyful just by wishfully thinking, "Now I am very sad, but something will happen." As if joy might fall from the sky. Buddhism says we have to do it ourselves. Then something will happen. The following story gives a good example of that.

A mother bird nested in a field and hatched her chicks. When the chicks had come out of the shell, the mother went away every day to fetch food and came back in the evening. One day, she found her children deeply worried. In a great flurry they told her, "We have to leave immediately. We are in big danger! The farmer has been here with his son. They said they want to reap the grain tomorrow, so they are getting all their neighbors in the village to help them." The mother reassured them, "Don't worry. Just sit here quietly. Nothing will happen." The next day, she went out as usual and her words proved to be true. Upon her return, again the chicks were very excited and told her, "The farmer and his son have been here once more and said they will now harvest the grain tomorrow. Since none of the neighbors had time, they are going to ask all their relatives for help." Again the mother soothed them and said, "Don't be anxious. Nothing will happen." When she returned the following day, the chicks were quite calm and relaxed. She had been right again. Nothing had happened. They told her, though, that the farmer and his son had been around again and had mentioned that, since the grain still needed to be cut and since their relatives did not have time either, they would do it on their own the following day. Hearing this, the mother was alerted and said, "Get ready, we are no longer safe here. We will leave as soon as we can."

So our habits will not change unless we change them ourselves. In this context, our thoughts are the main objective, since they are the starting point for all our actions. Our thoughts determine whether we act in a right or wrong way, as well as what kind of person we become. As soon as we have the right thoughts, our actions cannot go amiss. In the beginning, the attempt to reform our habits of thought will not prove so easy. We may have the impression that there is no progress at all. Yet there will be progress, as is illustrated by the meditation method that a great master gave to one of his disciples. He made the disciple get two bowls and two heaps of black and white pebbles. The master then told him to put a white pebble into one of the bowls whenever a good thought came to his mind and to put a black pebble into the other bowl for every negative thought that arose. During the first few months, the black pebbles piled up, while the white ones were very scarce. Then slowly, the picture changed. The black pebbles got less and less, and the white ones increased, until finally the bowl for the black pebbles remained empty. This shows the way to reform ourselves and cultivate our motivation. We should try to be as aware as possible. It does not mean that we should feel guilty each time we have a negative thought. Simply by being aware and by continuously exercising this awareness, our negative thoughts will gradually decrease and make way for more and more good ones.

Right Speech and Right Action

As far as right speech and right action are concerned, the way to develop them is similar to the method described in the context of right thought. All together, these three relate to the triad of body, speech, and mind, the three factors without which a human being cannot do anything. So we should try to act in a positive way with all three of these. Good verbal and physical action is whatever is beneficial to ourselves and to all our fellow beings. So we should do our best to cultivate this kind of activity and to increase it to an ever greater extent.

Some people think that when anger arises, for instance, it should be expressed and let out. Otherwise, it might be suppressed and eventually develop into an illness. There is a certain truth in that. If we keep something in our heart and cannot let go, if we do not speak of it but think about it all the time, we suppress whatever emotion is there. Yet if, on the contrary, we do not hold on to it, if we simply get angry and that is it, there is neither suppression involved nor is there any need to let the anger out. Here we should look into the question of where our anger comes from. Some people seem to think that it exists in the body, as if there was a little bag of anger that we take from when we need it. Our emotions, though, are not stored within us. As long as we do not get angry, there is no anger. By thinking that it exists permanently, we will make it stronger whenever it arises.

It is therefore quite important to understand that our emotions are not constantly present. For this reason, we should not be too upset when anger arises. If we get angry, all right, leave it at that. Do not take it further. It has happened so many times before. It is nothing unusual. There is no need to feel guilty about it. Feeling guilty, we will also hold on to our anger, we will keep it alive and prolong it, thus making more out of it than is actually there. The important point is to acknowledge the fact that we have become angry, but then not to keep it and make it stronger. The right way of taming anger and the other negative emotions is to try to cultivate their opposite sides. The antidote to anger is loving-kindness. The more we develop loving-kindness, the less our anger will become.

The same is true of jealousy. The more we indulge in this feeling, the more it will grow in power. Whereas, the more deeply we can understand how useless it is and how harmful it is to ourselves and others, to the same extent it will be weakened and gradually decrease. This applies to everything. The more extensively we train in something, the more strongly it will develop and eventually turn into our own experience. We must therefore submit ourselves to a certain amount of discipline. If, for example, we are inclined to talk in a very harsh way, or talk too much, or chatter meaninglessly, we should try to use speech that is beneficial to ourselves and the people we meet, and thus create a better atmosphere. When we talk to someone, whether or not that person gets angry does not depend so much on what is expressed, but rather on the way it is said.

We should therefore try to discipline ourselves to not do or say just whatever comes to mind all the time. Instead, we should try to see clearly which way of saying and doing things will be beneficial to ourselves and our fellow beings and what course of action would create a lot of problems. We are free to choose our own behavior. We do not have to be dominated by our emotions. We should be under our own control and try to change for the better.

Right Livelihood

The difference between right action and right livelihood is that the latter refers to the manner we earn our living. Ideally, this should not be harmful at all, but of utmost benefit to ourselves and to all sentient beings. Very often, though, there is not so much opportunity to choose our livelihood. In this situation, we should do whatever we can to act as beneficially as possible. Whenever there is no way for that, we should at least do our best not to cause any harm to ourselves and to other sentient beings.

Right Effort and Right Mindfulness

Right effort and right mindfulness are needed to cultivate all the other branches of the Noble Eightfold Path. Frequently, we do not use our energy in the right way. Often, we are willing to make a great effort for things that are not worthwhile at all, but not for things that would be beneficial for us. Right effort, therefore, means to control our actions and direct our energy in the right way.

Once the right course of action is understood, mindfulness is needed to apply this understanding correctly. The degree to which we can do something meaningful depends on the degree to which we are mindful. As long as we are not mindful, we will fall into our habits and just follow our usual ways. To avoid this, we have to bring ourselves back to the present and try to remind ourselves constantly of the best thing to do. Bringing our mind back to the present moment, we prevent it from being scattered. This is the main issue of practice. Toward this aim, effort is needed, since we are not used to doing positive or beneficial things. For this reason, we will not always like it and will not always find it easy. We will often prefer to idle away our time, just walking around or spending the day gambling and drinking.

To counteract our habits, it is therefore necessary to exert a certain amount of effort. We set our mindfulness and awareness against them. Doing this again and again, we will carry the practice of Dharma into our daily lives. There is no special technique to apply. It is simply done through mindfulness and effort. How much we practice in this way depends entirely on ourselves. As has been said earlier, we ourselves are the practice. There is no other practice apart from ourselves, and practice is not assigned to a special time. The whole day is practice. We constantly face all kinds of difficulties and emotions. Whenever we manage to be mindful in dealing with these, we practice. In this way we can turn each aspect of everyday life into practice.

Right Concentration

All the different kinds of Buddhist meditation can be categorized into either of two techniques. In Sanskrit these are called *shamatha* and *vipashyana*; in Tibetan they are called *shiné* and *lhakthong*. *Shi* means "peace" or "tranquility" and also "subsiding." *Né* means "stable abiding." Thus, *shiné* can be translated as "calm abiding." *Lhak* means "extraordinary," and can also mean "clear" and "vivid" or "without any obstruction." *Thong* means "seeing." *Lhakthong* therefore is "clear seeing" or "special insight." Of the two aspects of meditation, *shiné* is the means to make the mind calm, stable, and peaceful, and *lhakthong* will lead us to clearly see the truth, the true nature of everything. All meditations are included in these two.

There are different traditions regarding the order in which these should be practiced. Some say that *shiné* has to come first, otherwise, it will not be possible to see the true nature of mind. Normally our mind is in too much turmoil, too confused, rough like a wild churning sea. First, the mind has to become calm and thereby eventually clear. When the mind is calm and clear, this forms the condition to see its true nature.

Then again, it is said that there is a danger in just letting the mind dwell in calmness and clarity for too long. The ego can get attached to this state, which is experienced as being so nice that it can result in falling into the extreme of tranquility. If this happens, no further progress will be possible. Thus a second tradition says that one should not try to completely attain *shiné* before beginning to practice *lhakthong*. Once a certain level of *shiné* is reached, it is advised to take a break and proceed to *lhakthong* meditation. According to a third tradition, one should train in *lhakthong* first, since a certain amount of understanding is needed as a prerequisite to any practice.

In my view these differences in approach are not that important at the moment. It is vital for all of us to make our mind calm and clear, not only as a means to see the truth, but to enable us to deal with our emotions and to be more relaxed in our everyday lives. Furthermore, once the mind is calm, there is a greater chance of seeing clearly. How much is then seen depends upon the extent to which we look and know how to look. Both aspects are necessary, and in the end they should be in union.

As for *shiné* meditation, the main idea can be described as follows. If water is clouded by dirt, an easy method to clarify it is to leave it undisturbed and to let the dirt settle by itself. Similarly, if the mind is left to itself without interference, its waves, confusions, and bubblings will slowly subside, and it will become calm and clear. The technique, therefore, is very simple. Nothing at all is done. Then again, not doing anything is not that easy. So we have to start by doing something to occupy our mind very lightly, occupying it only to the extent that not too many things can take place within it.

For *shiné* meditation it is traditionally said that the physical posture is very important, since body and mind have a very deep relationship. The posture of the body affects the mind in many ways. Once the physical posture is correct, its effect on the mind will be very positive. There is a story in the sutras in which a group of monkeys watch some arhats meditating in the woods. Later these monkeys were seen sitting in the same posture. Through this, they actually attained the state of *shiné*.

The correct posture for *shiné* meditation is called "the seven-point posture." Once one is used to it, it is very comfortable and meditation can be sustained for long periods without feeling physical pain or discomfort. Of the seven points, the first is most important: the back should be as straight as possible. The other six points are just aids to facilitate this. If we are able to do so, we should sit cross-legged, ideally in the full vajra-position. If we find it too difficult, we should just sit on a chair and not worry—Maitreya himself, the future Buddha, sits on a chair.

The hands should be in the so-called *dhyana mudra*, the right hand on top of the left and the thumbs slightly touching each other. This helps to balance the shoulders. The shoulders should not lean to the right or to the left, since the first will promote the arising of desire and the second the arising of anger. The hands can also sometimes rest on the knees. The chest and the shoulders should be expanded to allow the breath to flow in and out as deeply as possible. The neck should neither be held to the back nor to the front too much; it should just slightly bend forward so that the Adam's apple is not seen.

The mouth should be relaxed. If this area is too tight, it will almost always create tension. The teeth should be a bit apart and the lips slightly parted as well, so that it is possible to breathe through them if wanted. The tongue should touch the upper palate and be placed flatly against it. This is a very good way to prevent having to swallow saliva too often.

The central point is to relax the eyes. As soon as the eyes are relaxed, the body and mind are relaxed as well. Without relaxing the eyes, there is no way to relax the body and mind. Some people prefer to close their eyes, but according to the Tibetan Buddhist tradition, the eyes should not be completely closed. They should be left slightly open, neither looking too far away nor too close, and not getting cross-eyed either. This can be seen from buddha images or from the photographs of great masters. Though the eyes are not closed, the gaze should not be tense or focused on anything in particular. The eyes should be just lightly open. Again, this is a general rule, so it does not always apply. Sometimes, when the mind is very active, it can be better to close the eyes. At other times, the mind may get so sleepy that the eyes will close involuntarily. In this case, it may be advisable to open them quite wide and even look up high into the sky or into the far distance.

In *shiné* meditation, the posture of the mind is what is truly essential. The mind should be completely relaxed. To achieve this relaxation, we should first try to feel our body being totally relaxed. Although we sit in this posture, which is slightly tense, within it there should be looseness and spaciousness. When the string tying a bundle of straw is cut, the tension is released and the pieces of straw immediately fall into a perfect circle: there is total release and total order at the same time. Similarly, we should feel this relaxation from the core of our being, and then let the mind be. That is the main point. As long as we are in the present moment, we are relaxed.

In *shiné* meditation a widely used practice is to be just lightly aware of breathing. This is a very suitable method, since breathing happens automatically and we are never without it. Being aware of our breathing we will be here and now, aware of the present moment. That is the central issue. Not being involved in the past or future, we should take a vacation from our hard work and just relax. We should allow ourselves to think, "For fifteen minutes I will be off duty, away from my usual routine of being immersed in my past and future worries." This is possible in all kinds of situations, while sitting in our room or in a railway station, wherever we have a bit of time. There are many methods to just sit and relax. The essential point is to be here and now, in the present moment, neither in the past nor in the future.

When using the "breathing method," we should not concentrate on the breath in the literal sense. Our concentration should be very light, since the aim is to loosen our tension while trying to be calm and clear. If we concentrate too much, we will counteract this and build up tension. For this reason, there should be just a light awareness. The mind is allowed to be aware of the process of breathing in and out. This only forms a kind of basis for the mind to settle upon. The eyes and ears are not closed. We are not trying to cut off or avoid anything. When, for instance, a car passes by, this is all right. We should not pursue the event thinking, "This car disturbed me." The passing of the car is just one moment, and then it is over. There is no need to think about it. We should just be with our breathing without wondering, "How do I breathe in and out?"

We could occupy our mind with anything in this way, not only with breathing. The aim is to be aware of the present moment and not to think about it. Thinking means to bring something that already happened back through our memory and to analyze it. As soon as we think, we are no longer here but elsewhere. We should let it flow. Whenever we hold on to something, we interrupt the flow.

In learning how to do *shiné* meditation or any other meditation practice, mere struggle and deliberate trial are of little use. Too much trying is not very helpful. Although a great amount of effort is needed, this effort should consist merely of the willingness to do the practice again and again. There is no real technique, in the sense of something being taught and learned and then applied accordingly. We learn through doing. This can be compared to the way swimming or riding a bicycle is learned. Someone who knows how to do it will say, "Just be flexible and relaxed and don't forget to pedal." Then you sit on your bike and tell yourself, "I have to be flexible and relaxed." But this will not prevent you from falling off. If you keep at it, though, a point will be reached when you find, to your astonishment, that you do not fall down any longer. You have learned how to do it, but do not know how it happened. Once it has happened, there is no more struggle. Almost the same process is true of meditation.

In the Tibetan tradition, the experience of meditation is sometimes described through three characteristics: *dé, lhö,* and *yang. Dé* means "comfortable" and refers to just sitting comfortably at ease without any pain or discomfort. *Lhö* is the opposite of tightness, and describes a state of total relaxation. *Yang* means "spacious," and it is saying that we should be very open and wide. Meditation is not equivalent to controlling our mind, to putting it into a small box or narrow canal. There is no need to shut our eyes and other senses. We should be open to such an extent that we almost dissolve into and merge with everything. This is not brought about through deliberate trial. Thus these three important features of meditation—feeling comfortably at ease, relaxed, and spacious—may not be achieved very easily. They have to come one by one.

Just in order to learn how to relax, a lot of exercise is needed. We will not find it easy. Just letting go, letting everything be, not doing anything is totally opposite to our usual way of behavior. Once we are able to give in a bit, to relax our muscles, our stomach, our shoulders, and finally our eyes, that in itself is already meditation. Doing a yoga exercise can be helpful. First one feels the total relaxation of the trunk and then gradually the relaxation of the feet, ankles, calves, knees, and thighs. From here, one slowly feels the intestines relax, the kidneys, liver, and so forth. Then one proceeds to the hands and shoulders, to the face and mouth, until one finally arrives at the eyes. The relaxation of the eyes is most vital. According to Buddhism the eyes are directly related to our heart. They are said to be the doors to the mind. Once we can relax our eyes, we can really relax. This is quite difficult, since almost all our tensions are channeled through the heart. In order to learn how to relax the eyes, we should neither fully close nor fully open them. This point is very important.

So, *shiné* meditation in its actual sense means not doing anything, just letting ourselves be. For this reason, even though a focal point—such as breathing, an image, a light, or a letter—is used to settle the mind, these things are not necessary as such. They are just used when one finds that the mind is too turbulent or distracted. In this situation, it is sometimes helpful to have something that allows the mind to settle down, something that lightly occupies it. This is the only reason why these means are applied, and one could make use of anything that serves this purpose, not just breathing, an image, and so on. In Tibet, pebbles or sticks were sometimes taken as a focus in meditation. The main thing is to know when we are distracted. As soon as this happens, the mind should be lightly settled back on whichever focus is used. Whenever we find that the mind is not really there, we simply bring it back. Meditation is just a means to make ourselves calm, relaxed, and spacious, and thereby eventually clear.

In this context, two faults can arise. One is distraction, a state in which the mind is not present. The other is sleepiness or dullness. Both are not meditation. When distracted, one should apply a bit of introspection. One should either be more alert or more relaxed, whichever proves necessary to bring the mind back to focus. When having fallen into dullness, we should be more alert. We should look up or make ourselves slightly tense. Machig Labdrönma described the right balance in meditation with the example of how to produce thread from yarn by twining the yarn, alternately tightening and loosening it. Similarly, when meditating, there should be a certain tension and a certain softness as well.

There are many different meditation techniques, just as there are many different types of human beings. Depending on the individual, one method will be more suitable than others. Apart from that, it does not matter very much which technique is used. Each will lead to three experiences—to bliss, clarity, and nonconception. I feel that one should not talk too much about these experiences, as it might arouse expectations that would kill the meditation. One technique, which can be combined with breathing, is to concentrate on the area four fingers below the navel and to imagine some warmth there, a kind of vibrating comfort that is then totally spread throughout the whole body. One feels very comfortable and blissful, very nice and warm. When this feeling is there, just remain within it. It is much easier to concentrate on something nice than on something that is not agreeable. Feeling blissful, comfortable, happy, and warm is therefore quite a good method. Different techniques can also be alternated, such as focusing on the breath for five minutes and then resting five minutes without any focus, just being within the sensation of our blissful nature.

Sound is another good object for *shiné* meditation. When a mantra is recited, for example, this is nothing other than concentrating on sound. In Hinduism, sheer concentration on sound is practiced much more widely than in the Buddhist context. One can concentrate on the sound of the syllable OM for instance. Just saying it slowly will keep the attention. Some individuals have a "sound nature." Especially in the West, many people say that they find visualization quite difficult and that it is far easier for them to remember a sound than a form. Concentrating on the syllable OM—the origin of all sounds and words—is also a method of meditation. In the same way, one can use a mantra—no matter which one—such as the mantra of Avalokiteshvara: OM MANI PADME HUNG.

As was mentioned before, we have to learn how to meditate by ourselves through trial and error. We have to fall down and get up and do it again. Recently I learned how to swim. In Tibet the opportunity did not arise, and there is no chance to do that in Sikkim where I live. The rivers come down like swords. Last year, I spent some time in Barcelona and was taken to a very nice beach where I was taught how to swim. I did not do very well. I was told that I had to do this and that. Yet, whatever I tried did not work. I always went down head first. Then the people teaching me said, "If you just lie on your back, you will float." That did not work either. At last, I was a bit frustrated and said, "Let it be whatever happens." Then somehow, my ears went in but the rest did not. I floated. It was the most wonderful feeling. And it was actually fear that was preventing it. When there is no fear, we can float. As soon as it comes back, I will go under again. I can float when I know I am in touch.

This captures the way we learn how to meditate. In the beginning, we will often find that we cannot completely relax, we cannot be totally tranquil and peaceful. Sometimes we may even feel that during meditation more disturbances occur than when we are not meditating. Then we may think we are getting worse and worse, but actually this is said to be a good sign. It does not mean that we are more distracted; rather it means that we are more aware of how busy our mind usually is. If we have the feeling that more things come up in our mind, that it is more agitated and unable to be peaceful, this does not mean that meditation is not taking place. During this time many people give up, thinking, "This is too hard. I can't get any peace!" In this situation, patience is needed to be able to carry on. If we patiently continue, we will find it gets much better.

One may wonder whether it is possible to reach enlightenment solely through *shiné* meditation. Though this is not possible, *shiné* is indispensable. We may not get enlightened just by being peaceful and clear, but the other part, the part that brings about enlightenment, will almost arise spontaneously once a good and strong state of *shiné* is reached. This other part is *lhakthong*, or insight, seeing the truth. Once the mind is calm and clear, and we do not get stuck in the experience of calmness and clarity, all we need to do is to look. This is called the union of *shiné* and *lhakthong*. This union will result in enlightenment. Shantideva has said in this context, "Insight born from strong *shamatha* is what totally destroys all the negative emotions." For this reason, *shiné* is the foremost practice.

Shiné has to lead to insight, or *lhakthong*, which is seeing things as they really are, seeing the truth. This is not comparable to the way we see with our eyes. It means being in sheer awareness. This will be explained later, in the context of Mahamudra. Within Mahamudra practice, *lhakthong* is the main issue. *Lhakthong* is seeing things vividly, knowing the truth, not just intellectually but directly, without any confusion. This is what really cuts through ignorance, the root cause of all our problems.

There is a traditional Tibetan drawing that depicts the development of *shiné* and *lhakthong*. It shows a road winding upwards with various different scenes. At the beginning of the road, there is a monk carrying a hook and a rope, chasing after a huge black elephant that has run wild, and is being led on by a monkey. The rope and the hook represent mindfulness and awareness, the main instruments used in meditation. The wild black elephant, led by an equally wild monkey, represents our mind in its present state. A wild elephant is very dangerous. It goes everywhere and cannot be easily controlled. Being so big, it crashes into everything. On top of that it is led by a monkey, an animal that cannot sit still even for a single instant. In the same way, our mind is always busy and totally distracted, as if it were being led around by a monkey. It is wild like an untamed elephant and also dull and confused, which is represented by the elephant being black. Meditating and meditating, we run after the elephant trying to use our tools on it.

After some time, distractions will slow up a bit, and there will be a certain amount of clarity. At this point, the elephant and the monkey are still there, but they are no longer running. This image should not be taken too literally though. While meditating, we should actually not run after anything. The less we run the better. Meditation means to know how to be, how to sit and let things be. We cannot run after our mind. Trying to do so is like trying to

The development of *shiné* and *lhakthong*

catch water with our hands. Especially if we try to hold on tightly, everything goes away. What is needed is a very skillful way of letting be and letting ourselves relax. When we can do that, we know how to meditate. This is only learned through doing, like learning how to swim or ride a bicycle. It will not be achieved through thinking or reading a book about it. Once we get the rope of our mindfulness onto the elephant, we hold it. We are able to hold on to our mind for a little while. At this point the monkey is still with the elephant, but it is not really leading anymore. This will come and go from moment to moment, but as long as we have a grip, the monkey's leadership is broken.

Then, a new problem comes up. This is represented by a rabbit sitting on top of the elephant. A rabbit may, in the midst of running, suddenly duck into hiding. It can fall into a kind of trance lasting for quite a long time. In this state, one can even touch it. So the rabbit signifies subtle dullness. So far, we have been trying so hard to get our mind settled. Now that it has happened, the idea comes up, "I am very peaceful. At last I have got it, I am a great meditator!" But maybe we are just doing the rabbit thing. That is the extreme opposite of agitation. The mind is not distracted anymore. It is there, but more or less sleepy, in a kind of trance, a dull stability. This is not the right kind of meditation. If we enter into this type of state and cannot get out of it, we will not advance any further. It is therefore regarded as an obstacle. To go beyond it, we need to rouse ourselves. Once we have overcome agitation and are able to concentrate on one thing, we must be aware of this subtle dullness and work on it by means of creating more clarity. This process is represented by the elephant starting to lose its black color and becoming progressively whiter. This means that clarity increases. We are not just stable but also becoming clear.

Next the practitioner is not only using the rope, but the hook is also on the elephant. He has gained real control, walking in front and leading the elephant. Distraction is lagging behind. The monkey still tries to keep up, but is very tired and almost unable to do so. Soon, it is seen being dragged along on all fours, desperately holding on to the tail of the elephant. The meditator walks ahead and does not even need to use the hook on the elephant anymore. We are now able to practice in our daily lives and not just in meditation sessions. Even when not meditating, the mind will follow. It is more settled and clear.

This is getting very near to the actual and final state of *shiné*. The elephant is almost completely white and just walking. There is no need to lead it, and the monkey is left behind. Distraction is gone. Then the elephant is totally white. Whatever we do, the mind follows. A state of nonmeditation is reached. When we sit, it sits. When we walk, it walks. This is *shinjang*, a suppleness and flexibility of body and mind that is the final state of *shiné*. The mind is completely trained, totally under control. It has reached the utmost level of peace and clarity.

From there onward, we just have to look. Then *lhakthong* comes. The last scene in the drawing shows the monk being surrounded by flowers, as he sits on the completely white elephant and holds a flaming sword. Riding the elephant and wielding the sword of wisdom, we are prepared to eliminate ignorance. Our flaming sword can burn and cut through the root of ignorance, thus destroying the causes of suffering.

So the technique is very simple. We just use mindfulness and awareness as our instruments in meditation. When meditating, we have to deal with distraction and dullness, implementing mindfulness and awareness to overcome them. We just need to do it. *Shiné* meditation is really working with our mind. It is not something that we can measure in terms of time or counting, such as saying, "Now I have done a three-year retreat. Now I have completed one hundred thousand mantras of Tara. Now I am great!" It is not like that. *Shiné* meditation means working on ourselves. The only measurement is how much experience there is. We cannot cheat. We have to be honest and just see ourselves. For this reason we will sometimes feel that it is quite difficult. It is said, though, that if one is really able to do it, *shiné* meditation is not hard at all. If we only practice twenty minutes a day, we may not be able to reach that stage. We must therefore try to integrate it really into our daily lives. Sitting for thirty minutes in a quiet place may be helpful, but making it part of our lives will have a far greater effect.

How should mindfulness and awareness be applied in our daily lives? This has to be done with a sense of proportion. I know a Buddhist institution where people are so mindful and aware that you cannot get an answer to your phone call! The person in charge hears the phone ring and is then mindful and aware of everything that is happening: "The telephone is ringing. I must be mindful and aware. Now I am standing up. Now I am walking toward it." By the time they are ready to pick up the receiver, the telephone has stopped ringing quite a while ago. One of my German friends said, "Mindfulness is great. But this is maybe going too far."

To bring mindfulness and awareness into our daily lives means to be mindful and aware of what we are and what we are doing. A Zen master said, "When I eat, I eat. And when I sleep, I sleep." This is not what we usually do. I brush my teeth and do not know where my mind is. I eat and cannot remember what I have eaten. We are not there. Our elephant has run away. We should therefore try to be at one with whatever we are doing.

If we are there the moment we are doing something, we can deal with it much more clearly and efficiently. Then as soon as we leave it, we should leave it. We can rest. We are not forced to carry something in our mind all the time. This is the reason why we have so much stress and tension. We continuously carry a problem in our mind. So when we are doing puja, we should be doing puja. When we are working, we should be working. There is no need to bring problems into it. If we have to deal with a problem, we should deal with the problem. Once we can apply this principle to our lives, there will be a lot less problems.

Many problems are also created by postponing what ought to be done. For instance, I have a tendency to not answer letters very quickly. To counteract this I wrote, "Eliminate procrastination!" on a sheet of paper and put it on a wall in my room. One day, while I was away, a very good friend came by and wrote underneath, "From tomorrow!" When I get a letter I usually think, "Oh, very nice. I will reply to it tomorrow." After a week I say, "I must really do it." In this way, all these letters pile up and are always in my mind. To actually answer them would maybe take two hours. Instead of doing it, I think about it all the time. In this way, I get very tense but still never do it. So knowing how to do it is very simple, but actually doing it is not that easy.

PART TWO

MAHAYANA

The Thirty-seven Practices of a Bodhisattva

To GIVE AN OVERVIEW of the Mahayana path, I will discuss a short but very important work entitled *The Thirty-seven Practices of a Bodhisattva*. This was written by Ngulchü Thogmé, a highly acclaimed scholar and saint who was known as a genuine bodhisattva because he truly practiced what he taught. He composed some important texts on the bodhisattva practices, including a commentary on Shantideva's *Bodhicharyavatara*. *The Thirty-seven Practices of a Bodhisattva* presents the content of the *Bodhicharyavatara* in a concise form to make it convenient to remember and practice.

The Tibetan title of the text, *Gyalsä Laglen*, is sometimes translated as *The Conduct of the Sons of the Victorious One*. This is not entirely satisfactory, since the reference to "sons" might incorrectly suggest that women cannot be bodhisattvas. *Gyal* is short for *gyalwa*, which means "the Victorious One," an epithet of the Buddha. The Buddha is called "the Victorious One" since he overcame all obstacles, defilements, and negative forces. *Sä* is the honorific word for "child," either male or female. The term *gyalsä* does not refer to a small child but suggests a prince or princess who, by becoming enlightened, will be the Buddha's successor, his heir or heiress.

In Western languages there is considerable emphasis on gender, and different words are used for men and women, whereas in Tibetan this distinction is hardly made, and is especially absent in honorific speech. For instance, the nonhonorific pronouns *kho* and *mo* are the words for "he" and "she," but the honorific pronoun *khong* refers to both. It is quite important to bear this in mind when translating Tibetan Buddhist texts, as otherwise the false impression might be created that Buddhism belittles women.

Ngulchü Thogmé starts his work with the Sanskrit phrase *Namo Lokeshvaraya*, which means, "I bow down to the Savior of the World." Following the ancient Indian tradition, Tibetan Buddhist scriptures begin with words of homage and what is called the "promise to write." When the teachings of the Buddha were translated into Tibetan, the translators usually kept the title and homage in Sanskrit to remind the readers of the source of the teachings and to show respect for the language of the Buddha's home country. For the same reasons this tradition was later continued in compositions that originated in Tibet.

Ngulchü Thogmé's homage is addressed to the bodhisattva of compassion, called *Avalokiteshvara* in Sanskrit and *Chenrezig* in Tibetan. *Loka* means "world" and *ishvara* means "lord" or "savior." Avalokiteshvara is called "the Savior of the World" because he embodies shepherdlike bodhisattva activity and is one of the greatest and most courageous bodhisattvas.

A bodhisattva is someone who says from the depth of his or her heart, "I want to be liberated and find ways to overcome all the problems of the world. I want to help all my fellow beings to do likewise. I long to attain the highest state of everlasting peace and happiness, in which all suffering has ceased, and I want to do so for myself and for all sentient beings." According to the Buddha's teaching, anyone who makes this firm and heartfelt commitment is a bodhisattva. We become bodhisattvas from the moment we have this vast and open heart, called *bodhichitta*, the mind bent on bringing lasting happiness to all sentient beings.

Buddhist literature defines three types of bodhisattvas: the kinglike bodhisattva, the captainlike bodhisattva, and the shepherdlike bodhisattva. A kinglike bodhisattva is like a good king who first wants everything luxurious for himself, like a big palace, a large entourage, a beautiful queen, and so on. But once his happiness has been achieved, he also wants to help and support his subjects as much as possible. Accordingly, a kinglike bodhisattva has the motivation, "First, I want to free myself from samsara and attain perfect enlightenment. As soon as I have reached buddhahood, I will help all other sentient beings to become buddhas as well."

A captainlike bodhisattva would say, "I would like to become a buddha, and I will take all other sentient beings along with me so that we reach enlightenment together." This is just as the captain of a ship crosses the sea, he takes his passengers with him, and they reach the far shore simultaneously.

A shepherdlike bodhisattva is inspired by thinking, "I want to help all sentient beings to reach enlightenment and see the truth. Only when this is achieved and samsara is emptied will I become a buddha myself." In actual fact it may not happen this way, but anyone who has this motivation is called a "shepherdlike bodhisattva." In the old days, sheep were not kept in fenced pastures, and the shepherds had to bring them down from the mountains to protect them from wolves. They would follow behind the sheep, guiding them into their pen and lock them in. A shepherd would take care of his sheep first, and only then would he go home and eat.

The bodhisattva Avalokiteshvara developed this shepherdlike motivation and is therefore considered to be the most courageous and compassionate of beings. He vowed, "I will not attain complete enlightenment until I have led all sentient beings to liberation without leaving a single one behind." Because of this utterly selfless and far-reaching promise, Avalokiteshvara is called the "father of all bodhisattvas," "the main bodhisattva," and "the embodiment of compassion." So, to begin this text on how to practice the bodhisattva's way of life, it is appropriate to pay homage to him. The text says:

Namo Lokeshvaraya

To the supreme guru and protector Avalokiteshvara,
Who sees all phenomena as being devoid of coming and going
And yet solely strives for the welfare of beings,
I always bow down in deep respect with body, speech, and mind.

This stanza describes the understanding of a highly realized bodhisattva. With such a realization one sees the true nature of oneself and everything else. In light of this understanding, nothing has any coming or going. Usually, we believe that we come and go, that we are born and die, and that everything keeps on happening. In this frame of mind, when something good happens, we like it very much, and when something bad happens, we do not like it at all and become afraid of it. We view everything as positive or negative, and as long as we maintain these two ways of seeing, we are driven by aversion and attachment. Aversion, in particular, is the main source of all our fear. Once we are afraid, we try to run away from what is fearful, and we cling to whatever might prevent the object of our dislike from getting too close. We become attached to the apparent protection we envisage, but this is no solution, as our aversion is still there. This dualistic way of reacting is regarded as the basic source of all our suffering.

When it says here that all phenomena are devoid of coming and going, this means that an enlightened bodhisattva sees the truth, the way things are. This is seeing directly without adding any concept or philosophy. Within this clear vision there is not the slightest doubt about anything, so there is no need for clinging or running away. A realized bodhisattva has no dualistic view.

Within this sheer and naked seeing, spontaneous compassion arises. Once we no longer feel compelled to cling to ourselves and fixate on our own problems all the time, we can look around and see everything clearly. We can perceive others' lives and understand how and why they experience their problems. Although we see that others are suffering greatly, we know that their suffering is almost needless. They are not doomed to be in pain, because their suffering just comes from a wrong way of seeing and reacting. If they could see how things truly are, they would not suffer anymore. This is the understanding of an enlightened being.

Genuine bodhisattvas are not disturbed by whatever occurs, although they see what is happening. Their vision gives rise to a strong and spontaneous wish to help every sentient being who has not attained this seeing. This aspiration will result in spontaneous actions to help anyone who suffers. A bodhisattva who sees the truth has no aversion and clinging, and therefore no fear and attachment either. So, the problems of others are seen as being illusory and based upon ignorance. At the same time, a bodhisattva sees the extent to which all these beings suffer. Knowing how easy it is to step out of the vicious cycle of ignorance and the suffering ensuing from it, a bodhisattva has the sole wish to relieve them from all their pain.

For this reason, Ngulchü Thogmé praises a bodhisattva as someone who knows that phenomena are devoid of coming and going, and yet strives solely for the welfare of beings. When we pay homage to someone, it reflects our appreciation and desire to follow and be like that person. So, the first stanza expresses the intention of being a bodhisattva, which forms the beginning. At the same time, it describes the main objective when following the bodhisattva path. This is seeing the truth, since bodhisattva motivation stems from seeing one's own and others' problems as they really are, and results in the wish to do something about them.

A bodhisattva's quest for truth is a kind of research based on personal experience. It is not a scientific approach, however, like when one tries to find the number of particles in an object or to measure the distance from the earth to the moon. On the spiritual path, seeking the truth means to try to see the nature of things, especially in relation to our own problems and surroundings. We try to see the phenomenal world as a whole and to sense its texture and nature.

Above all, our search is directed toward our mind, because when we feel problems and suffering, they are part of our own experience. We search for the facts of life, for the truth in our own experience. We question ourselves and ask, "What are my problems and how do they occur? How does my suffering arise? How do I become fearful? What can I do about my problems? What is it that I do not know about them? To what extent am I creating my problems myself? How much is due to my conditioning? What part does my own confusion play? To what extent am I ignorant and seeing reality in a distorted way? What is it within me that feels all this attachment and aversion, fear and excitement?"

The way to find the truth is to see reality clearly and precisely. So, a bodhisattva will deeply penetrate these questions and seek to gain a correct understanding. This understanding is then used to find solutions, not only for oneself but for all sentient beings. In this context, compassion for others and working for their benefit is not only the objective. It is also the path and method to see the truth.

The first step toward this goal is to try to open up. Usually we are so preoccupied with our problems that we cannot see anything else. There is a story about a princess who had a small eye problem that she felt was really bad. Being the king's daughter, she was rather spoiled and kept crying all the time. When the doctors wanted to apply medicine, she would invariably refuse any medical treatment and kept touching the sore spot on her eye. In this way it became worse and worse, until finally the king proclaimed a large reward for whoever could cure his daughter. After some time, a man arrived who claimed to be a famous physician, but actually was not even a doctor. He declared that he could definitely cure the princess and was admitted to her chamber. After he had examined her, he exclaimed, "Oh, I'm so sorry!" "What is it?," the princess inquired. The doctor said, "There is nothing much wrong with your eye, but there is something else that is really serious." The princess was alarmed and asked, "What on earth is so serious?" He hesitated and said, "It is really bad. I shouldn't tell you about it." No matter how much she insisted, he refused to tell her, saying that he could not speak without the king's permission.

When the king arrived, the doctor was still reluctant to reveal his findings. Finally the king commanded, "Tell us what is wrong. Whatever it is, you have to tell us!" At last the doctor said, "Well, the eye will get better within a few days—that is no problem. The big problem is that the princess will grow a tail, which will become at least nine fathoms long. It may start growing very soon. If she can detect the first moment it appears, I might be able to do something about it. But once it has come out, no one will be able to prevent it from growing." At this news everyone was deeply concerned. And the princess, what did she do? She stayed in bed, day and night, directing all her attention to detect when the tail might appear. Thus, after a few days, her eye got well.

This shows how we usually react. We focus on our little problem and it becomes the center around which everything else revolves. So far, we have done this repeatedly, life after life. We think, "My wishes, my interests, my likes and dislikes come first!" As long as we function on this basis, we will remain unchanged. Driven by impulses of desire and rejection, we will travel the roads of samsara without finding a way out. As long as attachment and aversion are our sources of living and drive us onward, we cannot rest.

There is no way to find peace as long as we maintain the momentum of our selfishness. "My" and "I" are all-pervading. I feel I am the center of the world. Everything is mine. Even bad problems are not just bad problems, they are *my* bad problems, and that makes them worse. Whatever we experience is seen as *my* cold, *my* fever, *my* friend, *my* enemy, *my* everything. "My" is the nucleus of our attention. According to Buddhism, we have been doing this for countless lifetimes. As long as we continue in this way, we will never be free from suffering.

The only alternative and way to freedom is to look outward, to open up and think, "Not only I, but also the others." This may feel hard in the beginning, since we are so used to the other way. Yet, by training ourselves little by little, we will open up to our surroundings and gradually broaden our vision. Instead of being stuck with our own problems, we will see others' difficulties. Even on a very basic level this will make a great difference. Gaining a more realistic outlook and putting ourselves into the context of all sentient beings, we will loosen up and become more open. We are only one of countless sentient beings. They have problems just like we do, and in comparison, theirs may be far more serious. Once we recognize that, we will not be blinded by every little thing and will be able to deal with what we have to face. Sooner or later we may discover that our problems are not such a big deal. They are due to reacting with attachment and aversion, and once that changes, there is no problem at all.

When we have no aversion, we have no fear. When we are not afraid, even something generally regarded as negative may not affect us too much. This shows the way to become a bodhisattva. If we appreciate the bodhisattva ideal, we need to train slowly and gradually to see the truth as it is. This will make us feel more open and less selfish in relating with others. Coming to know reality as it is, we will see everything more clearly, which will make us increasingly more altruistic. Our compassion will grow simultaneously with seeing the truth, and the more compassionate we become, the more clearly we will see.

Thus, the bodhisattva path is not only good for others, but is good for ourselves as well. I once heard His Holiness the Dalai Lama say, "Being altruistic is an intelligent way of being selfish." When we stop thinking about ourselves all the time, we achieve our own good, because we feel happier and more whole, less bothered by small things. Both our wisdom and compassion grow, and we continuously become better people. So, in a way, we achieve our own selfish goal as well.

It is important to see that the bodhisattva path of understanding and altruism is the best way for us to live. It is possible to view altruism as a burden, as something taxing, or as something that takes away from our own happiness. But this is a totally mistaken approach. Instead, we need to see that through compassion and altruism our mind will become clearer and more spacious, and that these will lead us to experience a greater degree of happiness. We will become sane and whole and capable of living in a better way.

This transformation happens when we become able to see the problems of others. We will come to appreciate our fellow beings, sympathize with them, and try to help whenever and however we can. Sometimes we will manage to do something and at other times it may not be possible. We do not have to satisfy every need of this world. We are grateful, though, when we can help in some way. With this understanding we will not fall into an attitude of thinking, "I am so great and special! I am so kind to help these poor people." We will see that helping others is actually helping ourselves to become saner and happier. This will make us feel grateful and deeply obliged. As we see more clearly, our gratitude grows and our compassion progresses to deeper levels, and we become more realized beings.

In brief, Ngulchü Thogmé's opening stanza of homage conveys the principal objective and training of a bodhisattva. The next stanza contains the promise to compose the text. This accords with the ancient Indian tradition adopted by the Tibetan authors of beginning a text by stating the subject matter and reason for writing. This stanza says:

The perfect buddhas, the source of all welfare and happiness,
Have arisen from accomplishing the sacred Dharma.
As doing so depends on knowing how to enact this Dharma,
The practice of the bodhisattvas shall be explained.

According to Mahayana Buddhism, it is necessary to become a bodhisattva before becoming a buddha. The practice of a bodhisattva leads to buddhahood and is the preparation for full enlightenment. The Mahayana teaches nothing other than the bodhisattva path, giving detailed explanations of its philosophy, meditation, wisdom, and conduct. At the beginning of this text, Ngulchü Thogmé promises to explain the practices of a bodhisattva, because all buddhas of the past and present have reached enlightenment in this way, and all future buddhas will do the same.

Here, the question might arise of why anyone would want to become a buddha. The reason is that the enlightened state of mind is the total opposite of the samsaric state of mind. In it every mark of samsara is absent. There is no struggle or delusion, and consequently, there is no unhappiness. Mind manifests as boundless clarity and compassion, or the union of wisdom and compassion. The enlightened mind is free from afflictions and totally at peace. While we are caught in the samsaric frame of mind, there will be little satisfaction and even less peace, since we will always experience various states of fear, expectation, struggle, and panic. Once we clearly see what samsara is, we will wish to be rid of our confusion and attain the complete peace, wisdom, and clarity that mark the state of a buddha. Once we know that we are no different from others, and that everyone else likewise wants to be free from suffering, we will not limit this wish to ourselves. We will want to attain buddhahood to fulfill the purposes of all sentient beings. Our view, our seeing of the truth is the central point. We are able to overcome our confusion and improve our knowledge by seeing the truth of ourselves and of everything around us. There is no reason why we should not discover that wisdom of seeing the truth, since it does not come from outside. It is ingrained within us, and is no more than our own true nature, which is just waiting to be seen and is therefore called buddha-nature. So, our learning can expand limitlessly until we see everything completely clearly. Nothing else is needed besides opening our eyes. This is what enlightenment or buddhahood is all about; there is nothing further to it.

The word "buddhahood" can carry a somewhat mystical connotation. It may seem far away and not really connected with us. In fact, the word "buddha" is derived from the Sanskrit word *bodh*, which denotes understanding and knowledge. Thus a buddha is someone who sees the true nature of everything to the fullest extent. The Tibetan equivalent is *sanggyé*. *Sang* means "awake," and refers to opening up completely and seeing oneself as one really is. The word "buddha" is always defined by awakening.

Awakening means getting up from sleep. While sleeping we have all kinds of dreams, but the moment we wake up they all prove to be illusions. Whatever happened during the dream, whether good or bad, does not matter, since it never truly existed. Likewise, enlightenment is waking up from the sleep of unknowing and seeing everything as it is. When we see all our confusion and problems clearly and fully, without any delusion, we will be enlightened. Our false ways of acting will be exhausted and our attitude will be changed simultaneously. The same is true of our energy. As long as we are subject to all kinds of problems, we will be stressed and afraid and our inner energy is blocked. Once we gain complete certainty and see reality as it is, there will be no more fear, and every blockage will be relieved.

The main reason we are able to attain enlightenment is that it is not something external that we have to achieve. We do not have to climb Mount Everest or discover something valuable that other people would want to steal. Enlightenment is just discovering ourselves, clearly and fully. Once we open up and see our true nature, nothing is a problem and we are buddha. For this reason it is said that we have buddha-nature. It is not something separate from us; it is not like a cabbage containing at its core a bright crystal called "buddha-nature" that is reached by peeling off all the leaves. Buddha-nature is our own mind, our own state of being, which only needs to be seen without our usual confusion, without our habitual tendencies and distorted views.

There is no hindrance except ourselves. Our belief in an existing self and our wrong views, habitual patterns, and negative attitudes are the only obstacles. All these are our own creations. In a way, we have created what we cherish and hold on to as being our "self." Thus, there is no reason why we should not be able to discard it and reach enlightenment.

When everything is seen clearly as it is, compassion manifests; this is because we realize that we do not need to protect ourselves any longer. Once there is no reason to feel insecure or fearful, there is nothing to prevent us from being compassionate. We become the embodiment of compassion. When we rediscover our own true nature precisely and fully, limitless compassion manifests spontaneously within the very moment of seeing.

Thus, enlightenment is not something far away. It is very close and present to be seen. The Vajrayana teachings, which expand the Sutra-Mahayana level of instructions dealt with here, give four reasons why we do not recognize the true nature of our mind. The first reason is that it is too near—it is just ourselves. Usually we think of buddhahood as something very distant and different from us, which might be gained after aeons of practice. It is nice to hear about buddhahood as the state of total freedom from suffering, but our personal situation is not like that, so it must be very far away. The true nature is so near that we cannot see it or imagine that it is actually within our reach.

The second reason is that it is too easy. Recognizing the nature of mind is merely seeing our true self. We do not have to dig up the earth or do something drastic to discover it. It is so simple that we cannot believe it. The third reason is that it is too good. Being so accustomed to having problems, we feel it is too good to be true. How can there not be a problem? Something must be wrong! The fourth reason is that it is too deep or too vast. Our ordinary perspective is very small. We miss the totality, the whole phenomenal world as it is. Always perceiving in terms of "this" or "that," we make things rigid and see them through the filter of our concepts. We label things as black or white, good or bad, and evaluate everything we encounter. We have to open up and shatter our ideas. Our usual thinking cannot fathom what needs to be seen.

These are the four reasons why we ignore the truth. It is possible, and even likely, that we can reach enlightenment, since it is so close and easy and good and deep. Right now our small conceptual mind is unable to grasp it. Once we know we have this capacity, we need the conviction that enlightenment is the state we want to achieve, being the only antidote to the suffering of samsara, and the final solution to all our problems.

Then we will see the point in becoming a bodhisattva. This basic understanding is of central importance. Lacking this perspective we might still decide to follow the bodhisattva path; then, even though we might take the bodhisattva vow, our decision would rest on shaky ground. Without firm and justified certainty we would still wonder whether it was worthwhile, whether it would truly benefit ourselves or not.

Now, we come to the first of the stanzas telling us how to proceed on the bodhisattva path. Through the opening verses of the homage and the promise to write, we have seen the view and objectives of a bodhisattva, and why it is possible to become one. Now we will begin to look at how to go about it, how to start and gradually progress on this path.

The first step is to accept that we have not yet reached a very high level and that we cannot expect to be real bodhisattvas right away. We need training but we are able to reach this goal through thorough training. A bodhisattva is someone whose entire being is bodhichitta, whose mind is bent on enlightenment. Bodhichitta has two aspects, aspiration and action. We are on the level of aspiration when we admire and appreciate the bodhisattva's way of life and maintain the wish, "May I reach enlightenment and be able to help all sentient beings to become enlightened. May I do everything necessary to accomplish this aim." Then, once we actively express our motivation, we are on the level of action. Bodhisattva activity needs to be developed gradually. Ngulchü Thogmé teaches us how to transform our samsaric state of mind into its enlightened equivalent, stage by stage, starting where we are now. So, to begin with he says:

> Now that the great vessel of leisure and endowment, hardly ever
>   to be found, is obtained,
> We should take ourselves and all other sentient beings across the
>   ocean of cyclic existence.
> Toward that aim we should listen, reflect, and meditate day and night.
> Doing so, not falling to slothfulness, is the practice of a bodhisattva.

In all Buddhist practices one of the first things to reflect upon is the preciousness of human existence. The expression "leisure and endowment" is another way of saying "the precious human body," as it is frequently called in Buddhist literature. The precious human body is the one we have right now, and it is important to appreciate it. The first step in the quest for truth is to look at ourselves and see how we are right now. Most of the time we underestimate ourselves and undervalue our situations. This is a major source of problems among human beings. We usually look forward to something else we believe will fulfill our needs and wants. We think, "Once I have that, everything will be wonderful and I will be happy from then onward." We rarely turn back and say, "I am so happy now. What I have is wonderful."

This causes us many problems because if we cannot appreciate what we have, it might as well not be present. As we do not care about it, we just waste it. This is what we usually do. We might have many good things, but we take them for granted and do not see their value. Only when we have lost them do we fully appreciate what we had. Yet, by then it is a bit too late. When we realize that we have missed the point, our remorse will increase at our wasted opportunity.

From among the different types of existence, human existence offers the greatest opportunity. Even if we have nothing else, if we are in poverty, without the slightest achievement in life, having done nothing great or fantastic, it is still so good to be what we are at this moment. A human being has tremendous potential. We have a great number of qualities making our existence far better than that of animals. We are intelligent and able to communicate. We can do many things for ourselves and also for the good of others.

Of course, this is true of the negative side as well. We have the capacity to act in positive and negative ways that most sentient beings do not have; we are free to choose our courses of action. If we can understand what a great opportunity and capacity this human life offers, we will not be depressed anymore. We have everything necessary to start with. There is no need to feel incapable and worthless as many people do nowadays. Once we deeply feel that this sheer and naked human birth is good enough in itself, we will have understood a central point. Insight into the preciousness of human existence can give us the courage to go forward and not neglect ourselves anymore. We will know we are worthy of doing something while we have the chance.

Sometimes people laugh at the teachings on the precious human life, saying, "Well, it's not that precious— there are billions of human beings. In India the same number as the entire population of Australia are born every year. What value is there in being human? There are too many people already!" If we do not understand the value of our existence, we can easily waste it by feeling incompetent and discouraged. Being without confidence is a total waste. The same is true of looking for excitement, for some temporary thing to enjoy. We may enjoy it for a while, but eventually it will pass and leave us dissatisfied and more miserable than before. This is also a vain pursuit, since it does not bring any lasting benefit.

Because of our potential to do good or bad as we choose, human birth is like a great ship that can take us wherever we want to go. So we should use this life for something that is truly meaningful in the long run. The best we could do is to discover the truth and find a way to overcome all our problems and others' problems as well. Once we discover our true nature, all our problems will dissolve. Since the enlightened state is within us, we will be able to find it. We can set out on a quest that will result in lasting happiness, rather than just providing some short and futile excitement. Then, we would be doing something truly meaningful and great.

Human beings are capable of so much endeavor, even in small matters. People spend their lives trying to measure the height of mountains or the depth of the sea. These provide useful information, but they may not prove significant in the long run. For example, we Tibetans could never understand why people climbed mountains for no reason. The mountaineers would say, "I am doing an expedition on Mount Everest," as if it were the most important thing in the world. They would spend so much time and money; they would even risk, and sometimes lose, their lives. We would wonder if they were mad, and ask, "What do you get when you reach the top?" They replied, "Oh, it is just wonderful!" We would say, "What is so wonderful in that cold wind?" The answer was, "Oh, it is so exciting!" It might seem wonderful, but it will only last a short time, and it is only wonderful if you consider it wonderful. Someone else might think that the most wonderful thing is being curled up, warm and snug, in a cozy bed. To me, for instance, that is much more wonderful.

Seeing how people are willing to risk their lives for minor goals, when we see that there is a way to totally transform ourselves and overcome the suffering of samsaric existence, we really should do our best to accomplish it. This is not simply a way to experience good feelings or energy for a short time. It will result in everlasting happiness, whatever the circumstance and situation. If we decide to devote most of our lives to this purpose, it will be truly useful for ourselves and others.

To achieve this we need to listen, reflect, and meditate. Listening means to study the teachings written down in the past and the instructions received in the present. In this way we can learn from the authentic experience of others. Then, we must search open-mindedly within ourselves and compare our findings and experiences with those of others. When we do this, we will receive all kinds of information that needs to be processed internally. This is the stage of reflection. Using our own logic and intuition, we have to investigate whether or not the information we have received is genuine, and then we must digest it personally.

We have to understand what we have learned, at least intellectually, so that there is no conflict and everything falls into place. Teachings are given from different angles, and as long as they have not been integrated, there will be fragments of understanding that may easily clash. Reflection means forming a full understanding and putting everything where it belongs. If we know the different viewpoints from which teachings are given, we will not have doubts when they seem contradictory. When we have assimilated them, we do not have to agree with everything, nor do we have to disagree, either.

Our understanding should be whole and well rooted so that it provides the ground for meditation. Meditation turns everything that has been intellectually understood into personal experience, mixing it with our entire being and integrating it into our daily lives. Understanding one thing but actually feeling and doing another is not very useful. This is the approach of many academics. They may have extensive intellectual knowledge, even regarding meditation, but they have nothing to do with it in their personal lives. That kind of knowledge is just information. If we want to know exactly how it is, we have to put it into practice and turn it into genuine experience. We should do whatever serves the purpose of making the mind calm and clear so that we can see things directly. This is the aspect of meditation.

This stanza conveys the message that our life is so precious and holds so much power that it should not be wasted. We should actualize its purpose and try to find what will solve all our problems. This is enlightenment, not only for ourselves, but for all sentient beings. Toward this end we should strive in a systematic way by means of study, reflection, and meditation. Applying these three tools is the first endeavor of a bodhisattva.

Learning, contemplating, and meditating should always go together in Buddhist practice. Although this is very important, it is often overlooked. At the present time in the West, there are two different groups of people interested in Buddhism. One group is based in universities and the other in Buddhist centers. Those in the first group adopt an almost exclusively academic approach, and many of them have a vast knowledge of Buddhism and read Sanskrit and Tibetan. Having read many sutras and tantras and their translations, they have various ideas about their content, but their views are often their own invention. Although they are very interested, they keep their distance from Buddhist practice.

Some of the professors I have met went so far as to tell me that if one wanted to study Buddhism properly, one should not become personally involved; if one became a Buddhist practitioner, one would become biased and no longer able to study it. Maybe there is some truth in this approach, but how can Buddhism be really understood if one remains completely separate from it and does not see anything personally relevant in its teachings? This approach is a little extreme.

On the other hand, there are those who only want to practice and do not want to learn much about it. As soon as a tiny bit of study is introduced, they do not want to participate and say, "Ugh, that is just this academic stuff!" This kind of attitude is found in many Buddhist centers. There is a tendency to say, "We have too much information already. We are fed up with it and don't need anymore. All we need is practice."

In fact, both study and practice are needed. There is a Tibetan saying, "Trying to understand without meditation is like climbing a mountain without fingers. Trying to meditate without understanding is like shooting an arrow in the darkness." Without meditation there is no way to develop true understanding, and without study there is no way to know where the meditation is going. Real understanding is not intellectual, but since we are intellectual beings, we need to pass through the level where we have doubts. Most of us begin by asking questions and having doubts. Certain fortunate individuals are able to follow the path with simple devotion and faith, but they are rather scarce. Intellectual people like us should first gain a proper understanding, and then proceed to practice. Study and meditation should be in union; neither should be neglected at the expense of the other. This is the middle way that is usually recommended.

To integrate our Dharma practice into our life situations is very important, especially as far as meditation is concerned. If we do not manage to do that, meditation is useless. The Buddhist view is that any practice, whether it is study, reflection, meditation, or another type of training, is meant for our life and should become part of our everyday activities and pursuits. If not, our Dharma practice has no real effect.

The statement that we should integrate Dharma practice into our daily life may seem to indicate that meditation and the rest of our life are two different things. In fact, it is not like that. Meditation takes place on an inner level, and while meditating we do not become another person or leave the world, even though in retreat we may not see anyone. We are the same people we always were, with all our thoughts, emotions, and reactions.

Meditation is a way to work with ourselves in a calmer setting, without too much outside disturbance. When thoughts or negative emotions arise in the mind, it offers techniques and a more conducive setting for overcoming them. We have an opportunity to learn in a somewhat protected situation how to make our mind calm and clear, and to see how everything really is and how we usually react. We practice in order to learn how to overcome all our problems. Whatever results we achieve should be carried into our life to an increasing extent and applied to any difficulty we face. We must try to put our experience into action. This is the real test of our progress. If we can manage difficult situations well, we have passed; if not, we need to go back to our cushion.

The second stanza says:

> Attachment toward friends and kin flows like water.
> Aversion and hatred for enemies burns us like fire.
> Ignorance causes oblivion of what to adopt and to renounce.
> To leave our dark homeland is the practice of a bodhisattva.

This verse seems to say that to become a bodhisattva we must leave the place where we live, but this is not the point. Even if we did move, it would not make a great difference. What we need to forsake is our confusion. We have to see that aversion, craving, and ignorance are the basic causes of all our suffering. We must find ways to dissolve the solidity of our hatred and craving, and of the ignorance that is their root. Anything we can do to reduce their impact, even a little bit, is real practice and a bodhisattva's way of life.

Here the advice is to stay away from places, situations, and entanglements that entail a lot of aggression and attachment. Once there is hatred, there is also some craving, and ignorance in terms of forgetting what is right and wrong underlies these all along. This stanza does not teach us how to deal directly with the mental poisons, but advises us to be aware and not get involved in situations that draw us deeply into them. We are so determined by our circumstances that we can easily fall under negative influences. While a great practitioner can deal with anything, a beginner needs to be careful and avoid situations full of negative emotions.

The third stanza says:

> By forsaking harmful places the poisons will gradually decrease.
> In freedom from distraction the wealth of virtue will naturally grow.
> Through lucid awareness firm conviction in the Dharma is born.
> Relying on solitude, therefore, is the practice of a bodhisattva.

This stanza describes the type of place and situation most conducive to diminishing negative reactions and strengthening positive qualities. This is practical advice, because as beginners we are strongly influenced by our surroundings and life situations. For this reason, it is recommended to take every opportunity to withdraw into solitude, not only in the outer sense, but in the inner sense as well.

When we manage to stay in both mental and physical solitude and use meditation techniques to make our mind peaceful and clear, our afflictions will gradually diminish. Once we leave adverse situations where we get caught in aversion, craving, and ignorance, our mental poisons will be easier to deal with. There will be fewer distractions, and wholesome activities will naturally increase. With less distractions and negative emotions, the mind will become more pure, and clear awareness and trust in the Dharma will be born.

For this reason, beginners on the bodhisattva path should train in solitude, taking every opportunity to practice in retreat. When we feel we are becoming strongly involved in negativity, we should try, as much as our time allows, to get out of that situation and practice in a solitary place. In this way we will find some rest and a certain distance from unwholesome entanglements.

Ngulchü Thogmé's fourth instruction teaches the importance of understanding the nature of impermanence:

> From beloved friends and family with whom a long lifetime was
>   shared we must finally part.
> Wealth and possessions we achieved with effort and strife will be lost
>   without leaving a trace.

> From the rest house of the body where it was guest the consciousness
> will depart.
> Then, to let go and be rid of concern for this life is the practice of a
> bodhisattva.

The more we are able to understand impermanence, the more we will see through the tremendous attachment we have for things that hold little benefit or value for us. For instance, we will usually expend enormous effort to develop friendships or gain wealth. Many people practically risk their lives for such things, not recognizing that they are quite meaningless in the long run. Wealth can easily be lost and will definitely be of no help when we die. Even the friends and relatives we love so much and do not want to lose will be separated from us at the moment of death.

Generally speaking, most problems in friendships and families come from thinking that relationships and situations will never end. Tiny problems become big problems, and we start fighting over them because we fear that they will last forever. "I'm not going to give in! I will not wash the dishes tonight, because if I do, I will always have to do them!" If we know that something will last only a short time, we do not mind; but if we think it will last forever, it is too much. Most problems among people, and even among countries, are attributable to the illusion of permanence.

One of the Jataka stories—the stories that relate the former lives of the Buddha—shows how important and fruitful it is to have a deep understanding of impermanence. There was a family consisting of an older couple, their grown-up son and his wife, and their grandchild. The family lived closely together, and they loved and respected each other so much that they became an example to their whole village. Everyone thought they were a model family. One day the grown son died. The neighbors were shocked and said among themselves, "This is terrible! His old parents and wife must be devastated."

The neighbors went to console the family, and when they arrived they found, to their astonishment, that the rest of the family was acting as if nothing had happened. Neither his parents nor his wife were in mourning, everything seemed quite normal. No one could believe their eyes and they asked the father, "What is this? Your son died, didn't he?" "Yes, my son died," the father said. His neighbor asked, "How is it possible that you are not sad and mourning for him? We thought that you had a wonderful family who loved each other dearly, but we must have been wrong."

The father said, "We were very affectionate and never said or did anything hurtful to each other, because we always knew that our being together would not last. We knew that each of us could die at any moment and we would be separated. With the understanding that we had only a short time together, we were able to be close and kind to each other. My son has gone, but I knew that this might happen anytime, so it is not a shock. Of course, I am not happy. But during the time we lived together, we did whatever we could to help each other. Now, my son has died, but I have no regrets. I am thankful to have had this opportunity."

Of course, it was the Buddha who made this statement in one of his former lives, and it is not so easy to develop this attitude. But when we know in our hearts that by having come together we will naturally be separated sooner or later, there is neither reason nor need to fight. We should use the opportunity of being together as best we can. If we try to create good conditions, and love and help each other, we can have a good time, but we will not appreciate it if we start fighting. This is true of every situation.

If we truly understand impermanence, we will be able to relate to people more wisely. Our minds will be clearer and we will be closer to seeing the way things are. We will know that sooner or later any relationship will end.

The same applies to possessions and wealth. We may gain or lose them— it is uncertain. There is no reason to be proud when we have something or to be depressed when we hardly have anything, since our material situation may change at any time. In my life this has happened several times. When I was born, my family was quite rich. Then we lost everything and were totally impoverished, and after a while we somehow managed again. Although we are not rich now, we are doing well, so I am not very concerned about these things. They may be lost again in the future.

If we hold on tightly to something, we will have problems to the same degree that we cling to it and fear its loss. A Tibetan proverb says, "If you possess the riches of a god, your problems are at the level of a god; if you possess a horse, your problems are at the level of a horse." This does not mean that the divine wealth or the horse are problematic in themselves, but the more we hold on to what we have and the more we want to possess things, to that very extent our problems will increase. The real problem is the importance we attribute to ourselves and the things we want.

Ngulchü Thogmé points out that we will be separated not only from our possessions and friends, but also from our body, in which our mind is just a guest. Our body is made from the five elements, and being compounded, it will definitely disintegrate when the time of dissolution has come. Even our bodies are not permanent.

Once we understand impermanence clearly, our clinging and samsaric way of seeing ourselves and everything else will dissolve somewhat. We will not feel so bound by our desires, and we will be able to be more open and expose our hearts. Our personal interests will not prevail over others', and we will not need to impose so many conditions upon our loved ones. Being less selfish and touchy, we will not feel so hypersensitive and vulnerable to being hurt. We can rid ourselves of concern for this life by seeing impermanence in every aspect of worldly existence. Loosening our clinging, particularly to ourselves, is one of the basic ways to act as a bodhisattva.

The fifth stanza reads:

> When our friends are such that in their company the three poisons
>   increase
> And indifference to the task of learning, reflection, and meditation
>   arises,
> When they cause the loss of love and compassion until these are
>   no more,
> Then to discard such misleading friends is the practice of a
>   bodhisattva.

Most of us are easily influenced by others. There are very few people who are so virtuous that they would not be negatively affected by bad company, and very few people who are so unvirtuous that they would not be positively affected by good company. Most of us are somewhere between these two and we easily change our behavior depending upon our environment and circumstances. As beginners on the bodhisattva path we are therefore strongly advised to protect ourselves from negative influences and carefully watch how we are affected by the people with whom we spend our time.

For a Dharma practitioner, evil or misleading friends are those who cause our mental poisons to increase. If we feel more anger or craving or confusion around certain people, that means they are not a positive influence. The same is true for someone with whom our efforts to study, reflect, and meditate decline. When we notice that our peace of mind and clear vision are getting weaker and we are becoming less compassionate, we should abandon the circumstances and friends that cause this.

One might wonder whether this instruction conflicts with the bodhi-sattva ideal of helping and supporting everyone. There is no contradiction because a bodhisattva's training must be a gradual process in accordance with individual capacities. When we take the bodhisattva vow, we make an inner promise: "Just as the buddhas of the past generated bodhichitta, I will do likewise. I aspire to full enlightenment, so I will gradually practice the path." To be willing to proceed carefully, step-by-step, is of utmost importance. As an aspiring bodhisattva, we want to help all beings, but we have to prepare ourselves to give such far-reaching support.

If we become worse for the sake of doing a small service for someone, this is unwise and unhelpful. The instructions on the bodhisattva vow include forty-two criteria for bodhisattva activity. For instance, they state that it would be wrong to give something when our personal loss would be far greater than the benefit derived from the gift. The aim is to be of greatest possible help to as many beings as possible. We should not try to help in a way that adversely affects or weakens our ability to do so in the future. Whenever we think we can give some assistance that will not harm ourselves, we should do whatever we can.

The main point of this verse is to be aware of how we are influenced by others so that we can continue on the path. What is called "compassion" is sympathetic feeling for people in bad situations, for people who are often unable to do anything positive. They are unhappy and cannot become happy because they are not doing the good actions that would cause happiness. Thus, their suffering is inevitable, and we should be sympathetic. We should pray for anyone stuck in a negative situation, and help such persons in any way we can. However, this does not mean that we have to become like them.

The sixth stanza is related to the fifth, as it describes the positive influences we should seek:

> When we rely on someone whose company eliminates all faults
> And who causes our qualities to increase like the waxing moon,
> Then to cherish this genuine spiritual friend more dearly
> Than even our own body is the practice of a bodhisattva.

A good friend is someone who helps us diminish our negative tendencies and increase our positive qualities. If we are fortunate enough to associate with people like this, we should deeply appreciate them. Just as it is important to avoid bad company, it is even more important to rely on virtuous friends. A genuine friend gives spiritual guidance and is most important for following the bodhisattva path.

The concept of a "spiritual friend" is not limited to teachers, but acknowledges the influence of our companions and the society in which we live. The importance of the Sangha comes in here. By being in a conducive environment, among good, devoted people who practice well, we will be influenced to develop well ourselves. Similarly, being in situations that lack positive influences makes progress on the path extremely difficult.

The seventh stanza describes taking refuge:

> Those who themselves are fettered in the prison of cyclic existence,
> Like worldly gods, to whom can they grant protection?
> When we seek shelter, to take refuge in the rare and sublime jewels,
> Who will not fail, is the practice of a bodhisattva.

When we take refuge in something, the object of refuge should represent the best thing we could achieve. For instance, if we were to take refuge in political power or wealth, we would believe them to be the greatest things we could obtain, the things that would fulfill all our wishes. When the verse mentions worldly gods, it refers to anyone or anything that is within samsara and not free from its fetters. Such beings or things cannot give us complete protection or a way to reach the final solution to all our problems. If we seek refuge, it should be in something that embodies the ultimate truth and is free from bondage and fear. The authentic and unfailing refuge is represented by the Buddha, Dharma, and Sangha, called "the three jewels."

Buddhahood is not something that we can find outside ourselves. It is the unlimited, ultimate reality within us. A buddha is someone who has realized this state and is no longer controlled by anything or anyone. A buddha is not trapped in any circumstances whatsoever and thus is totally free from fear. Having seen the truth to its full extent, he or she has limitless wisdom and compassion. This is therefore the best model for us. We will wish to follow this example when we understand that we are actually able to reach buddhahood. This understanding comes from knowing that buddhahood is not something out there, but will be revealed once we rediscover our true basic root, clearly and fully.

Taking refuge in the Buddha means to have a firm intention, thinking, "I am capable of becoming a buddha, and this is my deepest wish. I am going to awaken just like the buddhas of the past. I will follow their way and become a buddha myself." Taking refuge in the Dharma, one would say, "To become a buddha I will follow the experience of the previous buddhas as expressed in the Dharma. I will try to learn from their experience and follow the path with their guidance." Taking refuge in the Sangha consists of thinking, "Having opened up, I am ready for the help of others who are also trying to reach buddhahood. I am ready to be influenced by good friends who have received the teachings of the buddhas from the past until now. I will work on my own, but I also would like to receive the assistance of others, as much as I can."

If we have this understanding and take refuge in this way, nothing else is needed. Atisha said, "In Buddhism, there is nothing other than taking refuge." Fully understanding the meaning of seeking refuge in Buddha, Dharma, and Sangha, we can understand the whole of Buddhism. Buddhism means becoming a buddha, and becoming a buddha is the refuge. Therefore, taking refuge is one of the foremost practices of a bodhisattva.

The eighth stanza is about karma:

> The sufferings of the evil wanderings, so difficult to endure,
> Are evildoing's fruit, so the Buddha said.
> To never commit a harmful deed, even though life is at stake,
> Is therefore the practice of a bodhisattva.

Karmic cause and effect is one of the Buddha's main teachings. The quality of our lives and everything we experience, whether good or bad, is not imposed upon us by someone up in the sky, but is due to our own actions. Every action has a reaction. If we do something good, there will be a good result, and if we do something bad, there will be a bad result. We reap what we sow. This is the theory of karma.

Understanding karma thoroughly and being convinced of its validity, we will naturally avoid sinful actions since we do not want to suffer. Likewise, we will try to be good to others, not solely out of compassion, but also because we want to be happy. In this way the understanding of karma provides a double protection. We refrain from negative actions for our own sake, and we help others for their sake as well as our own. Being compassionate and helpful serves a dual purpose. Trying to do only beneficial things, knowing that good actions bring happiness and evil actions bring suffering, is the way to act as a bodhisattva.

The ninth stanza says:

> Happiness in the three realms is like dew on the tip of a blade of grass.
> In a short moment's passing it fades away.
> To strive for the supreme state of liberation that is forever unchanging
> Is therefore the practice of a bodhisattva.

In Buddhism one of the most fundamental practices is called "the four thoughts that turn the mind from samsara." These are contemplations on the preciousness of the human body, impermanence, the law of karma, and the shortcomings of samsara. This verse emphasizes the importance of seeing the nature of samsara. We normally regard the pleasure and happiness of cyclic existence as extremely important. Yet, as long as we are in the samsaric state of mind, there will be no true or lasting happiness. Even when we have everything we need or want and nothing is going wrong, we still fear that something will happen and cause our experience to end. There is constant insecurity in the back of our minds, an underlying fear that prevents us from being completely happy.

For this reason the verse says that happiness in the three realms of existence is like dew upon grass. The three realms are those under the ground, on the ground, and above the ground. These represent the whole of existence. Any sense of well-being or excitement that we experience within the confines of samsara is not permanent—something else will happen that may not be as pleasant. The only thing that will never change and that brings true, everlasting happiness is total liberation from the samsaric mind.

Liberation is achieved by eliminating all our misconceptions so that we see everything as it is, without confusion. This is the real purpose of meditation. Dharma practice is not just for the sake of generating good experiences and having a better life. Even good meditation experiences, though they may be blissful, should not be our final aim. They are good in that they are signs on the path, but they are not as good as we may think they are. They are ephemeral like everything else, and we can easily become attached to them and fall into yet another trap, even trickier than the ones before.

Meditation should lead us to the recognition that ultimately there is no difference between good and bad experiences. Being able to respond to them in the same way is what the Buddha called "equanimity." Once we are able to see that bad experiences are actually no worse than good experiences, we will be beyond fear and clinging and will be totally free. When we understand this deeply, we will no longer be attached to or bothered by little things. We will strive for the supreme state of total liberation in which we finally transcend all hopes and fears.

As long as we are in the samsaric state of mind, we have to accept that we will always have one problem or another. Once we see this clearly and understand that enlightenment is possible, that it is the true state of our mind, we will make the achievement of enlightenment the purpose of our lives. This is the real practice of a bodhisattva.

The tenth stanza reads:

> When our mothers who loved us since beginningless time are
>   suffering,
> What is achieved by our own happiness?
> Giving rise to bodhichitta to liberate all beings, limitless in number,
> Is therefore the practice of a bodhisattva.

The preceding two verses said that acting positively and not acting negatively are an important basis for experiencing happiness in this life and our lives to come. We need to liberate ourselves from all the causes of samsaric existence and attain the state of permanent happiness. In this verse Ngulchü Thogmé clarifies that our individual release is not enough. We are not alone in this world, so we cannot leave it at that.

We should bring this to mind by thinking, "I am not the only one who suffers. There are millions of sentient beings like me, equally longing to be happy and to be rid of all their problems. From beginningless time I have been born in samsara to a father and mother, and in turn I have been a parent to children. Every being must have been either my parent or my child, and just as I love my family in this lifetime, I have a reason to feel connected with all sentient beings. Whatever goodness I wish for those close to me now, I wish the same for everyone else as well."

Once we feel toward all other beings the way we feel for those we love dearly in this life, we will not just seek our own benefit and leave nothing for them. Looking carefully, we will understand that everyone needs to be liberated and find everlasting happiness just as we do. With this insight we will be able to develop bodhichitta, the aspiration and willingness to help anyone. Enacting bodhichitta is the main practice of a bodhisattva.

We have to admit, though, that often our compassion for others is not very strong and needs to be cultivated. This is to be done gradually, first through the understanding, "Just as I wish to be happy forever and free from all my problems, everyone who is caught in the samsaric state of mind, the countless beings throughout the universes in endless space, have the same desire and the same right to reach final liberation. However, most of them do not know how to fulfill this wish. Now that I am learning how to do it and making an effort to see the true nature of everything, I must help others to do the same. If I do not share whatever I learn, my life has little purpose."

This is the motivation of a bodhisattva. The more our motivation grows, the more confidence we will have in the path and the enlightened state. As our confidence increases, we will want to share what we have learned with all other beings. This is the way we develop our attitude.

The eleventh stanza says:

> All suffering without exception springs from our desire for personal happiness.
> A perfect buddha is born from a mind set on accomplishing the welfare of others.
> Truly exchanging our happiness for the suffering of others,
> We will therefore engage in the practice of a bodhisattva.

Our problems are mainly due to excessive self-cherishing, which expresses itself in too much attachment to our personal happiness and in an equally strong aversion to whatever could undermine it. As long as "I" and "mine" are the central figures, we view the whole world as something potentially harmful. By putting our desires and dislikes first, we are in the samsaric state of mind, and cannot solve our main problem at all. The only way to do that is to open our hearts and put others first.

We should try to face our fear and aversion, and accept what we do not like. And we should try to share what we have or desire, whatever seems most important to us. This is the practice of *tong len*, which means "sending and taking." In *tong len* practice we take upon ourselves the negativity and suffering of all sentient beings, and in turn send out all that is positive and joyful.

Although this is one of the most important practices of a bodhisattva, it does not mean that we have to do it in real life right away. This is the ideal, of course, as Shantideva says in the *Bodhicharyavatara*, but the practice of exchange is carried out first in a meditative way through visualization. The more this practice enables us to open up, to become less selfish and diminish our aversion, the more freedom we gain. We become more liberated, compassionate, and fearless.

The practice of *tong len* does not mean that when something goes wrong, we should grit our teeth and think, "I am a great and compassionate bodhisattva," and then try to live up to the ideal. The practice needs to be worked upon slowly and gradually. The Buddha said that if we can give a bowl of curry without regrets, then we should give a bowl of curry. When we have become less selfish and more courageous and are able to give our lives for others without any regrets, then we should give our lives. Not to respect our capacities and limits would be a totally mistaken course of action.

Once there was a man trying to be a bodhisattva who promised to give everything he had to anyone who asked for something. Being very rich, he started a kind of public campaign and made his promise known far and wide. Many people came and asked him for money, food, seeds, and all kinds of things. He gladly fulfilled their wishes and made everyone happy, and his fame increased. Then, one day a rather nasty Brahmin came along and asked, "Is it true that you will give whatever you have?" The rich benefactor said, "Oh, yes, totally! I am a bodhisattva!" "In that case, give me your right hand," the Brahmin requested. Without any hesitation the bodhisattva took out his sword, cut off his right hand, and offered it to him. Of course, now the bodhisattva had to use his left hand. In Eastern countries this is considered as being outrageous. So the Brahmin rejected it, saying, "What! I cannot receive something from your left hand. You are disrespectful!" This was too much for the bodhisattva, and he totally renounced his ideal.

This story shows what can happen if we are not sufficiently skillful. The skillful way to become a bodhisattva is to start in a small way on our own level and slowly enhance our capacity. At a certain stage we will have no difficulty in giving even our own lives for a truly beneficial cause. Until then, and especially at the beginning, we should engage in the practice of *tong len*.

In this practice we combine visualization and breathing. While breathing in, we invite all the negative things we usually reject, such as the bad karma, sickness, and misery of all sentient beings, to enter our body in the form of black smoke or dirt. At our heart center we purify that negativity, and in the form of white light breathe out to others everything positive, like good karma, health, love, and happiness. In this way we gradually improve.

The twelfth stanza says:

> Even if someone, driven by excessive greed, robbed us of all our
>   wealth
> Or instigated others to commit such a deed, we should offer him
>   our body,
> Possessions, and the virtues of the three times.
> Such dedication is the practice of a bodhisattva.

This and the following verses clarify that being compassionate to all sentient beings is not an easy task. Being under the power of negative emotions, such as desire, hatred, jealousy, and ignorance, people are not always pleasant. They can misbehave at times, and when we have been good to them, they may harm us in return. To be a bodhisattva may be our main intention, but in everyday life there will be many problems, and it will not always be easy to be loving and free from aversion.

The example given here is of someone driven by great desire who steals all our possessions. What should we do in such a situation? Should we hate the person, or should we try to understand why he or she acted that way? People who do negative things are truly ignorant of what is right and wrong. They are like someone who is sick or has gone mad, since they do not realize that their actions will bring negative results to themselves. If we develop a strong understanding of this, we will not feel a need to punish them. When they harm others, they are harming themselves and creating a cause for their own future suffering.

Of course, this does not mean that we should encourage people who commit negative deeds. When we see, however, that they are not accomplishing their own interest, but are doing the opposite out of ignorance, we will feel that they need to be treated with sympathy and compassion, rather than hatred. The extent to which we can react in this way depends on our level of spiritual development, but we should try as much as possible.

If someone steals from us or hurts us and we hate this person, this does no good for the evildoer and no good for us, either. Feelings of anger and hatred burn our own hearts and cause us much pain. Being consumed with anger, we cannot sleep and lose our good energy. So, instead of nurturing negative emotions, we should try to dedicate the stolen property to the thief. Of course, we should try to get it back, but if it cannot be recovered, we should mentally give it to the thief along with any good actions we have ever done.

Once there was a Zen monk in retreat in an isolated place, and he kept some money in a wooden box. One day when he was not there, someone came, pried open the box, and took the money. When the monk returned and found his money gone, he realized he could not get it back, and so he decided to dedicate it. He said, "I dedicate this money to whoever took it. May it benefit him greatly and may this dedication turn him into a good person." With this prayer the incident was over for the monk.

Some time later the police arrested the thief. They brought the money-bag to the monk and asked, "Isn't this your stolen money?" The monk said, "Yes, this is my money, but he did not take it. I freely gave it to him." At that the police could do nothing and had to set the man free. The thief was deeply stirred by the monk's noble-mindedness. He came back to the monk and offered him the money-bag, saying, "Please take this. I never knew that there could be anyone generous enough to forgive someone like me. You must be my guru." From then on, the thief became a student and totally reformed his way of life.

We may not be able to act like this monk, but at least we should try not to harbor any negative feelings, no matter what happens. Keeping hatred alive is harmful for ourselves as well as for anyone we meet. We should try to let go of whatever we have lost and dedicate it to the one who caused the loss, wishing that it may turn into utmost benefit for that person. In this way our deprivation transforms into generosity. If we cannot get it back anyway, isn't it better to give it away? The most important thing for a beginner to learn from this verse is not to nourish resentful feelings.

The thirteenth and fourteenth stanzas are similar and can be explained together:

> Even if someone severs our head,
> Though we did not cause it by the slightest fault,

Being compassionate and taking his evils upon us
Is the practice of a bodhisattva.

When someone wounds and slanders us
And his evil words resound in three thousand worlds,
To proclaim his qualities in return with loving mind
Is the practice of a bodhisattva.

These and the next few verses describe situations in which people are ungrateful or do harmful things to us. In such circumstances, we try to develop compassion. As long as everybody is pleasant, there is no need to generate tolerance and forgiveness. At the college where I worked several years ago, people sometimes said to me, "You never seem to get angry." I would answer, "Why should I get angry when everyone is so nice to me?" When people are unpleasant, though, we have to work at it. The first of these two stanzas describes an extreme ideal, and yet it relates to a true event in one of the life stories of the Buddha.

One time in a past life, the Buddha was a hermit called Drangsong Zöpa Mawa, who meditated in solitude in a beautiful forest. One day the king came to hunt in this forest, accompanied by his queens and entourage. While the king and his men went hunting, the queens and their attendants stayed behind and wandered into the forest to pick flowers. When the queens came upon the hermit sitting silently in meditation, they were impressed. They made offerings and asked him for teaching, which he granted.

The king returned to find the camp empty and all his queens gone. He had not been fortunate in his hunt, and in a mixture of anxiety and dormant anger he went looking for his queens. He found them sitting around the hermit in what seemed to be a somewhat intimate situation. This aroused his anger and he shouted, "What is this? What are you doing here with all my queens?" "I am not doing anything," the hermit replied. "I am just sitting here, meditating on patience."

The king, who had a nasty streak, took out his sword and cut off one of the hermit's limbs. He demanded, "Are you still patient with me?" The hermit replied, "Oh, yes. I have no hatred for you. You are ignorant and do not know what you are doing." The king struck him again and it continued in this way. While the king dismembered him, the hermit prayed, "This king is cutting my body and I feel nothing negative toward him. May I not only forgive him, but once I am enlightened and have gained the necessary wisdom, I pray to be the first person to cut his ignorance, all his misunderstandings and problems, just as he cuts me now."

His prayer was so sincere and strong that it came true. When the Buddha reached enlightenment and taught his first five disciples, one of them, Kaundinya, was the first to gain true insight. The Buddha explained that Kaundinya had been this king. Of course, the king had undergone a great deal of suffering for many lifetimes, but eventually the Buddha's compassion led Kaundinya to become enlightened before anyone else.

The most important point for us to learn from this Jataka story is that whenever people act negatively to our good actions, we should try to see their situation. Why would they be angry at us? Since people are not angry as long as they are happy, their anger means that they are unhappy and act negatively because of that. They feel trapped and try to take it out on other people.

Once we understand that, we will not have so much hatred. Even though we may not be able to help them, at least we will feel some compassion. Of course, people do evil things out of greed, anger, jealousy, and ignorance. Because of these faults they suffer in samsara. Overpowered by negative emotions, they are not free and continue to commit acts that perpetuate their own suffering.

This is why a bodhisattva wants to help all sentient beings. If we, as followers of the bodhisattva path, hate negative people instead of wanting to help them, it contradicts our own logic. We may not have the strength to fully love them the way a buddha or great bodhisattva would, but if we can see them in this light, our anger and hatred will lessen. We will feel some sympathy and it will be easier to forgive their mistakes.

In my view, to be able to do this is the main point and the real test for the genuineness of our compassion. Otherwise, we might be compassionate in theory, praying for all sentient beings and even shedding tears for their welfare, but as soon as someone would hurt us a little bit, we might be totally up in arms. If so, we would not be much of a bodhisattva. The way we react, when put to the test by someone who harms us in return for our kindness, is the moment of truth as far as compassion is concerned.

The fifteenth stanza reads:

When someone reveals our hidden faults and speaks ill of us
In the midst of a gathering,
To show him great respect, viewing him as a spiritual friend,
Is the practice of a bodhisattva.

This verse suggests a particular reaction to someone who tries to harm us for no reason. We usually get angry, but a better way to deal with such situations is illustrated by the example of Atisha Dipamkara, or Atisha as he is called by the Tibetans. Atisha, an eminent Indian pandita who lived in the eleventh century, was invited by the Tibetan king Thrisong Detsen to revive Buddhism in Tibet. When Atisha took up the king's invitation, he brought with him a monk who was the most awkward and short-tempered person imaginable. No matter what anyone said or did, invariably the monk became angry and spoiled the whole atmosphere. People said to Atisha, "You are such a compassionate and peaceful lama. Why did you bring along this nasty man who is always fighting with everybody?" Atisha replied, "Oh, he is my teacher; he tests my patience." If, rather than getting angry, we can view someone who hurts us as a spiritual friend, his or her behavior will turn into an instruction, giving us a lesson in patience. We should try to act in this way.

The sixteenth stanza describes a situation in which it is especially difficult not to react with hatred:

When beings whom we nursed and protected, loving them like our
    only child,
Turn against us as if our enemies,
We should love them even more, as a mother will when her child
    has fallen ill.
This is the practice of a bodhisattva.

If someone we love and trust turns on us and treats us in a hateful way, we will naturally be much more affected than by a person we are not close to. Unfortunately, this can happen quite often. So, how should we react in such a situation? Keeping alive our feelings of hurt and resentment is no solution, as we will not get any peace of mind. Our feelings will become more painful and cause us ever more suffering.

If we look carefully, we will find that the worst enemy we could have is our own hatred. It causes us much more harm than the outer enemy who provoked it. Hatred can be said to be the worst of the negative emotions. Instead of trying to eliminate our external enemies, we should do our best to get rid of our hatred, for our own good and the good of others. The only way to do so is to generate compassion, and compassion arises through understanding.

The situation described in this verse is particularly difficult. It is extremely hard to endure someone we dearly love suddenly turning into our enemy. Here again, we should try to look at why the person is behaving so negatively. It must be because he or she is caught in distress, which manifests in cruel ways. For instance, if someone who is drunk or crazy does something bad to us, we will not be greatly affected. There will be no hatred nor even much anger. We will brush it off, saying to ourselves, "Oh, he is drunk," or, "This person is mad," and will simply try to keep out of his way.

Ngulchü Thogmé uses the example of a child who has fallen sick. How would we feel if one of our children was overpowered by a serious disease and did some terrible things without knowing what he or she was doing? We should try to view someone dear who suddenly hurts us in the same light. If we can see that person is out of control and sick with negative emotions, we will not feel so much hatred and disgust. There may be resentment, and we may not be able to love that person more than before, but almost automatically there will be a certain sympathy that will lessen or end our hatred and allow us to forgive.

Trying to increase our love, particularly when someone is hateful, is one of the main practices of a bodhisattva. For this reason, the preceding five stanzas strongly emphasize ways to cope with this situation. The most important point is not to nourish feelings of resentment, hatred, and hurt, as these are the most powerful negative forces and obstruct anything positive. These emotions should therefore be dealt with first. Once we overcome feeling wounded and are able to forgive, positive qualities will be much easier to develop. We will naturally progress in becoming more wholesome.

The seventeenth stanza teaches the value of humility:

When someone who is equal or inferior to us
Contemptuously scorns us driven by pride,
Then to install him respectfully on our crown
As our guru is the practice of a bodhisattva.

Pride and jealousy are also big obstacles for a bodhisattva. The example given here is our peer or someone of lesser qualities who is jealous or proud and tries to put us down by insulting or slandering us. A bodhisattva's way of acting in such a situation is to regard the person as a teacher and his or her behavior as an instruction. A bodhisattva would think, "This person is giving me a lesson, manifesting as my guru and showing me a living example of how feelings of pride and jealousy are negative. They can blind us so that our perception is distorted and we cannot see things as they really are."

If we can take it that way, our reaction will be appropriate and we will avoid becoming puffed up and proud. When someone who is inferior to us in many ways tries to put us down, we would ordinarily assert ourselves, saying, "This person has no right to do that. I am much better." That would inflate our own jealousy and pride. If we can see the experience as a teaching, we will become more humble.

One of the main signs of bodhisattvas is the degree of their humility. The more we truly understand and practice the Dharma, the more humble we will become. This has nothing to do with feeling lowly or timid. We become more humble and at the same time more confident. The mark of a good practitioner is not being proud and showing off, but being humble and respectful to everyone. Someone who knows how to practice sees the good in everybody, and tries to view others' negative actions as an instruction rather than an insult. If we take it this way, we will not act as they do and at the same time will not feel insulted.

You may have heard of Vivekananda, an eminent Hindu teacher who lived during our era. One day he was traveling by train in India. Those who have been there know what Indian railways are like. At the stations there are enormous crowds, and everyone pushes to get on. One time, when the train left, Vivekananda found himself stuck with an extremely angry man who shouted at him for a long time. All the time he was shouting, Vivekananda did not say a word. Finally, when the man was exhausted and could speak no more, Vivekananda calmly said, "Suppose you give a present to someone and he does not accept it. With whom does the gift remain?" "With the giver, of course," the man said. Vivekananda replied, "Yes, and I do not accept your insults."

The eighteenth stanza teaches us how to cope with extremely adverse conditions:

Even though we be living in misery and constantly subject to others'
    scorn,
Even though we be stricken by incurable disease and haunted by
    evil spirits,
Then to take the negativity and suffering of all sentient beings
Upon ourselves without despair is the practice of a bodhisattva.

At times we may find ourselves in very difficult situations, such as not having the necessities of life, being lowly and abused by other people, or falling
seriously ill. Even if the conditions of our lives are the worst imaginable, we
should not lose confidence, but use the circumstances as a means to purify
ourselves and work for the benefit of others. This will give our difficult situation a purpose.

For instance, if we are sick, we could say, "I would like to relieve all sentient beings from this kind of sickness. May all their illnesses be gathered into
mine and totally healed." Likewise, if we are very poor, we could pray, "May
my poverty suffice to clear away the karma of poverty of all sentient beings.
May all their deprivation be absorbed in mine, so that no one is poor anymore."

In this way, a bodhisattva can try to take on the afflictions of others and
purify their negative karma, which at the same time would purify his or her
own karma as well. Usually, this is not the way we react. If we are poor, we
resent others who are better off. If our own material situation becomes really
hopeless, we easily develop hatred toward rich people.

However, if we employ the method described here, which is a kind of *tong
len* practice, we will gain the courage and confidence to take the ill fortune of
all beings onto ourselves. Anything adverse that arises in our lives will gain
a purpose when we actively transform it into the path. In doing so, our resentment toward our own situation will lessen and there will be a greater ability
to accept what is there. Our negative conditions may improve, but even if they
do not, we will be healed of the mental agitation that usually accompanies
them. The practice described here is a very important cure.

The nineteenth stanza shows how to deal with the opposite condition:

Even if we had won renown and many a man reverently bowed
    before us,

Even if we had acquired riches equaling the treasure of the god
    of wealth,
Seeing all the world's splendor and fortune as essenceless
And not becoming arrogant is the practice of a bodhisattva.

It is often seen that human beings can endure problems quite well, but
cannot endure success. When we are successful and have everything we
desire, it can easily go to our heads. There is a great danger of losing our common sense and becoming careless and arrogant. As it is said, "Nothing cor-
rupts a person more than power." Very powerful people sometimes become
so proud that they no longer care about their actions or about the effect they
have on others. Losing any sense of right and wrong, they create severe problems for themselves and everyone else.

Even if we have all the success we could dream of—fame, wealth, and so
on—we must understand that these things have no real substance. Attachment does not come from having things, but from the way our mind reacts
to them. It is fine to participate in good circumstances, provided we can see
that they have no real essence. They may come and they may go. When seeing this, we will not become so attached. Even if we lose our wealth we will
not be badly affected, and while it is there we will enjoy it without being
senseless and arrogant.

This and the preceding stanza describe the importance of maintaining
stability regardless of our situation. No matter whether we are the lowest of
the low or the highest of the high, we should keep our sanity and sense of
right and wrong, our humility and confidence. Otherwise, when our for-
tunes increase we will become arrogant, and as soon as they decline, we will
feel utterly lost and dejected. There should be inner strength in which we
remain stable and independent from outer circumstances.

This kind of strength arises from understanding. No matter how rich or
famous we are, these things can vanish in a very short time. Being lowly is
also not permanent. There is no real essence. Anything can come and go.
Even if adverse conditions cannot be changed for some time, we can deal
with them if we have the necessary confidence. A bodhisattva can handle
any situation in a stable manner. As long as we lack this capacity we will go
up and down like a yo-yo. Gaining inner strength is not only the right practice for a bodhisattva, but for anyone who wants to become a good human

being. With it, we will be able to help others as well as ourselves and follow the path in a steady way.

The twentieth stanza teaches the priority of overcoming our own anger and hatred:

> If we do not subdue the enemy that is our own hatred,
> Fighting outer enemies will only increase their number.
> Therefore, taming our mind stream by mustering the hosts
> Of love and compassion is the practice of a bodhisattva.

The *Bodhicharyavatara* says that to avoid being hurt by thorns and brambles, we might consider covering all the mountains with leather. That would be impossible, but putting on shoes would serve the same purpose. Similarly, if we tried to subdue all our outer enemies, we would never succeed. Once one was eliminated, another would rise against us. While doing this, our anger would continue to breed new foes. The only way to overcome our enemies is to turn inward and kill the real one, which is our own hatred.

The importance of this recognition is shown by the life of Ashoka, the great Indian king. In his early years as king he was very combative and waged war against his neighboring countries, killing thousands of people. One day while traveling, he heard someone shouting, "At last I have won. I am a great victor!" Ashoka ordered his men to find out what was happening. They found a man shouting by the bank of a river, into which he had thrown his sword. They brought the man before the king, and Ashoka asked, "Why are you making such a noise? What have you won?" The man answered, "For a long time I was filled with hatred. I had many enemies whom I tried to kill one by one. Eventually, I realized that for each enemy I killed another one arose, and as long as I nurtured hatred and the thirst for revenge within me, there would never be an end to my enemies. Since then I have been trying to overcome my anger, and I have finally succeeded. I have thrown my sword into the river. From today onward I will kill no more." His words kindled a spark in Ashoka's heart, and he thought, "So, it can be done!" Later in his life Ashoka embraced nonviolence, and played a major role in spreading Buddhism in Asia.

This example shows how we must work on our aversion. As long as our mind is filled with anger and revenge, everyone seems to be an enemy. Everything aggravates us and is viewed as being potentially harmful. However, the more our hatred decreases, the more our surroundings seem benign, since it is mainly our mind that determines what kind of experience we have.

One of my favorite allegories is about a wise shepherd who used to graze his sheep near a mountain pass above his native village. One day a stranger came by and inquired, "What kind of people live down in that village?" The shepherd asked in return, "What kind of people live in the village you came from?" "Oh, they are horrible," the stranger replied. "They are nasty and inhospitable." The shepherd said, "Well, the people down there are just the same. They are quarrelsome and totally lacking in hospitality." Hearing that, the stranger turned back and went somewhere else.

Some time later another traveler arrived and asked the same question. Again the shepherd inquired, "What kind of people live in the village you came from?" "Oh, they are wonderful," the second stranger replied. "They are warmhearted and friendly." To him the shepherd said, "Well, you will find the people down there are just the same. They are very good and hospitable to everyone." So, the traveler continued on to the village.

Why would the shepherd say two completely different things about the same place? He knew that the man who found everything bad where he came from would find the same thing anywhere he went, while the one who found everything good where he came from would encounter the same goodness elsewhere. The way we experience our environment depends on our reactions and habits. Since wherever we go we take ourselves with us, we will meet, more or less, the same kind of people everywhere. Therefore, we should do our best to tame our own mind.

The twenty-first stanza teaches how to deal with attachment, especially for negative things:

> What attracts our desire is like saltwater.
> The more we drink, the greater our thirst will grow.
> Abandoning this very instant what causes attachment
> Is therefore the practice of a bodhisattva.

Whenever we have a strong craving for something negative but do not give it up because we like it or are used to it, we should view this attachment as being like saltwater. The more you drink, the thirstier you become, and eventually you could die of thirst. Similarly, the more we consume what we crave, the more our clinging will grow. It will never be completely satisfied. The only way to satisfy and end our craving is to stop indulging our passion. For instance, if someone has a drinking problem and is in danger of becoming an alcoholic, drinking more and more is no solution since it just increases the urge. One has to stop drinking, and this takes a firm decision based on recognizing how harmful it is and the further problems it will cause.

Once this is seen, one has to say, "I want to give it up and I will give it up right now." As long as we wonder about our ability to do so, there is no chance, since we have too much doubt. The moment we are strongly resolved, we simply do it. After all, it is our decision, so then we are able to carry it through.

This is true of any addiction we may have. When we are habituated to something, at the beginning it is not easy to change and more problems may seem to arise. However, our craving will slowly diminish until it is gone. Whenever we notice that we have become addicted to something, we must understand how harmful it is and give it up immediately with great resolve. This is the crucial point. Of course, we will need some determination and stability, but once we have entered this process, our habits will gradually weaken until there is no problem at all.

While this verse emphasizes giving up attachment, it does not mean that we should not enjoy anything. For instance, quite a few people think that Buddhists should not eat good food. This is a misunderstanding. There is nothing wrong with sense pleasures as such. We can enjoy our lives, and the better we manage to do so, the better it is.

A problem arises only when we become strongly attached to something, as this causes anxiety about losing it and aversion toward what threatens it. Being caught in the chain reaction of wanting something so much and loathing its opposite is the main source of our problems. Attachment, therefore, needs to be abandoned, but in doing so we should not become uptight. Once we are aware of being attached to something and we resolve to overcome our craving, we should not feel guilt and panic if we give in to it again. We have had our habits for a very long time. Getting caught once more does not make us worse. We can only improve, and should do so slowly and gradually, yet with firm resolve.

The twenty-second stanza says:

All appearances are our own mind.
Mind itself is free from conceptual elaboration since beginningless
   time.
To know this and not ideate perceived and perceiver nor charac-
   teristics
Is the practice of a bodhisattva.

This is a central verse for succinctly describing how to see the true nature of the mind. The statement "All appearances are our own mind" is a little difficult to understand. It does not mean everything "out there" is my mind, or all of you are my mind and I am your mind. However, whatever we see around us is not quite as solid and real in nature as it might seem. Everything is interdependent; everything is a cause and an effect at the same time. The things we perceive are just appearances. There is no single thing with a real independent existence of its own.

Appearances are our own mind in the sense that whatever I think something is, however something appears, is my own perception. When I see or hear something and like it very much, I will want to have it, and then I may become so attached that I feel I cannot live without it. Then, when I lose it, or fear losing it, I get into trouble. On the other hand, I might not like it at all. I might despise it and try to get away from it. When I do not succeed, I am also in trouble.

The way I perceive any object of the senses is my own perception and my own contribution. There is no one telling me, "This is pleasant and that is unpleasant; this is like this and that is like that." Whatever I experience is my creation and my view. For example, if I like to have a fair complexion, I will avoid the sun and will feel good in a place with forests and snow. Or I may long for sunshine, and find it a hateful place with its cold snow and wild animals in the forest. All these judgments are my own doing; they come from my mind.

From there attachment and aversion arise. When I have aversion to something, it means nothing to me and I cannot see any good coming from it. Attachment is more tricky because we tend to think that the object itself is truly pleasant, and it causes us to experience a very good feeling. Looking more closely, though, there is a problem. For example, if I like a place very much and want to stay there forever, if I cannot imagine being anywhere else, what will happen when I have to leave? Wherever I go I will be unhappy, longing to get back. Once my return is almost within reach I will be agitated and counting the days. Even after I have returned, my longing and pain will not dissolve. Knowing I cannot stay as long as I would like, I will be anticipating my departure and again counting the days, "Today is already Saturday and I have to leave on Monday." Whenever I become really attached to something, I cannot see anything else. I make it the most important thing and nothing else will suffice to make me happy.

However, if I do not have attachment, I can enjoy my stay in a cold place, but I can also go to India or anywhere else and enjoy that, too. There is no problem. The problem arises when we become fascinated by a particular thing, in either a positive or negative way. Our Dharma practice should lead us to overcome these reactions.

All attachment and aversion come from what we have mentally created. We have made an image and that is our mind as we normally experience it. In order to solve this problem in a more profound and permanent way, we have to look at our mind and see its true nature. In our innate, unfabricated nature, which is the basic state of our mind, there is no problem. We make all our problems by creating concepts and all kinds of mental conditioning.

Seeing the true nature of mind means experiencing the way the mind is when we do not fabricate and contrive anything. We need to look at our mind when it is devoid of our creations and free from mental elaborations. If we can see this state of mind, there is no grasping, no grasped object, and no subject doing the grasping. There is simply perception or seeing, which in itself does not cause a problem.

When the true nature of mind is seen, there are just appearances without any evaluation. One thing arises in the mind and then another thing arises. The arising that is pleasant is no better than the one that is unpleasant. They are simply different manifestations of the mind. There is no need to grasp one and reject the other. Once this is seen clearly, we see the true nature of mind. This is something that we need to experience directly. When we see the truth, we become liberated from our struggle within the nets of aversion and attachment.

This complete freedom is the goal of all Dharma practice. The real purpose of practice is not to gain good experiences, but to reach the level where whatever happens is good. When there is no aversion to anything, everything is utterly good and there is no more reason for fear. When we reach this state, we will always be fearless and joyful, finally freed from all our prob-

lems. Our practice will reach fruition when our suffering has permanently
dissolved. We will have seen the truth and liberated ourselves forever.

In a brief form, this stanza contains the entire understanding of our ultimate nature. Once we understand clearly that attachment and aversion create the samsaric state of mind and the entire cycle of existence, then actual
practice begins. The teachings recommend different ways of dealing with
attachment and aversion. The first stage is taught in the Shravakayana system. At this level we counteract the mental poisons by creating their oppo-
sites. When feeling hatred, we try to generate loving-kindness. When feeling
attachment, we try to generate nonattachment. When feeling confused, we
try to develop understanding.

The next two stanzas, verses 23 and 24, describe the second stage, the
Mahayana way of dealing with negative emotions, in which we view the
absolute nature of our objects of attachment and aversion:

> When encountering attractive objects, they are as rainbows
>   in summer.
> Though they appear to be so beautiful, not to view them as being real
> And to abandon attachment and yearning
> Is therefore the practice of a bodhisattva.
>
> All the various sufferings are like the death of one's child in a dream.
> Taking illusory appearance as being truly existent—what a fatigue!
> When meeeting with adverse conditions, to view them as delusion
> Is therefore the practice of a bodhisattva.

Whenever we are very attracted to something we consider beautiful and
whenever we suffer from something we consider horrible, we should try
to look at those objects and see their true nature. Everything, no matter
how good or bad it may seem, is in fact emptiness. This means that when
we look at something and examine whether it is permanent or impermanent, it will always prove to be impermanent. It is always changing. When
we examine whether something is independent or interdependent, it will
always prove to be interdependent. There is nothing that exists on its own.
When we examine whether something is one or many, it will always prove
to have many parts. Nothing is just one thing which is unitary, independent, and permanent.

Although we may perceive any object in those terms, in reality it does not have any independent existence. It depends upon many different factors and is therefore changing all the time. It cannot remain forever, and while it is there, it is not a single thing. For example, we can look at a glass and think that it is one thing, but in fact it is made of many parts; it does not have an existence of its own. Nowadays, this way of seeing is established by scientific methods. When examined through an electron microscope, a glass consists of all kinds of molecules, atoms, and so forth. Looking deeper, we find that it is made of energy, and energy is near to being nothing at all. Even though we see it as a solid glass at the very moment we look, it is actually not there; it is made of almost nothing.

We can understand this intellectually and say, "This glass lacks inherent existence," but at the same time continue to think, "This is *my* glass; I do not want anyone else to have it!" As long as our understanding is only academic, our problems will not dissolve. If we can see the nature of emptiness more deeply at the level of our hearts, we will feel how everything really is and we will no longer be addicted. We are also like this glass. Everything exists in this way. Once we see this clearly, we will see that there is no need to be so strongly involved or to feel so much passion or aversion. Then everything will be seen as being like a rainbow or a dream.

Suppose that something terrible happens in a dream, like the death of our only child. If we can recognize that we are dreaming, we will know it is not real and we will not be as affected by the dream. Of course, it is not easy to see our lives in this way. Toward this aim, we have to study, reflect, and meditate. The more we can see this way, the lighter everything becomes. This is one of the main practices of a bodhisattva.

Attachment and aversion are closely related, like two sides of a coin. When we are afraid of something and do not want it, we look for its opposite and desire that with equal intensity. Once we have it, we become attached to it and fear its loss. Everything else threatens it and generates aversion. Whenever we have one of these impulses, we immediately create its opposite as well.

Of course, everyone has some attachment. The problems arise when it becomes too strong. This is easier to understand from the viewpoint of aversion. The smaller our aversion, the less problems we will have, and when there is no aversion at all, there will be no attachment either. When it is said that we should not have attachment, there is a tendency to think that we should not like anything. That is not what is meant. For instance, if I do not have aversion to any place, I can like a particular place and enjoy my stay there, but I can also enjoy staying anywhere else. Yet if I am strongly attached to this particular place, all other places are not good enough and I will not want to be there. So, the less aversion I have, the happier I will be.

For this reason it is said that without aversion everything is experienced as compassion, loving-kindness, and joy. Once we have freed ourselves from aversion we will experience a great amount of joy, which has nothing to do with strong attachment. If we cling intensely to a particular thing or person, our feelings may easily turn into resentment or even hatred. Being fixated, there is no space for anything to change and we feel completely stuck. For someone who is filled with compassion and joy, the situation is very different. There is no attachment. We simply like something and that is good. Eventually we will not dislike anything. Then we will reach the kind of limitless, great equanimity described in the prayer of "the four limitless wishes":

> May all sentient beings come to meet with happiness and the causes
>   of happiness.
> May they be free from suffering and the causes of suffering.
> May they be inseparable from true bliss devoid of any misery,
> And dwell in great equanimity beyond lust for the near and hatred
>   for the distant.

Great equanimity is different from not caring for anyone or not having feelings. It is freedom from attachment and aversion, since without them everything becomes clear and there is no problem. With such equanimity we will be joyful and compassionate regardless of circumstances. When there is no attachment, nothing is rejected. Equanimity is very important, but it is sometimes hard to understand.

The next six stanzas describe the practice of the six perfections, or *paramitas*, which are the active practices of a bodhisattva. The six perfections are generosity, discipline or moral conduct, patience, diligence, meditation, and wisdom. The twenty-fifth stanza deals with generosity:

> As wishing for enlightenment one must even give one's body,
> The giving of external objects needs not to be mentioned.

Engaging in generosity without nourishing hopes for reward
Or good karmic fruits is therefore the practice of a bodhisattva.

This verse describes the final achievement of enlightened bodhisattvas who have developed generosity to the extent that they give up their own bodies to fulfill the aims of sentient beings. Accounts of this capacity are found in the Jataka stories of the former lives of the Buddha and in similar scriptures. When enlightenment is reached, there is no attachment to anything and everything is done solely to benefit others.

As beginners, we have to start gradually and proceed step-by-step. We need to practice generosity to open ourselves up. Presently, we are focused so strongly on our desires and needs that we find it hard to give and be open to others. At this stage we can develop generosity by being more bighearted and concerned about others. As a first step we need to overcome our possessiveness and strong attachment to things.

An example of this comes from one of the Buddha's disciples, who was later known as Anathapindada, which means "one who is generous and altruistic." He was a rich businessman who attended the Buddha's teachings with great enthusiasm. But whenever the Buddha spoke of generosity, Anathapindada found himself unable to relate to it. One day he addressed the Buddha and said, "I like your teachings very much, but whenever it comes to generosity, I find it totally beyond me. I cannot give anything away. Even the thought of it is painful."

The Buddha replied, "If you practice, you might become more generous." Anathapindada said, "How can I practice? It is impossible for me to give anything." The Buddha asked him, "Can you give something to yourself?" When Anathapindada said he could, the Buddha said, "Take something in your right hand and give it to your left hand. Then, have your left hand give it back to your right hand. Keep doing this and it may make you more generous."

Anathapindada followed his advice; he went home and took a piece of gold and gave it to his left hand and said, "Take it!" Then, he gave it to his right hand and said, "Take it!" In this way, he slowly became more generous, until finally he was one of the greatest benefactors of his time, setting up houses throughout the country to feed and shelter the poor.

This shows that generosity is not just a matter of giving. It means being rid of our overwhelming attachment to ourselves and whatever we have. That is the main point. Generosity is being spacious and openhearted. When people say that someone has a big heart, this usually means that the person is generous. Opening and expanding our heart is a gradual process. While we develop generosity we should respect our own capabilities. As the Buddha said, we should give a bowl of curry when we are able to give a bowl of curry, and give our lives when we are able to give our lives. In this way we will continue to become more bighearted.

As long as we remain concerned only about ourselves and our belongings, we become isolated to the point that we are almost alone. To the extent that we harden ourselves against everything else, our world becomes more cold, miserable, and lonely. This reminds me of a book written by an Egyptian mystic who described a vision of hell in which a person born there was surrounded by everything desirable, but was totally alone. There was no one to talk to or see his riches. He sat there all day, watching and protecting his possessions, without enjoying them or doing anything further with them. This shows what can happen when we are self-centered.

We should dissolve this attitude by starting slowly but never relenting. This verse shows the best way to practice generosity. Ideally, we should not hope for any reward. Yet in the meantime if we speculate on immediate positive results or eventual karmic fruition, it is all right. The main thing is to start opening up. This process is limitless, and eventually our attitude and actions will become the perfection of generosity. At that point there will be no more attachment and anything can be given. However, this is a very high level and we should start from where we are at the moment.

The twenty-sixth stanza describes the perfection of moral conduct:

> If, lacking discipline, we even fail to accomplish our own benefit,
> The wish to fulfill others' benefit is a joke.
> Guarding our moral conduct without longing for worldly existence
> Is therefore the practice of a bodhisattva.

Right conduct is based on understanding karma, on seeing what is right and wrong. Whatever is beneficial to ourselves and others is right, and whatever is harmful to ourselves and others is wrong. Discipline means acting accordingly. First, a bodhisattva should refrain from harming others in any way—this is discipline in its actual sense. Going further, a bodhisattva makes great effort at helping others, which is the main feature of generosity.

The twenty-seventh verse teaches the perfection of patience:

> For a bodhisattva seeking the delights of virtue, all who afflict him
> Are like a treasure mine. Becoming acquainted
> With patience toward all, without resentment or wish for retaliation,
> Is therefore the practice of a bodhisattva.

Developing patience means to see situations with more understanding, and to forgive people instead of harboring hatred and resentment. This makes us more free and able to generate loving-kindness, compassion, and other positive emotions. The most important point here is to forgive. The Buddha has said, "There is nothing worse than hatred, and no practice stronger than patience." To free our minds from hatred and the feelings of hurt and resentment that are born from it, we should try to understand others' point of view and see the true nature of things. Using these means, we should do our best to overcome our hatred and become more patient. Once patience has developed to the point of being spontaneous, the perfection of patience has been achieved.

The twenty-eighth stanza describes the perfection of diligence:

> When shravakas and pratyekabuddhas, whose aim is just their own
> benefit,
> Are seen to strive with the zeal of one trying to quench a fire on
> his head,
> To persist in diligence, which is the source of all qualities,
> For the welfare of all beings is the practice of a bodhisattva.

The Buddhist notion of diligence is to delight in positive deeds. Its opposite, called le lo in Tibetan, has three aspects. Le lo is usually translated as "laziness," though only its first aspect refers to laziness as we usually understand it. The first aspect is not doing something because of indolence, even though we know that it is good and ought to be done. The second aspect is faintheartedness. This comes about when we underestimate our qualities and abilities, thinking, "I'm so incompetent and weak. It would be good to do that, but I could never accomplish it." Not having the confidence of thinking, "I can do it," we end up doing nothing. The third aspect refers to being very busy and seeming diligent, but wasting time and energy on meaningless activities that will not accomplish anything in the long run. When we do many things for no real purpose, we fail to focus on what is truly worthwhile and our path has no clear direction. When we refrain from these three aspects of laziness, we are diligent.

This verse uses a slightly pointed example based upon the fact that shravakas and pratyekabuddhas, who follow the two paths of the first vehicle, aim at reaching individual liberation and do not follow the bodhisattva ideal. Nevertheless, they engage in very purposeful activities that are highly beneficial to other sentient beings as well. In contrast, we may find that we often spend a great deal of time and effort, sometimes even risking our lives, on things of little value. If we find a real goal that is in our best interest, such as reaching enlightenment, we should really make the effort. This is all the more true of bodhisattvas, who do not practice for their sake alone, but to relieve the suffering of all sentient beings. Having discovered and conceived such a great and noble purpose, shouldn't we start working on it with all our effort? Cultivating this understanding is a way to generate more enthusiasm and diligence in practice.

The twenty-ninth stanza deals with meditation:

> One must gain the understanding that special insight well endowed
>   with calm abiding
> Will utterly vanquish the mental poisons.
> Becoming familiar with meditative stability truly transcending
>   the four formless states
> Is therefore the practice of a bodhisattva.

All Buddhist meditation is included in the two aspects of calm abiding and special insight. Calm abiding is the method that makes our mind calm and clear, while special insight is the means to gain experiential understanding of the nature of mind and all phenomena. The first step is to make the mind calm. It is usually so busy and polluted by different thoughts and emotions that we cannot see clearly. Practicing calm abiding eliminates our confusion and makes the mind naturally clear.

Once calmness and clarity are present, we can try to look at our mind to gain deep insight into its nature. When this is achieved, we see the true nature of everything. Whatever perceptions we have are due to our mind. When we see our mind and the way it functions very clearly, we will also see what our mind sees and understand the nature of all phenomena as not being different from the nature of our mind. There is no obstacle, since that which sees everything is our own mind. Once we clearly see one thing, we will understand everything else. Special insight is just a way of looking, which is born from our own experience. When we understand this way of looking, we can apply it to anything. This is similar to scientific analysis. Once we have found a valid method to analyze one chemical substance, we are able to analyze other substances in an equally valid manner.

When we have full control of our mind and understand it totally, there are no more problems, and we will reach enlightenment in the highest sense. This verse points out that calm abiding and special insight, the two meditations that lead toward this goal, need to go hand in hand. When insight is based on strong and unwavering peace of mind, it overcomes all mental poisons, such as hatred, attachment, jealousy, ignorance, and so on.

These defilements are temporary and removable habits that are based on misconception. Since we lack valid insight into the nature of things, we create concepts about what we perceive. We see everything in a hazy manner, which leads us to assume things and react incorrectly, and this creates all kinds of problems. All the negative emotions stem from an initial distorted perception. This brings about a chain reaction of habits that condition our mind and behavior. If we see this clearly, the whole construction vanishes and we see everything as it is, without falling into our usual pattern of reacting with attachment and aversion. Once we do not react that way anymore, we will be liberated. The way to achieve liberation is to overcome all negativity through clear insight into the fundamental nature of everything.

The verse refers to the "four formless states," which are stages of meditative experience where the mind has become extremely stable and clear. At that point, if there is no genuine insight as well, the meditation is still worldly and cannot transcend samsara. These formless experiences are very pleasant because one is absorbed in utter peace, joy, light, and the absence of any reference point. But if one does not pass beyond them, one will not make any further progress and will not reach the realization of the enlightened mind.

Once there is firm insight, enabling us to perceive the true nature of ourselves and everything else, we will not get stuck in the four formless states and we will reach the path of seeing. The Buddhist teachings describe five paths or stages of spiritual development: the paths of accumulation, junction, seeing, meditation, and no more learning. During the second path, junction, there is a genuine touch of the truth, but it is not yet seen directly. Feeling its warmth and light, we will strongly anticipate its presence, but we will not have a direct vision of it.

We actually see the truth at the stage of seeing. This is the first, small level of enlightenment. It is not comparable to being a buddha, yet our vision is beyond samsaric states of mind. Through the path of seeing we reach the first *bhumi*, or bodhisattva level. From then onward we travel the path of meditation, which consists of nine levels, or *bhumis*, during which our initial direct vision of the truth becomes increasingly refined.

At the stage of meditation, though we see things clearly, we still carry a lot of conditioning from the past—many habitual patterns and conventional ways of thinking. These must be gradually resolved. A single vision of the truth will not shatter these old habits all at once. They need to be worked upon slowly throughout the nine levels of the path of meditation.

Finally, a point is reached where no more effort is needed. This is the stage of buddhahood, called the path of no more learning. No more meditation is needed because everything is totally clear; even the subtlest traces of habitual tendencies are dissolved. The two aspects of meditation, calm abiding and special insight, are the means to attain enlightenment. They are the main tools to free ourselves from the samsaric state of mind.

The thirtieth stanza deals with the last perfection, that of discriminative wisdom:

> Without wisdom, through the five perfections alone, one cannot
>   attain perfect enlightenment.
> To cultivate the discriminative wisdom
> That is endowed with all skillful means and does not ideate subject,
>   object, and their interaction
> Is therefore the practice of a bodhisattva.

The wisdom referred to here is nothing other than the insight described in the preceding verse. Special insight meditation is impossible without *prajna*, or discriminative wisdom, which sees the nature of everything clearly as it is. This stanza stresses the fact that the first five practices are not enough to reach enlightenment. We may have developed generosity, good conduct, patience, diligence, and calm abiding, but without the discriminative wisdom that sees the truth we cannot be liberated.

This wisdom should be free from any dualistic view. Whatever arises in our mind is usually split into two or three aspects. There is a perceiving subject here, a perceived object over there, an interaction taking place between them; and all these are viewed as being real. As long as we see that way, we do not see the true nature of everything. Wisdom is very basic—it is not mystical or distant; it is just the vision of what is true. It is right here and knowable in every moment. Nevertheless, we find it difficult because we do not have the required openness and do not know how to look.

This is demonstrated nicely by a cartoon I saw in a Chinese magazine on Zen. It showed a big fish and a small fish in the middle of the ocean. The small fish asked, "Where is the sea? Everybody keeps talking about the sea, but I don't see it. Where is it?" The big fish said, "Oh, it's all around you." The small fish was bewildered and said, "But what is all around me?" The big fish replied, "You are in it. All around you, up and down, everywhere is the sea." The small fish said, "Well, what is it? I don't see any sea around me!"

Similarly, we are not trying to see something that is totally different or completely beyond us. We are trying to attain the wisdom of seeing ourselves and everything around us clearly. The question is, how do we do it? This verse says that wisdom should be endowed with skillful means, which refers to generosity, moral conduct, patience, diligence, and meditative stability. Without discriminative wisdom, these five practices will not reach perfection, but they do serve as steps to develop it. All of these are interdependent.

Why do we meditate and exert diligence? The sole reason is to reveal the wisdom of seeing the true nature of ourselves and all things. Even generosity leads toward this, because when we open ourselves to be generous, we see more clearly. All the first five perfection practices work together toward one goal. Together with compassion they are part of the aspect of skillful means, or method, which leads to authentic insight into the true nature of everything. When insight is achieved, the practices of method are united with wisdom to thus truly become "perfections," or *paramitas*, which literally means "gone beyond." Discriminative wisdom leads beyond duality or, strictly speaking, beyond the threefold concept of a subject performing a particular action, of an object toward whom or which that action is directed, and of an interaction taking place between them—all of which are believed to be truly existent. As long as this belief in the true existence of an actor, object of action, and an action unfolding between them is not eliminated, the five aspects of method, or skillful means, are called "perfections," but are not perfect as of yet. They are able to become perfect, though, once they are unified with the discriminative wisdom that directly sees emptiness. Until then, they are merely named after their fruit (with respect to this latter ability), as is frequently the case in Buddhist terminology.

Whenever we practice, we should include all six perfections. This can be done in a modest way to start with, until they become completely transcendent. For example, we can practice all six *paramitas* when we receive teachings. First, we pay respect to the teacher, offering a throne and prostrations. This is a form of giving. Someone filled with pride finds it hard to bow down. By prostrating we open up, we show respect and give up our pride.

While listening, we engage in good conduct by being mindful, sitting up straight, and not disturbing others. If we get bored and try to not fall asleep or show our boredom, this is patience. Being enthusiastic and wanting to learn more is diligence. Keeping our mind focused on what we are hearing is meditation, and trying to understand the actual meaning of the teachings is wisdom.

If we cultivate awareness of these practices, the six perfections will become part of our lives and we can practice them in any situation. Integrating the six perfections into all our activities leads to our own improvement and our increased ability to help others. It is therefore the foremost practice of a bodhisattva.

The thirty-first stanza says:

> Not analyzing our own delusion, we might assume the form of
>   a "follower of Dharma"
> And commit nondharmic actions.
> To always investigate our deluded motives and to abandon what
>   is seen as misleading
> Is the practice of a bodhisattva.

This verse stresses the importance of looking at ourselves and evaluating our actions and motives. This is an important point. Sometimes we look beyond ourselves too much. We start criticizing others and neglect looking at our own actions, or we might accept others' comments as a general judgment on our lives, thinking, "Oh, she likes me so much, I must be really great," or, "He said something bad about me, I must be a terrible person." We often judge ourselves through the eyes of others. In this way we do not get a completely clear picture, because we usually know ourselves much better than others do.

We can look more easily into our own mind than anybody else can. When we look carefully, we may find that although we claim to be a Dharma practitioner, our actions do not truly correspond to Dharma practice. We could be on an ego trip or deceiving ourselves. We have to open our eyes to see that; we ourselves have to judge the quality of our motivations and actions. Often we are not willing to do that, and content ourselves with just following a lifestyle conditioned by other people's ideas.

There is a story from India about this. Once a Brahmin was taking his goat to a nearby town. Four young men of doubtful character saw him coming and decided to trick him out of his goat. After they had laid their plot, one of the young men approached the Brahmin and said, "What a nice dog." For Brahmins dogs are impure animals, so it is not surprising that he was outraged: "This is not a dog; it's a goat!," he exclaimed. "Well," the young man said, "it looks like a dog to me." Then he continued on his way.

After some time another of the young men walked toward the Brahmin and asked him, "Where are you going?" "I am going to town," he answered. "Why are you taking that dog with you?," the young man inquired. The Brahmin said, "I am not taking a dog; I am taking my goat." "That isn't a goat," the young man insisted, "that is a dog. You are taking a dog." The Brahmin was bewildered by now and shouted, "No, you must be crazy!" The young man gave in and went away.

Then the third man passed by and the Brahmin asked, "Am I taking a goat with me?" "No, you are taking a dog," the man replied. By now the Brahmin was beginning to panic and hurried on. When the fourth man came his way, he said, "Come here! What is this? Do you see a dog or a goat?" The young man shook his head, "Of course, I see a dog." At that the Brahmin left the goat on the spot and ran away. So, the four men got his goat as they had planned.

This shows how misleading it can be when we rely too much on the opinions and statements of other people.

The thirty-second stanza says:

> If driven by our mental poisons we expose other bodhisattvas' faults,
> We cause our own deterioration.

So to never speak ill of anyone who is a follower of the Great Vehicle
Is the practice of a bodhisattva.

This simply means that we should not talk badly about others. Just as others do not have the knowledge to judge us completely, we cannot judge others correctly either. We should therefore try to not criticize others, especially other bodhisattvas. Due to a misunderstanding or some other reason, we may have heard something that is untrue about someone, and yet we make a negative judgment and talk about it. The person who is belittled may be a real bodhisattva. So, we should never speak ill of anyone.

The thirty-third stanza is mainly directed toward someone like a lama. It says:

By clinging to the households of friends and benefactors we may get
    entangled in arguments,
Being driven by our desires for gain and honor,
Whereas the true tasks of learning, reflecting, and meditating may
    increasingly fall into decay.
Abandoning that is the practice of a bodhisattva.

When we are attached to obtaining honor, fame, or wealth, we become involved in disputes and petty rivalries, and our true Dharma practice of learning, reflecting, and meditating decreases. We should therefore not become involved in situations where we think, "This is my benefactor, my sponsor. I should get more support and appreciation." As a bodhisattva we should not become entangled in this kind of worldly concern.

The thirty-fourth stanza says:

Using offensive words we disturb the minds of others
While our bodhisattva conduct deteriorates.
Abandoning harsh words unpleasant to fellow beings
Is therefore the practice of a bodhisattva.

This verse teaches the importance of right speech. Of course, the words we choose are mainly due to our state of mind. When we are angry or in a bad mood we use harsh and unpleasant words. But our manner of speaking is very important. Even if we have to say something of considerable impact, people will usually not take it badly if we speak reasonably, with respect and concern. On the other hand, we may unintentionally say something that really hurts people. There is a Tibetan saying, "Although words are not made of blades, they can pierce the hearts of others."

For this reason, we should watch carefully what we are saying and how we are speaking, and try to speak in a mild and respectful way. This is an important training for a bodhisattva. When we use disturbing words that hurt people's feelings, they are put off and we are unable to help them. This keeps us from being able to practice the bodhisattva's way of life.

The thirty-fifth stanza says:

> Once habituated to the mental poisons, we will find it hard to
>   reverse them by means of their antidotes.
> Arming ourselves with the remedies of mindfulness and
>   awareness, and defeating desire and so forth
> In the very moment they arise,
> Is the practice of a bodhisattva.

The only way to change our habitual ways of thinking and reacting is through mindfulness and awareness. We will fall into our usual patterns of hatred, attachment, jealousy, and so on unless we are mindful. Once strong emotions have taken over, it is hard to do anything about them since we are already overpowered. The only way to deal with them is to cultivate awareness and recognize them the moment they arise. When something happens in a situation or communication, we should try to be mindful of our reactions. Once awareness is there and we understand what is happening, we should put the techniques and teachings we have received into practice.

This is the time to do it. The various Buddhist practices are not intended just for retreat or our meditation cushion. These situations alone will not help us very much. Of course, they are very beneficial for training our mind, for gaining greater calmness and clarity, but most of us do not spend our lives in meditation. Ninety percent of what we do happens in worldly surroundings. So, the place to put Dharma into practice is in our everyday lives.

Day after day we do things like going to an office, driving a car, communicating with others, and all kinds of experiences happen. Some are pleasant, some are unpleasant, people's reactions vary, as do our own. Sometimes we are in a good mood and other times we are not. In all these situations and moods we should look at how we react. When we notice that a strong and totally useless negative emotion has arisen, we should ask ourselves whether we are behaving appropriately and then use the practices we have learned. We might make use of reasoning or one of the methods described in this text. Or we might be more experienced in Dzogchen or Mahamudra, and look at our emotion and its nature face-to-face. Whatever works best is most suitable.

Unless we practice being aware, we cannot change our habitual patterns. When it is said that Buddhism is a way of life, it means that its methods should be used every day. They should be applied to all our problems and emotions, using mindfulness and awareness. Otherwise, these methods are useless. When anger comes up, or jealousy, hatred, or strong attachment, we should identify them the very moment they arise. We should ask ourselves, "Is this good or bad? What are its consequences? Do I want to experience them?" Once we see our emotions clearly in this way, we will usually work things out. This will become almost automatic.

By being aware of our negative impulses, almost subconsciously we will become aware of our positive ones and diminish our negativity. In this way we can gradually change our attitude and tendencies through mindfulness and awareness.

The thirty-sixth stanza summarizes the advice given in the preceding verses:

> In brief, wherever we stay, whatever we do,
> We have to know the state of our own mind.
> Being continually in command of clear mindfulness and awareness,
> Hereby accomplishing others' good, is the practice of a bodhisattva.

This is similar to the preceding verse. We have to be mindful of what we are doing. We have to see whether it is positive or negative, and then behave appropriately. The most important point in this context is not to lose the bodhisattva attitude of trying to help all sentient beings, including ourselves, no matter what our life situations may be. We should never totally abandon this motivation, and continue to be mindful and aware.

There is a famous story about Geshe Ben, a Tibetan practitioner who used to say, "I do not carry out any practice other than looking at my mind." One day Geshe Ben was informed that some of his devotees were coming to see him. He cleaned his place carefully and prepared a table with abundant offerings. Then, he sat down and asked himself, "What am I doing and why am I doing it?" When he found that he intended to impress his devotees and was hoping for their praise, he immediately went to the fireplace, took a bunch of ashes, and threw them on his shrine. Then he sat down again and waited for his visitors. Word of what he had done spread, eventually reaching the ears of Atisha Dipamkara, who said, "That was the best offering he could possibly make."

At another time Geshe Ben was staying with a family in a village. He wanted to go into retreat in a cave, but had very little *tsampa*, the barley flour that is the traditional staple food in Tibet. However, the family had a big supply, and when nobody was around he thought, "Why not take a bit of their *tsampa* with me? They have so much and I have nothing." He fetched his *tsampa* bag and put his right hand into the family's big sack. At that moment he realized what he was doing. With his left hand he seized his right hand inside the sack and shouted at the top of his voice, "A thief has come! Thief! Thief!" Everybody came running and asked, "What is happening? Where is the thief?" Geshe Ben showed his right hand and said, "Here he is!"

This shows how we should try to catch ourselves and see whether what we are doing is right or wrong. If we understand that we are not doing the right thing and another course of action would be best, not only for ourselves but for everybody else, we should behave accordingly. That is how we create a positive habit. This is a key practice, which is done not only for a limited time but throughout our lives.

Practice is not merely visualizing Tara and Avalokiteshvara, or Zen sitting, or whatever else. We ourselves are our practice, so it is somewhat irrelevant what kind of formal practices we carry out. All of them are geared to help us become better people, to make our minds calmer and clearer, and to gain greater realization of the truth. Understanding that we are our practice, we have to see ourselves clearly, evaluating what we are doing and how we are doing it.

Training means looking at ourselves again and again, using introspection so that we are not overwhelmed by negative emotions and circumstances, but are able to control ourselves. Without discipline we lose our self-esteem. Confidence arises when we know how to control ourselves and do what we know is right. As long as we are under the power of small whims, we feel helpless and guilty. Why do people sometimes hate themselves? It is because they have no self-control, thinking, "I do not like the way I act, but I can't do anything about it!"

We should therefore take control. Once we know what is right and wrong, we should act accordingly. Of course, this is not always easy and we should not hold ourselves too tightly. If we try to do that, after a while the whole thing collapses. We should make an effort to change our ways little by little, seeing what we are doing and where we are going, in a broad-minded and relaxed way. We should develop discipline, and grant ourselves some space at the same time.

The last of the thirty-seven stanzas describes the practice of dedication:

> May the virtues achieved through striving in this way
> Dispel the suffering of all beings limitless in number.
> Dedicating thus toward the enlightenment of all, by means of the
>   wisdom
> That is totally pure of dualistic distinction, is the practice of
>   a bodhisattva.

Bodhisattva practice is never complete without dedication. According to the Mahayana, all practice should contain three sacred aspects, called *dampa sum* in Tibetan; these are pure aspiration, the pure practice itself, and pure dedication. It is said that the quality and effectiveness of any action or practice depends on the way it is dedicated. If we dedicate our positive actions toward a limited and petty goal, the results will be equally shallow. But when we dedicate even a small action for a far-reaching and worthwhile purpose, through the power of interdependence the merit will not be exhausted. It will continue until our dedication is fulfilled.

From the Buddhist point of view we should make the most noble dedication we can think of, even if our action is very small, like saying one mantra or one line of a prayer. Performing this kind of dedication is said to be like adding a drop of water to the sea. As long as the sea remains, the drop will remain as well. The highest dedication imaginable is to dedicate all our merits, no matter how great or small they may be, toward the full enlightenment of all sentient beings, without omitting a single one. We cannot do any better. This is not merely wishing them temporary comfort, such as a good meal or a nice time; rather it is a wish for their complete, everlasting awakening, which is the most supreme attainment a being can have.

This kind of dedication becomes dreamlike if it is made in the light of the discriminative wisdom of emptiness. This is the wisdom which sees that nothing is solid, that there is no separate "me" here or "you" there, that nothing is unchanging and truly existent, and that everything is interdependent. This unimaginable, great dedication can come true since it is not a real, existing thing. In a dream we can dream of anything. Nothing is impossible because nothing is real. Similarly, in the waking state anything can come to pass, there being nothing solid that exists on its own. As long as everything is viewed as being solid and real, nothing much can happen, since all these solid things must remain as they are. Once everything is known to be insubstantial and changeable, and we dedicate in light of this wisdom, our dedication will gain great power.

This does not mean that we should not dedicate our merit for a specific purpose. However, the Buddhist way is usually to proceed from the large to the small. First, we dedicate for all sentient beings and wish they will become fully enlightened as quickly and easily as possible. Then, we narrow it down and wish for our whole world to be peaceful, prosperous, and so on. From there we proceed to our own country, the place where we live, and ourselves. Dedication does not exclude ourselves. We can wish for our own well-being, health, and progress. But we do not limit it to that. We dedicate for a great and worthwhile purpose.

This concludes the thirty-seven stanzas describing the practices of a bodhisattva. Of course, the bodhisattva practices are not limited to thirty-seven, but Ngulchü Thogmé has summarized them in this way.

The following three verses contain the colophon.

> Based upon the meaning as expounded in the sutras, tantras, and
>   their explanatory texts,
> And in tune with the words of the saints,
> I composed these thirty-seven bodhisattva practices for the sake of all
>   those who wish
> To train themselves on the bodhisattva path.

Here the author explains how and why he wrote this text. He based his verses on the sutras and tantras of the Buddha's words and their commentaries, and combined these with the oral instructions of his teachers and his own personal experience. Since the sutras and tantras are extensive and there are many commentaries on them, not everyone following the bodhi-sattva path has the time and opportunity to study them all. So, to make them accessible for more people, he put the teachings on the bodhisattva path into a concise and comprehensible form of thirty-seven stanzas.

> I am aware that my intelligence is small, and lacking study I am not
>   learned.
> I have not mastered the art of language that will please the hearts of
>   the wise.
> Yet, having relied on the sutras and the words of the saints,
> I deem these bodhisattva practices to be unmistaken and true.

This verse contains an instruction on modesty, showing that truly learned people are free from pride and never boast about their knowledge. Ngulchü Thogmé puts his humility into words, saying that he is not learned and his writing may not please the scholars. Then, he points out that his instructions are based entirely on the authentic teachings of the buddhas, bodhisattvas, and masters of the past. This is a characteristic feature of the Indian and Tibetan Buddhist literary tradition. The writing is traced back to its sources and the author says that the instruction is not his own invention; all credit goes to those who composed the original, genuine teachings. This is quite different from these days when an author attaches great importance to the fact that his work is entirely his own and that he holds the copyright on it.

> Still, someone of small intellect such as mine can hardly fathom the
>   vastness of bodhisattva conduct.
> So I pray to all saintly beings
> To grant their forbearance and patience with all my mistakes, such
>   as contradiction in meaning,
> Lack of context, and other defects.

This is a continuation of the previous verse. It does not mean that Ngulchü Thogmé's words contain mistakes, but in case someone finds fault, he asks for forgiveness. This also implies that we should not take this text literally and consider it as an ultimate authority. Instead, we should examine it and if we find its teachings true and applicable, we should put them into practice.

The last stanza contains his own dedication:

Through the virtue that has arisen from this work,
May all beings equal the protector Avalokiteshvara,
Who by supreme bodhichitta, relative and ultimate,
Abides in neither extreme of existence or quiescence.

Ngulchü Thogmé prays that the merit resulting from composing this text will lead all sentient beings to develop the relative and absolute bodhichitta of compassion and wisdom. He wishes for them to go beyond the cycle of existence as well as the limited nirvana of peace, and reach complete enlightenment. This will enable them to work for the benefit of all beings and be at the level of the bodhisattva Avalokiteshvara, the embodiment of wisdom and compassion.

The text concludes with the author's personal colophon:

For his own and all others' benefit, this text was written by Thogmé, the master of scriptures and logic, while dwelling in the cave "Jewel of Silver Water."

Buddha Vajradhara

PART THREE

VAJRAYANA

THE VAJRAYANA is very vast and deep—it embraces the whole of the Shravakayana and Mahayana teachings, and complements them with a great variety of skillful means. It conveys a direct and unabridged clarification of all points and elucidates even the most subtle topics. To understand and practice it fully is therefore not easy. It is difficult to comprehend as a whole, since it is very much based on experience and practice, rather than intellectual issues. Thus, it is almost impossible to teach the Vajrayana without the basis of the general Buddhist teachings, and especially those of the Mahayana. In fact, without the Mahayana basis of genuine love and compassion toward all fellow sentient beings, the Vajrayana teachings are useless and might even be misleading.

This is illustrated by a famous story about a meditator and a ghost. Somewhere in Tibet in a cave there was a very good lama in retreat. He was practicing, when suddenly something appeared in front of him. He saw it as a negative, obstructing spirit. So he tried to say some mantras to drive it away. But it did not go away. It said mantras back. Then he visualized himself as a very strong, wrathful deity and again said mantras. In return, that spirit became even more strong and wrathful and said mantras back. After that, the lama realized that this was a spirit of someone who had practiced all those wrathful deities and mantras. When he understood that, he became very sad, and genuine concern and compassion arose for the person who had become this evil spirit after practicing the Vajrayana methods. Within this genuine concern and compassion, he forgot about his visualization of the wrathful deity, the mantras, and all those things, and his compassion overtook him. At that moment, the spirit began disappearing in front of him. It became smaller and smaller, until in a very weak voice it said, "That I did not have," and disappeared.

So the Vajrayana is the most inclusive of all the teachings of the Buddha, but some aspects are not that easy to comprehend. If the core of the Vajrayana teachings is not grasped, they can seem too religious or too cultural, perhaps too Tibetan or Indian, and too concerned with ritual. However, the instructions of the Vajrayana system are based on experience rather than on an academic or intellectual view. They are to be understood experientially and will result in a very personal realization. For this reason, it is somewhat difficult to discuss them in a way that they can be understood correctly.

During his lifetime, even the Buddha did not make these teachings very public. Instead, he taught individually. Thus, the lineage of the Vajrayana is very personal, and in many cases teachings have been handed on from one master to one disciple. For this reason, the Vajrayana is sometimes also called the "Secret Mantrayana." After the Buddha had passed away, its instructions continued to be taught in the same highly individual manner and did not become widely known for a very long time.

SECTION ONE
TANTRA

So I was not too sure how to approach this subject, but then I remembered that I have a book that might be suitable. This is a small book, which is compact and yet at the same time covers almost every aspect of Vajrayana teaching and is a broad outline of its content. It was written by a great yogi named Do Khyentse Yeshé Dorjé, whose unconventional appearance earned him the nickname "Crazy Khyentse."

Do Khyentse was not a monk and did not even look like a yogi, or *ngagpa*, as the nonmonastic practitioners of the tantras are called in Tibet. His dress was that of an ordinary man from Kham, in East Tibet. He wore this region's traditional black *chuba*, always carried a rifle, and rode on horseback. At times he would even hunt. He used to smoke a long pipe and had the appearance of a wild man. At the same time he was a great master and occasionally, though not very frequently, taught. He was the kind of teacher who inspired total and unwavering faith in some people, while others would have none at all and would regard him as an ordinary person, or worse.

One day Do Khyentse was staying near Dzogchen Monastery. As with most Buddhist monks, especially from Tibet, the monks there were somewhat sceptical and did not easily believe anything. Hearing that the renowned Do Khyentse was in the neighborhood, two of them decided to play a trick on him. "Look at this fool," they said, "he doesn't have any understanding whatsoever. Let's put him to a test!" Then one of them lay down in the road pretending to be dead, while the other ran up to Do Khyentse in apparent distress crying, "Khyentse Rinpoché, Khyentse Rinpoché, please come with me! My friend has just fallen down and died. Please perform *phowa* (i.e., the transference of consciousness) for him!" Do Khyentse turned his horse and followed him back. When they reached the "corpse," he rapped his pipe on the monk's head three times, knocking out the ashes, and said, "All right, it is done," and left. Then the other monk said to his friend, "You see, we were right. He is totally stupid. He can't even tell the dead from the living. Get up and let's go." His friend, however, did not get up. No matter how much he shook him, he did not move. Aghast, he realized that his friend was really dead. Now, he was very frightened and, full of remorse, ran back after Do Khyentse and in tears begged him, "Please forgive me, we were just testing you. Please come back and revive my friend." Khyentse said, "Is it true? He was not dead?" The monk answered, "No, he was not. We just pretended to put you to a test." At this Do Khyentse replied, "All right, if this is so," and once more went back with the monk to where the other was still lying in the road dead. Again, three times he knocked out the ashes of his pipe on the monk's head and rode away. Then the dead monk arose and complained to his friend, "Why did you ask him to bring me back? I was feeling so good in the pure realms."

Another time, three monks went to see Do Khyentse and asked him to accept them as his disciples. He said he would, provided they abandoned their guru for him. Otherwise, he told them, he would not grant any teaching. "Think about it well overnight," he said, "and if tomorrow you are ready to give up your guru, come back and I will give you teaching. If not, I will send you away." The following morning two of the monks said to each other, "Well, it is maybe just for some auspicious reason that he talked like that. It does not mean that we really have to give up our guru. Let's go and receive his teachings anyway." The third said, "No, I already have my guru, who has given me ample instructions. If I am required to forsake him to get more teachings, I do not need any further." Whereupon, he left. The other two went to see Do Khyentse and asked him for teaching. He looked intently at them and said, "So you are truly willing to give up your guru?" They both said, "Yes, we are." He asked them where their third companion went, and they told him that he could not accept the condition and instead had gone away. Hearing that, Do Khyentse took whatever dirt lay in front of him and threw it into their faces, shouting, "You fools! You think I would give instruction to a student who would abandon his teacher? Go immediately in search of your friend who has left and bring him to me. I want to see him." When the friend was brought back, Do Khyentse said that he had acted rightly. Subsequently, he kept him as his assistant. Sometimes he instructed him, but mainly he took him wherever he went and gave him a lot of trouble as well. After Do Khyentse had passed away, this disciple, popularly known as Aku Özer, assumed the task of compiling and editing the greatest part of his works.

Do Khyentse's main teacher was the first Dodrubchen. His main student was Patrul Rinpoché, who later composed the famous text known as *The Words of My Perfect Teacher*. When he met Do Khyentse, Patrul Rinpoché was already a very learned scholar and highly respected for his intellect. His main teacher had been a great khenpo called Nyushu Lungtog. In his younger days, Patrul Rinpoché was quite active in worldly affairs. He was a good negotiator and had a very strong personality. At times, he was maybe even a little proud. In one encounter, Patrul Rinpoché had camped nearby where Do Khyentse was camped. One day, Do Khyentse came along on his horse in a combative mood and shouted at Patrul Rinpoché, "Hey, Palgé Tulku, you old dog! You think you are really great? You are nothing! I challenge you. If you are brave, come here and fight with me!" Patrul Rinpoché thought to himself, "He is such a great teacher but must be drunk and confused to be acting like this." Do Khyentse came nearer and said, "You think I'm drunk? You think you're so great?" With that, he grabbed Patrul Rinpoché's hair and tossed him about, dragging him around, shouting, "You are a dog! You are nothing but a wretched dog! If you have any guts, get on your feet and fight with me!" With that he beat him up. Later Patrul Rinpoché said that this was the greatest introduction to his mind. Before he had some recognition and understanding, but it was only like dawn. This then was like the sun itself shining in the midst of the sky. Thereafter, he always considered Do Khyentse as his teacher and called himself "the tattered old dog," especially when composing a Vajrayana text. He would say, "This is my secret name, my tantric name, given to me by my master."

The text to be considered and explained here is not widely known. Do Khyentse Rinpoché wrote it in the form of a dialogue between a monk and an old yogi. The title is:

Babble of a Fool:
A Note on the Creation and Completion Stages

The text starts with the author's homage to his guru:

My supreme father, Rigdzin Jangchub Dorjé,
Kind Guru whose compassion is immeasurable
As it has reached the state of omniscience,
May you always keep me in your protection.

The next stanza is a traditional statement, which is the author's "commitment to write":

Your blessing with its splendor of a thousand light rays
Has inspired my mind to fully blossom like a lotus garden.
So I will now disperse the fragrance of well chosen words
That it may bring forth enjoyment for all fortunate bees.

Here the author uses a poetic metaphor. The blessing of his teacher is like the sun, which makes the lotus of the disciple's mind blossom through its rays and warmth. The blooming lotus emits a fragrance, which attracts the bees. This means that through the kindness of his spiritual master a certain experience has dawned in his mind, from which the teachings arise. These instructions were composed in order to be beneficial to people who have the karmic fortune of being able to receive them; they begin:

Once there was a monk who lived in a mountain hermitage called "Quite Pleasant" who boasted about practicing the "timely exercises of penance." Then there was an old *ngagpa* (or yogi) who was a holder of the lineage "Whatever Appears is Self-Liberated"; he was transforming the sense pleasures into the path. These two met in a town called "Appearance Grasped as Being Real."

In Tibet two types of sangha developed, called "the yellow sangha" and "the white sangha." The former consisted of ordained practitioners, monks and nuns, who wore red and yellow robes. The formal Buddhist robes worn for ceremonies were yellow, and it was from those that the name "yellow sangha" was derived. The white sangha consisted of Vajrayana practitioners who remained householders. Its members are usually called *ngagpas*. *Ngag* means "tantra" and *pa* is a syllable which denotes a person. So a *ngagpa* is a tantric practitioner but, of course, this does not mean that monks and nuns could not practice the Vajrayana as well. The term "white sangha" refers to the fact that *ngagpas* would dress in white, or at least wear a white shawl, for religious activities.

> The monk addressed the yogi and asked, "Old yogi, here in Tibet a lot of fuss is being made over tenets such as the earlier and later traditions, the old and new tantras, and so forth. Do you know the reason for this? Do you adhere to some particular tenet?"
>
> The old yogi replied, "Monk, as far as the Buddha's teachings in India are concerned, there were no such things as old and new. But you are right. Here in Tibet an increase and a diminishment of the teachings took place and therefore they are divided like that. The period of kings starting with King Lhathothori Nyenshal and ending with King Relpachen is called the 'Thirteen Happy Royal Generations.' The teachings of the Buddha that were spread in Tibet during this time are called 'the teachings of the earlier tradition,' and the teachings spread from then onward are called 'the teachings of the later tradition.' In the same way the teachings of the secret Mantrayana that were translated in Tibet until the lifetime of King Relpachen are called 'the old translation,' and those translated from then onward are called 'the new translation.' You may wonder about the reason for this. The answer is that between these periods King Langdarma did great harm to the teachings of the Buddha and caused their decline."

King Lhathothori was the twenty-seventh king of Tibet and lived in the sixth century. Relpachen was the last Tibetan king and lived during the turn of the ninth century. Today, in the West, Tibetan Buddhism is often distinguished in terms of the "Yellow Hat School" and "Red Hat School." This passage shows that, traditionally in Tibet, there were many ways of drawing distinctions: the earlier and the later traditions, the old and the new translations of the Vajrayana teachings, and various others. The old translations of the Vajrayana teachings are practiced by the followers of the Nyingma

School of Tibetan Buddhism. The Gelug, Kagyü, and Sakya Schools all follow the new translations of the Vajrayana teachings and thus, for the most
part, those three schools practice the same tantras. King Langdarma was a
brother of King Relpachen and was extremely hostile to Buddhism. He
destroyed most of the monasteries and refused to permit the monks and
nuns to follow the religious life, forcing them into the army or other lifestyles
that contradicted the vows they had taken. Some were able to escape his persecution, but many were killed. In this way numerous teachings of the
Dharma were lost. What remained were some teachings that had been held
and practiced by the yogis, or *ngagpas*, the nonmonastic followers of the
tantric tradition. This was due to the fact that the *ngagpas* did not wear any
special clothing but dressed like ordinary Tibetans and could not be identified as practitioners. This issue is quite interesting, and suggests that this
kind of noninstitutional tradition is important for the survival of Buddhism.

One may wonder, for instance, why Buddhism was wiped out during the
Muslim invasion of India, whereas Hinduism remained. Even now some
Hindus accuse the Buddhists of being responsible for the conquest of India
by the Muslim invaders. They claim that there were so many monks at
Nalanda University that they could have easily defeated the whole Turkish
army, if only they had each picked up a stone and thrown it. Yet the monks
used no violence and most were beheaded. It is true that in theory they would
have been able to prevent it. An account contained in the works of Muslim
history conveys an impression of the size of Nalanda University at that time.
It is recorded there that it took more than a year to burn all the books in its
library. Buddhism was so easily destroyed in India because the upholders of
the teachings were mostly monks living and working in a large number of
big monasteries and universities. Many of them were very learned and possessed profound experience as well, whereas the members of the lay Buddhist community usually contented themselves with having great faith in
the ordained Sangha and supporting the Buddhist institutions. Yet, the lay
Sangha lacked, for the most part, the knowledge and realization to be able
to uphold the Dharma by themselves. Buddhism, therefore, presented an
easy target to eliminate, since the monks and nuns were easily recognized
by their robes.

The conditions in Tibet were similar during the reign of King Langdarma.
Luckily though, there were some followers of the tantric tradition who did
not wear robes or live in monasteries, and for this reason were able to escape

his persecution. Maybe this could be a signpost for the future of Buddhism. Traditionally, the Sangha is considered the community of monks and nuns. In my view, it is very important that Buddhism in its actual sense reaches the households and is assimilated there. People living ordinary lives should not just be devotees but should also gain true knowledge and understanding. In this way, the Dharma will survive.

The division into two traditions of translation does not apply to the Sutrayana teachings. These were mostly translated during the first period and more works were added later. As for the Vajrayana teachings, there are two distinct sets of translations, which are called the old and the new translations, *nyingma* and *sarma* in Tibetan. Many great translators, such as Marpa, Drom, Drog, etc., brought different new tantras that they translated and taught in the later period. The old yogi continues:

> "Nowadays in Tibet there are very many scholars overly fond of their particular tenets. Yet in this old yogi's estimation the definitive meaning of all these tenets is contained in three great ways of expounding the Dharma, and there is nothing that is not included therein. You may wonder what these three are. The ground is Mahamudra, the Great Symbol. The path is Madhyamaka, the Great Middle Way, and the fruit is Maha Ati, the Great Perfection. As for myself, for generations my family has followed the earlier tradition, the old translation of the Vajrayana. But I do not have any knowledge of all the different tenets it involves myself. I just follow it blindly and practice its instructions as my father did."

Again the monk said in a slightly haughty way, "All right, old yogi, what are the scriptures of you followers of the old tantric tradition? What is your understanding of the teaching of the Buddha? How do you followers of the tantras practice according to your philosophical tenets?"

The old yogi replied, "Monk, do not be so foolish. You must surely know that the scriptures consist of the three *pitakas* and the four tantras along with the commentaries explaining their intended meaning. The scriptures of the followers of the earlier tradition contain the words of the Buddha and the three *pitakas*, as they have been translated during the time of King Thrisong Detsen. Then, if you wonder what the three *pitakas* and the four tantras are: the three *pitakas* are the Vinaya Pitaka, the Sutra Pitaka, and the Abhidharma Pitaka. The four tantras are Kriya Tantra, Charya Tantra, Yoga Tantra, and Mahayoga or Anuttarayoga Tantra."

All the Buddhist teachings as they are contained in the Kangyur, the translation of the direct words of the Buddha into Tibetan, can be divided into the three *pitakas*, or three baskets. Strictly speaking, the Vinaya Pitaka consists of twelve volumes. It deals with the way of life and code of conduct according to Buddhist ethics as it is observed by the ordained and lay community. This relates to the Shravakayana level, or the general Buddhist teachings. However, if the entire Kangyur is presented in terms of the three *pitakas*, the Vinaya Pitaka would also comprise those sections of the Mahayana and Vajrayana teachings that deal with the conduct of a bodhisattva in general and with the conduct of a tantric practitioner in particular. The Abhidharma Pitaka consists of the teachings that mainly aim at the development of wisdom and knowledge. They convey an understanding of the nature of things according to the Shravakayana, Mahayana, and Vajrayana levels. The Sutra Pitaka contains the teachings on meditation and consists, for the most part, of discussions between the Buddha and his disciples on various subjects.

Sometimes the teachings of the Buddha are classified in a slightly different way. Firstly, two parts are distinguished, namely Sutra and Tantra. Then, the Sutrayana level of instructions is divided into the three *pitakas*. According to this classification, the Vinaya Pitaka consists of some twelve volumes. The Abhidharma Pitaka comprises mainly the *prajnaparamita* sutras. And the Sutra Pitaka, which is very large, consists of some thirty-six volumes, containing discussions on various subjects.

The four tantras are Kriya, Charya (which is sometimes also called Upaya), Yoga, and Mahayoga or Anuttarayoga. They are contained in about thirty volumes of tantric teachings, and each is classified as belonging to one of these four levels. Accordingly, there are certain similarities and differences between them. In terms of practice, the four levels of tantra are ordered according to their profundity: the lowest being the Kriyayoga, the second the Charyayoga, the third the Yoga, and the fourth the Anuttarayoga, which is the deepest and most profound teaching.

The old yogi continues:

"The teaching of the Buddha has two aspects, the Dharma in terms of instruction and the Dharma in terms of realization."

The actual meaning of the expression "the teaching of the Buddha" is very difficult to render by means of a short English phrase. In Tibetan the phrase is *sang gyä kyi ten pa*. *Sang gyä* means "buddha," but *ten pa* does not just refer to his teaching, or his instruction. It is also the realization and experience we gain through the practice of his instruction. This realization does not come from somewhere else. What comes from the Buddha is like a trigger, which helps us to gain understanding, whereas the actual experience has to come from within ourselves. This point is unique and it is very important to understand it properly. For instance, a common prayer says, "May the teachings of the Buddha spread throughout the world." This sounds a little as though we were praying that the doctrine of the Buddha spread in the sense that monasteries be built and that everyone become a Buddhist. What it really implies, however, is the wish that all sentient beings may become compassionate and wise. This meaning is rather different. For the time being, there does not seem to be a better word than "teaching," but it is important to understand that the "teaching of the Buddha" has two aspects, instruction and realization. The old yogi describes these as follows:

"The Dharma in terms of instruction consists of the supreme words of the Buddha that he expounded in twelve different ways."

These are called "The Twelve Branches of the Supreme Speech of the Buddha." The names of these twelve branches are: discourses, songs, prophecies, poetry, commitments, stories, expressing realization, history, expositions of the lineages of great beings, full and complete explanations, descriptions of the wondrous deeds of holy beings, and reasonings. He continues:

"The Dharma in terms of realization is equivalent to the intended meaning of these supreme words within an individual's own stream of being. It depends upon the question of how many of the qualities resulting from the three trainings and from the creation and completion stages of the Vajrayana system have been fused with our mind. If you wish to uphold this Dharma, it is very important to exert yourself in the three aspects of study, reflection, and meditation, which constitute its cause. In the beginning you study and reflect upon the Dharma in terms of instruction. During this time you are called a student. When you then practice meditation for the sake of the awakening of the Dharma in terms of realization, you are called a practitioner. These days, though, it seems that there are many followers of the earlier and later traditions alike who reverse the order of these practices. This is a sign that the teaching of the Buddha is degenerating.

"You, as a monk, will surely know the three trainings. All the teachings of the sacred Dharma expressed in the Vinaya are the training in ethical conduct. The teachings expressed in the Sutra Pitaka are the training in *samadhi*, or meditation, and those expressed in the Abhidharma are the training in *prajna*, or discriminative wisdom.

"These three trainings are also taught by summarizing the sutras into the Noble Eightfold Path. I have heard that in this context the root of the sutras is taught as follows. Through the four topics right action, right speech, right thought, and right livelihood, ethical conduct is taught. Through the topic right meditation, the training in *samadhi* is clarified. Through the topic right view, the training in discriminative wisdom is elucidated. The two branches right effort and right mindfulness form the support of all three trainings and further their growth. For us yogis, there is a way to explain and practice these by combining them with the two aspects of the creation and completion stages. When you know how to do this, everything that is expressed in the sutras will be realized in an easy way by the Mantrayana.

"The actual practice of us old yogis as it accords with our tradition is carried out within the framework of the Four Great Streams of Transmission, which stem from the old translations. You may wonder what these are. The first is empowerment, the second is the creation stage, the third is the completion stage, and the fourth consists of the explanation of the tantras. In order to practice these, you have to bind them tightly within the framework of four mudras: the ground of practice is Karmamudra, what is to be practiced is Dharmamudra, the means of practicing is Samayamudra, and the result of practice is Mahamudra."

EMPOWERMENT

"As to empowerment, which forms the beginning, we followers
of the earlier tradition adhere to the lineage of Padmasambhava
and Nagarjuna. As a sign of this lineage you must practice while
keeping all three ordinations."

The three ordinations are the precepts of the Vinaya, the bodhisattva
vows, and those of the Vajrayana. There are slightly different views about
how an individual can observe these three sets of precepts together. According to one opinion they are observed separately but concurrently, just as the
sun, moon, and stars are separate from each other and yet present in the
same sky. Another view is that one set of vows will transform into the next.
For example, when one first takes the Vinaya ordination—meaning refuge
and the precepts observed by a lay or an ordained person—and then later
takes the bodhisattva vows, the Vinaya precepts are transformed into and
become part of the bodhisattva vows. In this context, though, these are just
minor differences in view. What is important, as the old yogi points out, is
that, according to the tradition of Padmasambhava and Nagarjuna, all three
types of precepts have to be observed. Even though one is a practitioner of
the highest tantra, the Vinaya and the bodhisattva vows must be taken as the
basis. Without these, one cannot practice the Vajrayana. He then continues:

"So the best foundation is to be either a fully ordained person or a
novice. Yet I, an old yogi, got lost in the faults of village life, and
thus did not meet with the right conditions to practice as a monk.
My foundation is that of a lay practitioner."

Within the system of the Vinaya there are basically three types of ordination, which are further categorized into seven or eight. The first is called
genyen in Tibetan; this is the ordination of either a male or female lay practitioner. The second is the ordination of a novice monk or nun, who are called
getsul or *getsulma*, respectively. The third ordination is that of a fully ordained
monk or nun, called *gelong* or *gelongma*, respectively. Then, there is a special
ordination between those of a novice and a fully ordained person, which is
only taken by women. In Tibetan, a woman who has taken this ordination
is called *gelobma*. This ordination is only taken for a year and was instituted

to enable women to find out whether they wished to become a nun, since a fully ordained nun has to keep more vows than a fully ordained monk. These are the seven types of ordination. There is a further set of precepts, which are observed just for a short period of one or two days and are called the *nyen né* precepts. According to the Vinaya, the five basic precepts to be observed by a lay practitioner are not killing a human being, not stealing, not telling seriously misleading lies, not engaging in sexual misconduct, and not becoming intoxicated. These can be taken all together and also separately in any combination, such as taking just one precept, or two, three, or four.

"Of the different *genyen* vows, I have only taken those of the threefold refuge. Thus, I exert myself with respect to three things to abandon, three things to adopt, and three things conducive to this practice. By means of this discipline I keep the precepts of a true *genyen*. On top of that, I have also taken the bodhisattva vow. In my practice the root of this vow is contained in the three sacred aspects: the sacred motivation, the sacred practice itself, and the sacred dedication. Within these as well, I also keep the vows of the Mantrayana, practicing the three sacred aspects within the framework of the creation and completion stages of meditation. This is how I try to get to the bottom of the three sets of vows in my personal life and practice. And this is also what I teach young yogis of small intelligence, so that they gain at least some basic understanding of the structure of the three ordinations.

"As for requesting the actual empowerment, the empowerment that ripens, there are many different ways it can be granted. Their root is contained in four aspects, which are the vase empowerment, secret empowerment, wisdom empowerment, and word empowerment. By the power and blessing of a compassionate lama and with the appropriate materials like the vase, nectar, portrait, and crystal, the empowerment is bestowed on a fortunate disciple's channels, essence, wind, and mind. As soon as this has happened, you practice the path, which consists of the two stages of creation and completion. This cultivation will lead you to attain the fruit, the state of the four *kayas*, in one body and lifetime. The four *kayas* are the nirmanakaya, sambhogakaya, dharmakaya, and svabhavikakaya."

What the old yogi expresses here is the fact that the three *yanas* are not considered to be separate from each other. They constitute one path, of which the Shravakayana forms the basis. When some aspects of the teachings contained there are expanded further, it becomes a Mahayana level of instruction. The Vajrayana, again, is not something that is totally different, but is part of the Mahayana. For this reason, it is not possible just to practice the Vajrayana and leave aside the teachings of the Shravakayana and Mahayana. Nevertheless, the Vajrayana has characteristics that make it distinct from the other vehicles; Nagarjuna describes these as follows:

> *In it there is not even one single point left unclear.*
> *Since it has many methods, it is not difficult.*
> *For someone who is highly disciplined and skilled,*
> *The Mantrayana teachings are especially excellent.*

There is no difference between the three vehicles as far as their final objective is concerned; their aim and purpose is the same. The difference lies in the degree to which the various aspects of the teachings are clarified and disclosed. The Shravakayana is composed of the Four Noble Truths and the Noble Eightfold Path. The teachings of the Mahayana and Vajrayana do not express anything in addition to this, but just explain these topics in greater depth. In the highest tantras and the instructions of the great Vajrayana masters, everything is clarified in an utterly direct and complete way. There is nothing left unexplained. For this reason, Nagarjuna has said that not even a single point is left unclear in the Vajrayana system.

In comparison with the Mahayana, the number of methods provided by the Vajrayana is far greater. It contains many different means of practice, such as using our own body—the channels, winds, and the essence. It applies direct ways of dealing with emotions to transmute everything that is negative into the positive, and so forth. The Vajrayana system is "not difficult" in the sense that it does not demand such a great amount of austerity and strictness of the practitioner, as is required in the context of the other vehicles. Discipline is another matter; this is needed to be able to practice any Buddhist method.

When dealing with strong emotions, for instance, a Vajrayana practitioner does not have to use deliberate means to stop them. Unlike in other systems, the Vajrayana provides very skillful methods so that the negative

emotions are used in order to transmute themselves. This is a very characteristic feature of the Vajrayana approach to practice.

In the Shravakayana context, effort is directed at counteracting our emotions. When, for example, strong anger or attachment arises, deliberate effort
is made to generate its opposite, like loving-kindness or nonattachment.
Once this is successfully achieved, the negative emotions have no opportunity to surface, since opposite emotions, like anger and loving-kindness,
cannot be present together at the same time. In this way, the negative emotions are reversed through giving rise to the corresponding positive ones.

Within the context of the Mahayana, the practitioner takes a further step
and seeks to understand his or her emotions and see their nature. When
anger comes up, we try to look at ourselves and our anger in order to see the
egolessness of our mind and the emptiness of that anger. There are different
methods that lead us to see the ultimate nature of ourselves and our emotions. Using these methods, we will understand that the nature of everything
is subjective. Anger, as everything else, is not something solid, something
truly and independently existing. Through this understanding, the negative
emotions are counterbalanced and positive emotions gradually arise.

Following the Vajrayana teachings, we do not give up or reject anything;
rather we make use of whatever is there. We look at our negative emotions
and accept them for what they are. Then we relax in this state of acceptance.
Using the emotion itself, it is transformed or transmuted into the positive,
into its true face. When, for instance, strong anger or desire arises, a
Vajrayana practitioner is not afraid of it. Instead he or she would follow
advice along the following lines: Have the courage to expose yourself to your
emotions. Do not reject or suppress them, but do not follow them either. Just
look your emotion directly in the eye and then try to relax within the very
emotion itself. There is no confrontation involved. You don't do anything.
Remaining detached, you are neither carried away by emotion nor do you
reject it as something negative. Then, you can look at your emotions almost
casually and be rather amused.

When our usual habit of magnifying our feelings and our fascination
resulting from that are gone, there will be no negativity and no fuel. We can
relax within them. What we are trying to do, therefore, is to skillfully and
subtly deal with our emotions. This is largely equivalent to the ability of
exerting discipline.

Generally speaking, to be able to apply the methods of the Vajrayana, a great deal of discipline is required, far more than is necessary within the context of the other vehicles. It is a matter of first knowing the technique to apply, and then of actually applying it. This is not easy, since whatever is there is dealt with directly. The negative emotions themselves are used. The process is almost like using poison as medicine. For this reason, a high degree of discipline is necessary. We need the awareness and courage first to see clearly whatever is there and then to accept and endure it, no matter how negative it may be. Strong anger, for instance, is a very intense and fierce emotion, and is usually experienced as being totally overpowering. It is not a minor thing, but constitutes a real challenge. If we are able to relax within that kind of feeling, we will be able to relax within everything. Once this capacity is acquired, it will not matter how strong our emotions are—it is even said that the stronger they are the better. Yet, if we are not skillful enough, we will not be able to apply these subtle methods.

Once we have gained the necessary knowledge and skill, this practice is very easy, since we simply make use of what we have and are at the moment. With the prerequisites at hand, this is not difficult at all. Whatever negativity surfaces, that is used as our strength, as our main practice. Nagarjuna's verse refers to someone who is highly intelligent and disciplined and at the same time very skilled and capable. To practice the Vajrayana, an individual must be able to face any negativity that comes up, and to use that negativity without losing control. This requires a high degree of intelligence, combined with an equal amount of discipline and skill. For such a person, the Vajrayana methods are more excellent than those of the preceding vehicles. These features, as expressed in Nagarjuna's verse, describe the uniqueness of the Vajrayana and its distinction from the other vehicles.

The old yogi next talks about the four empowerments, a central point within the Vajrayana system. Without having received empowerment, one is not allowed to practice any Vajrayana teaching. It is not that easy to illustrate the meaning of the four empowerments. Empowerment is a teaching, a very direct way of instruction, which conveys the very essence of all teachings simultaneously. It is also an introduction to the mind itself. During empowerment a strong condition is created such that the conceptualizations of the student are cut completely, and he or she can obtain a glimpse of the truth. For this reason, it is said that when a highly realized teacher grants empowerment to a highly developed disciple, the disciple can reach realization within that very moment. In this context, in traditions such as

Dzogchen one often finds statements such as, "When you realize this, if you meditate in the morning, you will be enlightened in the evening. If you meditate in the evening, you will be enlightened in the morning." This can happen, but it will not happen to everybody.

Empowerment involves many different aspects. It involves the quality of the teacher's lifetime of preparation and practice, as well as the quality of the student's own preparation. This latter aspect is most important. Empowerment depends upon the relationship between the master and the disciple. It relies on the firmness and completeness of their trust and confidence, since it is a transmission from mind to mind. It requires a very strong understanding and trust from both sides; this is called "blessing" in English, though this word is not a sufficiently accurate translation. The Tibetan is *jin gyi lab pa* and means to be transformed through a certain environment and influence. This is the meaning of "blessing" from the Buddhist point of view. It denotes a total transformation from the core of our being, which is induced by different things happening around us. Empowerment, in its actual sense, should lead us to receive this blessing and to undergo a genuine and complete transformation. The same is true for each of the different methods provided within the Vajrayana: mantra, meditation practices, visualization techniques, and so forth. They all have the same objective: the total transmutation of our body, speech, mind, and our entire being. Because empowerment involves all four of these, there are four empowerments.

The four empowerments are called "vase empowerment," "secret empowerment," "wisdom empowerment," and "word empowerment." The basic constituents that the empowerments work on are the channels, winds, and the essence, called *tsa*, *lung*, and *tiglé* in Tibetan. These three are used in connection with the mind. Thus, the first empowerment is related to the channels, the second to the essence, the third to the winds or energies, and the fourth to the mind. The purpose of the first empowerment is to awaken and reveal the nirmanakaya aspect of the disciple. In the same way, the second empowerment is meant to initiate the manifestation of the sambhogakaya; the third, the manifestation of the dharmakaya; and the fourth, the recognition of the svabhavikakaya aspect of our own being. When these four empowerments or initiations are received for the first time, they are called "seed initiations," since the teacher plants a seed, which is then cultivated by the disciple to gain an initial understanding and experience.

After that, the teacher will give all the instructions necessary to arrive at an actual and genuine realization. In Tibetan these are called *tri*. Generally speaking, the entirety of the Vajrayana teachings divides into three methods of instruction, called *wang, lung,* and *tri*. These are "empowerment," "reading transmission," and "explanation." Of these three, empowerment is the shortest and most direct manner of instruction. Thereafter, one should ask for the reading transmission, which is the means conveying the permission to practice. The teacher bestows this transmission by reading the text that is to be practiced to the disciple, who is supposed to listen carefully and one-pointedly. Finally, explanation consists of a very detailed, experiential, and word-by-word elucidation of the particular transmission. Once these three have been received, one can proceed to the application of the actual practice.

In the course of application the four empowerments are employed again and again. They are the heart of every Vajrayana practice and one applies them in the form of visualization. This is called *lam wang*, "the path empowerment." This term indicates that, in the context of the Vajrayana, empowerment actually constitutes the path. Practice is nothing other than the application of the four empowerments through which we purify body, speech, mind, and our entire being. We do this in order to realize the true nature of everything and to reveal true self, which emerges as the four *kayas*.

We may wonder what kind of preparation is needed to be able to receive empowerment in its actual sense. The first and most important prerequisite is to find a teacher we can trust completely and unwaveringly. In this context, blind trust is of no avail. Our confidence needs a foundation. The teacher has to be fully qualified, and the disciple's trust must be based on the recognition of this. In addition to that, every aspect of our previous Dharma activity—be it study, purification practice, accumulation of merit, or any other type of exercise—is part of our preparation. Even empowerment belongs to our preparation, as long as it has not led us to see the true nature of everything. The aspect of study plays an especially important role at the beginning. In order to be able to practice properly, a correct and clear understanding of the Buddhist teachings is required. We need to know how they relate to and build upon each other and where each instruction belongs. If we endeavor to gain this knowledge first, our practice will have a sound basis.

The life story of Naropa is a good example of the importance of study. Before he met his teacher Tilopa, Naropa was a great scholar and one of the most eminent professors at Nalanda University. He was especially skilled in the field of debate. At Nalanda, the four most proficient professors, each aided by four assistants, had the task of dealing with any outsiders who came to challenge the university in debate. These four, corresponding to the four cardinal directions, were called the gatekeeper of the north, south, east, and west. Naropa was the gatekeeper of the north, and responsible for meeting any challenge, question, or problem brought in from that direction. It was an enormous charge, since at that time debate was a sophisticated art, and new debates were brought forth every day. Furthermore, the tradition at this time was that whoever was defeated had to adopt the views of the winner, accepting the victor as their master. Thus, if Naropa had been defeated by a Hindu scholar, he would have been forced to become a Hindu and follow that teacher. Yet Naropa never lost to a challenger.

One day, Naropa was sitting on his veranda at Nalanda University reading a tantric text. While he read, he thought to himself, "I am really learned. I can understand everything, even this, without any doubt or lack of clarity." Suddenly, a shadow fell over his book. Looking up, he saw an old lady with a stick. Pointing it directly at him, she said, "You don't know anything!" Shocked that she could read his mind, he asked, "If I have no knowledge, then who does?" She replied, "Tilopa, my brother. If you want to gain true understanding, you have to find him."

At these words, Naropa was taken by such strong inspiration that he left everything immediately. He did not even wrap up his book, but went in search of Tilopa. All the study and learning Naropa had undertaken until this encounter had been a preparation. When he met Tilopa, he no longer needed any actual teaching, since he already knew everything. Many other things were necessary, though, and he followed Tilopa for many years. He learned from him through various signs and symbols, until finally Tilopa hit his shoe on Naropa's head, causing him to faint. Regaining consciousness, Naropa found that he had arrived at true understanding.

This example indicates that everything is a preparation. In this context, we cannot single out certain points. Whatever contributes to our total development—any understanding we gain, any study, purification, and so forth—is part of our preparation. This is even true of empowerment itself, as a practitioner will normally receive more than one. It is extremely rare that one's first empowerment results in total transformation. Especially in the view of the Tibetan tantric tradition, it is thought that one's first empowerment is usually not received in a complete way—it is obvious that most people do not become enlightened in the course of that same evening. According to this understanding, empowerment plants a seed that has to be cultivated through practice. In this way, empowerment is also a preparation, as is every aspect of our practice and activity in daily life.

The more we gradually gain understanding, the more our way of seeing things will be transformed. As we incorporate genuine experience and realization into our stream of being, as we become more mature, we will derive greater benefit from the next initiation. For this reason, we may receive a hundred or more empowerments before we reach the maturity required to be able to receive initiation in its actual and final sense. When this happens, all the preceding initiations, as well as all the other aspects of our practice, will manifest within it. Empowerment, in this true and ultimate sense, is not something that the teacher gives to the disciple. It comes from within and is equivalent to full realization.

Empowerment is transmitted in four different ways, described as "elaborate," "nonelaborate," "very nonelaborate," and "extremely nonelaborate." This indicates that empowerment does not necessarily involve a great deal of ritual. For those who have an affinity for ceremony and who attach great importance to outer form, empowerment can be conveyed in a very elaborate and ritualized manner. For a disciple who does not have this tendency or has an adverse affinity, the teacher can just use the environment, or even no outer support at all. No matter which kind of empowerment we receive, the most important points are our own preparation and state of mind.

So there is not necessarily a fixed routine in which empowerment is transmitted; it can be done in any manner. The initiation Drugpa Künleg gave to his brother is an example of this. Drugpa Künleg was a seemingly crazy yogi who never meditated in the conventional fashion, not even for a single day. He just wandered around the country and appeared to be mischievously fooling about and doing things that weren't totally respectable. For this reason, he was a source of continuous offense to his brother, who was his total opposite, a very proper and learned monk whose behavior was always impeccable. Yet, despite his outward appearance, Drugpa Künleg was a highly enlightened being.

Becoming increasingly annoyed with Drugpa Künleg's activities, his brother finally had enough, and said to him, "You act like a madman! This has to stop—you are a disgrace to Buddhism. You must withdraw into seclusion and meditate with me for at least a few months." With these words, he forcefully took Drugpa Künleg to his retreat place and told him to meditate in the adjoining room. To please him, Drugpa Künleg did as he was told. His brother was sitting in his room solemnly immersed in meditation, but soon his gaze fell on a white yak tail hanging from the ceiling and he began to day-dream, thinking, "Next time I go to Lhasa, I will take this nice yak tail with me and have it dyed red. Then, I will decorate my mule with it!" It was the custom in Tibet to fasten a red yak tail to the head of a mule and hang a big bell around its neck. A caravan of these mules was a very impressive sight. No sooner had this thought passed through his mind than his attendant knocked at his door. Slightly indignant, Drugpa Künleg's brother inquired, "What is it? Do not disturb me, I am in meditation." The attendant said, "I'm sorry. But this is very urgent. Your brother has just run away. He suddenly jumped up and left for Lhasa." Drugpa Künleg's brother was outraged and cried, "This is going too far. He cannot leave the retreat like that! Go imme-diately, and send some people to bring him back!" The attendant did as he was told, and as soon as Drugpa Künleg was brought back, his brother scolded him, "What do you think you are doing? We were meant to be in retreat for several months. How can you run away like that?" Drugpa Kün-leg replied in an astonished tone, "I thought the retreat was over." Unable to believe his ears, his brother exclaimed, "Where did you get that idea? This is just another of your follies!" Drugpa Künleg said, "Not at all. When I saw you go to Lhasa to have that yak tail dyed red, I thought the retreat was finished!"

Being such a proper lama in every respect, Drugpa Künleg's brother also possessed a set of very precious ritual implements. Made of silver and gold and manufactured with sublime handicraft, they were very dear to his heart. One day, Drugpa Künleg paid a visit to his brother's camp and said, "Today I have to request something very significant from you. I have to give an empowerment of utmost importance to my reputation. Would you lend me your ritual objects for just one day?" His brother was very suspicious and said, "You have never given any initiations. What is this supposed to be now?" Drugpa Künleg replied, "You are right. But today is a special occasion, and this empowerment is really very important. I must give it." "What is it called?," his brother inquired. "Its name is 'Untying the Knot of Miserliness,'" said Drugpa Künleg. At this, his brother grew even more suspicious. "I have never heard of any such initiation," he said, "you are joking." Drugpa Kün-leg insisted, "No, please. There is an initiation called 'Untying the Knot of Miserliness,' and I must definitely give it." Finally his brother gave in. "If this is so," he said, "I will lend you my ritual objects, but please take care of them and make sure they are not damaged." Drugpa Künleg promised, "Don't worry, I will secure them on my back and guard them with my life." Reluctantly, his brother handed him the box with the ritual objects. Drugpa Künleg fastened it on his back and immediately set out for a nearby mountain and started to climb. As soon as he had reached the top, he let himself fall and rolled down its steep slope. When his brother's attendants saw this, they cried, "Come quickly! Your brother has fallen down the mountain." Drugpa Künleg's brother was deeply upset. Thinking that Drugpa Künleg had met with an accident, they all ran to where he was lying. "What has happened," his brother cried, "are you hurt?" "I'm not hurt," Drugpa Künleg replied, "but look, all your precious objects are totally ruined. I'm so very sorry." His brother was relieved that he was unharmed. "Oh, don't worry about that," he said, "it's all right. As long as you are not hurt, it does not matter." In this way, he received Drugpa Künleg's empowerment "Untying the Knot of Miserliness."

To return to our text, the old yogi had said that his *genyen* vows consisted of the threefold refuge, which he kept by abandoning three things, adopting three things, and observing three things conducive to this practice. In the following he describes these further:

> "Then, what are the three things to abandon in connection with the refuge vow? Their root is as follows: Do not strive for protection by worldly gods. Do not seize an opportunity to harm other beings. Do not mistrust and belittle the members of the two types of Sangha.
>
> "What are the three things to adopt? Respect and revere any representation of the Buddha, even including fragments of a broken image. Respect and revere the scriptures of the Dharma, down to a single letter torn from a page. Respect and revere the members of the Sangha, even those who just adopt their outer style.
>
> "What are the three things conducive to practice? Rely on a teacher who is both learned and accomplished. Study and reflect upon the Dharma. And do not forsake the activities and precepts, which are the signs of the Sangha."

At this point the old yogi becomes a little playful and teases the monk who from the beginning has been so haughty:

"Nowadays, there are some of my old yogi friends who deem it sufficient to just have their lama teaching them practice. Propounding the story of the noble lineage of 'Non-Learning and Non-Reflecting,' they do not study the words and meaning of the creation and completion stages. Though followers of the secret Mantrayana, the path of skillful means, they do not see the slightest reason to wear the white yogic garb. They do not even see any necessity of wearing at least a cotton shawl. Meanwhile, they carry out prostrations until their foreheads are swollen with lumps, and they count the beads of their rosaries until their fingernails are splintered. Not the slightest sour drop (of alcohol) comes into their mouths. Not the slightest red bit (of meat) is seen by their eyes. Having carried on like this for many years, they assure each other that they are truly good practitioners who keep their *samayas* well. Come to think of it, though, they do not even understand the refuge vow, and thus may just be wasting their precious human bodies. You as a monk should speak up about this; they won't listen to the words of this old yogi!

"If you listen to me, I will tell you that you also need to know the three sacred aspects, which represent the meaning of the Mahayana sutras. What are these three? The first sacred aspect is the development of the pure aspiration toward practice. The second is the actual practice itself, which should be free from focus on the distinction between subject and object. The third is the pure dedication, which should form the end of any practice. Whatever Dharma practice and beneficial action I engage in, at the beginning I engender the wish, 'I accomplish this root of virtue so that all sentient beings may attain buddhahood.' This motivation is bodhichitta, the pure aspiration toward practice. As for the pure actual practice free from focus, I engage in whatever root of virtue I accomplish in light of the discriminative wisdom, which is free from grasping at the three spheres as being real."

The last statement of the old yogi is to say that the selfless nature of the three spheres, which are agent, object, and their interaction, is understood. Thus any practice or virtuous deed is carried out in a nondual way, free from any involvement in conceptualizing them as being solid or truly existent.

> "As soon as I have accomplished any root of virtue, I generate the wish, 'I dedicate this toward the end that all sentient beings attain the state of buddhahood.' This is the pure dedication. If our practice is not sustained by these three sacred aspects, its virtue will only lead us to attain the state of a god or human in a future life. But if we apply these three, our virtuous deeds will be conducive to total liberation and will cause us to attain the state of a buddha. So it is very important not to be mistaken as to this point. Especially for followers of the tantric tradition, if someone does not know how to turn the three sacred aspects into the path, that person will pervert the tantric practice and go astray on the path of Rudra. Even you monks, if you do not know this, you will go astray to an inferior vehicle. For this reason, please heed my words and do not forget them."

Here the old yogi points out that any practice carried out within the framework of the three sacred aspects corresponds to the Mahayana principle and, thereby, becomes a means to reach total enlightenment. Without these, any good deed will yield a good result in terms of more happiness, but it will still be harvested within the confines of cyclic existence. Actions that are merely beneficial will not lead us to overcome the samsaric state of our mind. Without the pure motivation, practice, and dedication, we cannot be a bodhisattva and cannot practice the tantric teachings either. If we should venture to do so, our activity will totally oppose the principles of the Vajrayana. It will be reversed, or perverted, tantra, and we will tread the path of Rudra.

The name "Rudra" goes back to a person who many *kalpas* before was the son of an extremely wealthy man. He lived a very long time ago, long before Buddha Shakyamuni. His name was later used symbolically to denote a person who perverts the tantric teachings. One day, he went to see a very eminent lama. He was accompanied by a servant, and they both asked for instruction. Having received the same teachings, they went back to study and practice them. Sometime later, they came together to discuss the experience and understanding they had gained. To their astonishment, they found that they did not agree on anything. Their viewpoints were diametrically opposed to each other, so they decided to go back to their teacher to find out who was right. Their teacher listened to them both and said that the servant's view was correct. At that, the master was extremely hurt. "You are no longer my teacher!" he exclaimed. "You are totally biased and even side with my servant. From now on, I will not listen to you or anybody else. I will be in my own command! I will follow my own judgment and do whatever I deem right." With these words, he left and practiced his own idea of the teachings. By doing everything as it should not be done, he gained a very strong negative power. A long time later, he was reborn as a person who was very powerful and at the same time extremely evil. At that time he was called "Rudra." He managed to conquer, and spread his negativity throughout almost the entire world. Even the gods trembled at his sight, and he held everyone under his sway, including the spirits. No one was able to stand up to him. In this situation, some people turned to his former teacher and servant, who by then had become highly enlightened beings. They asked them for help, saying that they were the only ones with the power to bring an end to Rudra's doings.

In light of their karmic connection from the past, they agreed and manifested in front of Rudra, who was engaged in his usual violence. They transformed into a horse and sow, and then entered his body; once inside, they expanded themselves, causing him unbearable pain. Since they were inside him, Rudra could not do anything against them. From within, they reminded him of his evil deeds. They exhorted him to repent and taught him the right course of action. Then, he remembered the former words of his teacher, and this time he understood. Out of heartfelt remorse, he offered his body to be an example of someone who can be very evil and suddenly transform into the positive. From then on, his outer appearance has been used as a symbol within Vajrayana practice. Once subdued, he himself became a protector of Dharma as a wrathful deity.

CREATION AND COMPLETION

Having completed his description of empowerment and of the three sacred aspects, the old yogi next turns to the creation and completion stages.

"For us yogis, the root of all vows and *samayas* is directly captured
in the two aspects of creation and completion. The essential point
and culmination of all vows is the creation stage, and the essential
point and culmination of all *samayas* is the completion stage. Yet,
strangely enough, although they must know this, even the lamas
do not talk about it, and although the disciples know how to apply
it, they do not put it into practice."

As mentioned before, all the different branches of the Noble Eightfold
Path are included in the two aspects of creation and completion. These are
the specific methods or skillful means used within the Vajrayana system.

The purpose of all creation and completion stage practices is to exercise
birth and death and to go beyond our fear of dying, thereby gaining access
to our own true nature, which is unborn and unceasing. I remember an inter-
view His Holiness the Dalai Lama gave. He was asked about his view on birth
and death; he laughed and said, "I am born and die six times every day." What
he was referring to was that by practicing the creation and completion stages
we train in being born and dying again and again. Our whole life consists of
first being born and then changing through growing up, aging, and finally
dying. But this very process is taking place all the time. Every year, every
month, every day, every moment we are changing, being born and dying.
But of course we don't perceive it this way. When thinking of our lifespan,
we always believe that it will last at least fifty, sixty, or seventy years. The purpose of the creation and completion phases of meditation is to purify our
distorted vision of and our relation to birth and death. Though the term "to
purify" is traditionally used, it should not be misunderstood in the sense of
something originally being dirty and later being cleansed. It means practicing the process of birth and death in order to see them for what they are, not
just theoretically but in a practical, experiential way.

The aim is to come to the understanding that the process of birth and
death is something very natural, something that is happening all the time.
They are not precisely defined events, which only happen once and then are
done. In order to realize and become used to this insight, we train in the practice of the creation and completion stages. This is a process of meditation in
which we create an image in our mind, then transform it into something else,
and finally dissolve it. This process is repeated again and again. Through per-
sistent training, we gradually loosen our usual concept of ourselves being a

fixed and defined entity. We become more open to change and thus lessen our clinging to viewpoints and opinions.

As a result of this practice, we should be able to let go of everything. Normally, we cling to so many things, such a large variety of patterns, including negative ones. We cannot let go of our memories, our hurts and hopes. Often we cling to them so desperately that they turn into our identity. The feeling of pain, misery, and dissatisfaction almost becomes the central focus around which we revolve. It snowballs to such an extent that we become totally stuck in it. Therefore, to learn how to let go is essential.

When we find that we can turn into so many things, when we are born and die, appear and dissolve, again and again, there is no need to stick to just one identity. We can change it repeatedly; we can become a deity. This is one of the main practices leading to the recognition that what we believe ourselves to be is just one option. "I am not Ringu Tulku any longer. I am something totally different, like Chakrasamvara, Buddha Shakyamuni, the Healing Buddha, or Avalokiteshvara." Then I identify myself with that. My tendency to hold on to myself as a fixed entity, bound up with all kinds of problems and insufficiencies, is gradually dissolved. This makes way for the feeling, "Who is this Ringu Tulku anyway? What have I got to do with all this rubbish?"

For this reason, it is said that Vajrayana practice is taking "the result as the path." What we aim to become or realize is used as our path and practice. If we want to become an enlightened being, full of compassion, wisdom, and goodness, we start by feeling that way. Normally, we tend to think, "At this moment, I have none of these qualities but I long to obtain them. I would like to be wise and compassionate, to be filled with good energies and joy, all of which I am not at the moment." Instead of nourishing this wish for future attainments, a Vajrayana practitioner develops the deep conviction, "I already have buddha-nature within me, the essence of an enlightened being. I am just slightly polluted on the surface; too much dust has settled on top. It does not touch the purity of my nature. All I need to do is to clean its surroundings, to wash the dirt away." This is the essential philosophy behind Vajrayana practice.

Enlightenment is not something that we gain from somewhere else. It just means to unfold what is already present, to open up to our own true nature, which is inherently pure and endowed with all the qualities of an enlightened being. Its manifestation is hindered by stains that are adventitious, removable like the pollution on the marble facade of a city building. All the qualities we wish to attain, such as wisdom, compassion, joy, and so forth, are not to be obtained from somewhere else. They are the expression of our own true nature, once it is revealed and fully exposed. In light of this understanding, we can try to actually sense it, we can try to become that kind of person. In the beginning, the attempt may feel slightly artificial, but as a way of practice it proves to be a very efficient approach. We try to develop and apply the insight that we have now to open what is already there but not yet manifest, in order to be fully enlightened. This is the main issue of any Vajrayana practice.

The Creation Stage

The old yogi describes the creation stage as follows:

> "If you were to ask this old yogi, the creation stage is as follows: it is connected with three types of *samadhi*. In order to purify the karmic imprints of the four modes of birth, there are four ways of creation, which are the detailed, medium, concise, and very concise forms of the creation stage. Once you understand the purpose of these four, the actual practice falls into seven parts. The first five of these are the preliminaries, which are means of training, familiarization, and stabilization. The sixth is the actual practice itself, and the seventh is the postmeditative training of transforming everyday life into the path."

In Vajrayana practice the process of birth and death is exercised through the visualization of a deity. Which deity is visualized will depend on each students's personal affinity and need, and therefore will depend on the individual instruction of his or her spiritual teacher. Depending upon different *sadhanas*, or meditation texts, the deity is either visualized in front of oneself, or above the crown of one's head, or one visualizes oneself as the deity.

Any visualization is preceded by three types of *samadhi*. During the first *samadhi* the mind is left in its suchness in order to allow the mind to manifest in its natural state, which is the union of emptiness and compassion. This manifestation is the second *samadhi*, from which birth takes place in the form of a seed syllable or a color. This initial creation forms the third *samadhi*, which then transforms into the particular deity to be visualized.

The purpose of any visualization practice is to purify the four modes of birth that we may have undergone countlessly during our various preceding lifetimes. Each of these has left karmic imprints in our mind that need to be cleared away. Nevertheless, it is important to understand that one thorough purification will take care of everything. Every Vajrayana practice is complete in itself. It is therefore not necessary to practice all the different forms of creation stage that the old yogi describes. These are mainly due to different *sadhanas*. Which of these is used individually again depends on the personal relationship between master and disciple.

Creation stage practice itself has seven parts, of which the first five are preliminaries, which will give rise to five experiences, those of movement, attainment, familiarization, stability, and final accomplishment. The preliminaries are: focusing on the deity, curing defects in the visualization, separating from the deity, bringing the deity onto the path, and mixing the mind with the deity. In their course, eight signs of clarity and stability will manifest, which are the sign that the highest stage of *shiné* meditation is achieved.

When these signs are present, one is prepared for the sixth point, the actual creation stage practice, called "Actualizing the Deity." It is carried out within the framework of "the four nails," which are the nails of *samadhi*, of mantra, of irreversible understanding, and of manifestation and absorption. These nails again form four stages, called the "approach" practice, the "close approach" practice, the "accomplishment" practice, and the "great accomplishment" practice. It is important to understand that the practice of creation stage is not something that is mastered easily. It may take a lifetime or even many lifetimes until the meditative capacity described as its result is achieved, being in fact the capacity of an enlightened being. Nevertheless, the Vajrayana takes the fruit as the path. For this reason, one trains in the full content of the *sadhana* to be practiced right from the beginning, thereby mastering the different aspects of creation step-by-step.

The seventh aspect of creation stage practice involves the way to carry its impact into every aspect of life. It teaches the view of utter purity and how to practice in light of this view during daytime, during sleep, and during dreams.

The old yogi then describes the three *samadhis*:

"You may wonder what the three types of *samadhi* are. The ground is 'the *samadhi* of suchness.' You let the mind rest evenly within its uncontrived true state itself.

"The path is 'the *samadhi* of overall appearance.' This means
that the unceasing radiance inherent in the uncontrived true state
itself shines forth as great compassion.

"The result is 'the *samadhi* of the seed.' The pure vivid manifestation of the inseparable union of emptiness and compassion
transforms into a seed syllable, into *Hung* or *Hri*, and so forth."

During the first *samadhi*, "the *samadhi* of suchness," the mind is allowed to
be in its actual uncreated state without making any changes or modifica-
tions. The mind is left the way it is, in its present state. It is allowed to abide
in the present moment without putting any concept onto it. This is the
ground *samadhi* that stands at the beginning of any creation stage practice.
One always starts with leaving one's mind in its suchness, in complete nowness, in its true uncontrived nature without adding anything to it.

When doing so, the nature of our mind itself proves to be radiant with
goodness and warmth, with all-encompassing compassion that manifests
in spontaneous bliss. This is the second *samadhi*, the *samadhi* of overall
appearance. Here the term "compassion" is to be understood in light of the
Vajrayana. It is not compassion in the sense of feeling sad and full of pity
upon seeing something negative happen. In the experience of the Vajrayana,
compassion manifests within spontaneous bliss. This is ultimate bodhichitta, the expression of the deep insight into the true nature of our mind
and everything else. Once everything is seen as it is, it is also seen that every
being suffers unnecessarily. Suffering is not the nature of sentient beings.
Their nature is the union of emptiness and bliss. Nevertheless, as long as this
is not understood, sentient beings suffer tremendously in various ways.
Upon seeing this, great compassion arises in someone who understands the
true nature of mind. This compassion is completely uncontrived and free
from any artifice, such as thinking, "I should be kind to my fellow beings."
This is called "the *samadhi* of overall appearance or manifestation." For a
beginner, though, who does not realize the nature of mind and of everything
else, this means to give rise to the feeling of compassion using the methods
taught in the Mahayana system.

The foregoing is to say that there are two aspects, completely inseparable
from each other. The first is emptiness, the experience of our own true
nature or of the way everything really is. This is totally unchanging and cannot be altered. The second is compassion, the radiance native to the true

nature of mind. The manifestation of their union appears in the form of the seed syllable, which can be visualized as a letter like *Hung*, or *Hri*, or it can be visualized as a color. This is the third *samadhi*, called "the *samadhi* of the seed."

The three *samadhis* described above are the essential points within any visualization, or creation stage practice. "Emptiness" can be spoken of in the context of the three *samadhis*, but this term should not be understood in its literal sense. It stands for the true nature of mind. The mind is allowed to rest in its natural state without adding or removing anything. Then, there is the flow of its natural spontaneous compassion and bliss. From this union of our ultimate nature and its radiance, also called the union of wisdom and compassion, the first birth takes place. The first thought that comes up is taken as the working material to create the visualization. When a thought appears in our mind, we usually think of something: a sound, color, or anything else. Instead of following our habitual pattern, we try to create something that is related to the deity and the visualization we intend to do. This is the seed syllable which then transforms into or gives birth to something else.

The old yogi then explains the four modes of birth:

> "The four modes of birth are being born from an egg, from a womb, from heat and moisture, and being born miraculously. These are what need to be purified. The means of purification are the detailed, medium, concise, and very concise forms of the creation stage. Of these, the detailed version of the creation stage purifies the karmic imprints of birth from an egg. The visualization involves five ways to generate from yourself and eight ways to generate from something else.
>
> "The medium version of the creation stage purifies the karmic imprints of birth from a womb. It is practiced through three, four, and five stages, called the 'three vajra rituals,' 'four awakenings,' and 'five awakenings.'
>
> "The concise version of the creation stage purifies the karmic imprints of birth from heat and moisture. It is practiced by means of just visualizing a seed syllable or by uttering a mantra, from which the entire form of the deity is born.
>
> "The very concise version of the creation stage purifies the karmic imprints of a miraculous birth. This is practiced in an

instantaneous way, the generation being accomplished by the mere thought of it."

As has been mentioned before, there are different ways of training in the creation stage according to different *sadhanas*. This is not the place to describe them further, so the root text is just given for the sake of presenting its full content. Each of these ways of training is complete in itself and will lead to the result that is to be achieved by creation stage practice. The forms most commonly applied in the West are the concise and very concise versions of the creation stage.

The important point in this context is the fact that all creation stage practices always consist of seven aspects, which the old yogi describes as follows:

"Once you have understood the nature of these four exactly as described, the path of the actual practice has seven parts. These are: (1) focusing on the deity, (2) curing defects in the visualization, (3) separating from the deity, (4) bringing the deity onto the path, (5) mixing the mind with the deity, (6) actualizing the deity, and (7) carrying everyday experience onto the path."

Of these the first five are preliminary practices that should lead to the achievement of the highest state of *shiné*. Using the image of a deity as the focus of meditation, we allow it to appear in the mind and let the mind be occupied by it. This is a very good way to keep our mind together. Otherwise, it is usually everywhere, totally scattered and blurred. Our own mind appears as the image of a deity, which is clear and yet not solid or real. It is just an image, but at the same time it is more than that. It radiates goodness, and is vibrant with all wholesome energies and experiences. Thus, our entire concentration is immersed in a positive side. In this respect, the practice of the creation stage, which is called "deity yoga," is not identical with just concentrating on our breathing or similar things but involves a bit more.

1. Focusing on the Deity
The old yogi describes the first of the five preliminary practices as follows:

"Whichever deity from among the three roots you want to practice, allow the form of the deity to arise and be reflected in your mind. It appears, and yet does not have any tangible substance. It comes into the mind like a reflection in a mirror. At that time, you should meditate, letting the mind look at this form. Sometimes, let the eye of the mind gaze directly and intensely at the deity. At other times, just let it be reflected and be at one with the appearance in your mind."

This describes deity yoga, or the visualization. Any visualization is usually of one of the three roots, called *lama, yidam,* and *khandro* in Tibetan or *guru, deva,* and *dakini* in Sanskrit, which are (briefly speaking) different visual expressions of enlightenment. Whichever expression of these we want to practice, first we give rise to the intention, "I want to visualize this deity." With this resolution, we collect our attention on this particular enlightened principle. We allow its image to appear naturally in our mind. It is a mere image, a lucid reflection, which just appears but is neither solid nor real. Then, we focus our mind on it and stay with the image, letting our mind be occupied by it. In the different *sadhanas,* each deity is described in terms of very specific features. At times we let the mind's eye look at these as if we were actually looking at something. At other times we do not even do that but just let the image be in our mind without looking at anything in particular.

"While you meditate alternating these, at first thoughts will come up in a turbulent torrent. This is called the 'experience of movement.'"

No matter what kind of meditation we do, whether it be calm abiding or any other kind of practice, we will pass through five levels of experience. These are the experiences of movement, attainment, familiarization, stability, and final accomplishment. The first is the experience of movement, turbulence, or fluctuation. In the context of deity yoga, this occurs when one first begins to try to focus one's mind on the visualized deity. Movement is described by the image of a wild mountain stream, gushing down steep slopes in a thunderous, unstoppable torrent. This is the first sign of the meditation having effect, though it will be experienced as quite painful. The mind is flooded by so many thoughts, all kinds of things coming up very strongly, that it becomes very violent and heavy. It becomes so turbulent and rushing that we feel there is no way to stop it. Thus, this stage is very difficult, yet very important at the same time. It constitutes the first level of progress.

At this stage we may feel that everything has turned for the worst, because

our mind has become much more agitated and wild and totally overpowering. But this is an incorrect perception. In actual fact, it is the first time that
we have created the conditions to experience the state of our mind as it usually is. We are normally so distracted and scattered that we do not notice how
many things take place in our mind, how busy it is all the time. Once we try
to be slightly less distracted and more concentrated, we become more aware
of what is going on. That is the first experience, the experience of the turbulent state of the mind, which is also the first achievement in meditation. This
stage is crucial, because a great deal of courage, determination, and faith is
required in order to be able to go on. Most people stop here; they feel it is too
painful and that there is no hope for progress. At this point, we need to work
hard and go forward.

> "After some time, not many thoughts will arise and the form of
> the deity will shine forth distinctly in lustrous radiance. This is
> called the 'experience of attainment.'"

While working on the experience of movement, we will gradually find
that not as many thoughts come up in our mind. All its turbulence becomes
somewhat quietened. During this process, the visualization becomes
clearer. At the end, the image appears very clearly, very distinctly and vividly,
in a splendid and lustrous way. There is just clarity and vibrating appearance.
When this happens, the second stage of meditation is reached. This is called
the "experience of attainment." This term should not be taken literally, as
this is not the final attainment. It refers to the stage in which, for the first time,
the mind has settled to a certain extent. The mind's turbulence has calmed
down, and it has gained some basic balance and a dawning stability. This is
focusing on the deity, the first part of the creation stage practice.

2. Curing Defects in the Visualization

> "Whichever features of the deity do not stand out clearly—the
> color of the body, the gestures, signs, expressions, and so forth—
> let your mind solely capture these particular aspects, so that they
> become clear."

The second stage of creation stage practice refers to the time when the image of the deity is present, but its features are not clear or distinct. To cure this, we should focus on a part of the deity, such as the body, the face, a hand, an ornament, a piece of clothing, and so forth, becoming ever more precise in this process. In this way, the clarity of the image is gradually improved and completed.

3. Separating from the Deity

"In one session, let your mind look precisely at the deity and meditate in that way, undistractedly, with intent effort. Then in the following session, do not meditate on the form of the deity, but solely heed and embrace your mind as it truly is. These two are cultivated alternately."

During this stage, we alternate two aspects of meditation. At times, we meditate with undistracted effort, focusing our mind directly and one-pointedly on the deity. At other times, we do not concentrate on the image of the deity at all. Letting go of our focus, we leave the image completely and let it get out of our mind. Then, we let the mind be as it is, in the protection of its true nature. We allow the mind to settle down in its true state without doing anything. We totally relax without being involved in any activity or creation. Thus, both deliberate effort and totally letting go are applied alternately in the course of the third phase of creation practice.

4. Bringing the Deity onto the Path

"Meditate making the deity very large and at other times very tiny. Let it perform a variety of actions and display many different expressions. In the course of this practice, no matter whether or not you meditate, the reflection of the deity will shine forth continuously. This is called 'the experience of familiarization, which is like the flow of a river.'"

At this point we change our visualization of the deity. Sometimes we make it very big. We visualize it as large as a mountain or a city, and let it fill the whole universe. At other times, we make it very small, so tiny that it is hardly to be seen. These changes are sometimes made quickly and sometimes slowly. At times the visualization is changed very rapidly, and the deity is given different actions, postures, or colors. In this way, we do not just concentrate on one fixed form, but we try to maintain our focus while the image is made to fluctuate. Before this point, we have mainly been deliberately controlling our mind. In the beginning this is necessary, as we must stabilize the mind and make it settled and stay with its focus. But now we apply a different technique, the purpose being to go beyond the need for deliberate control and to overcome the phase in which the image is dependent on our careful control and maintenance.

Through this exercise, we can gain complete mastery, and there will be no need to protect the visualization any longer. We can feel completely free with it. We can throw it around, let it be everywhere and do anything, without losing control. This is exercising stability in movement, which is one of the most important aspects in meditation. The aim is not just keeping the mind together in one place, but to find stability even while it moves and is distracted. We are aiming at a state where, although there is movement in the mind, it is not turbulent, but remains clear, calm, and stable. Concentration on a moving deity is a method of developing this ability. We can make a big or small deity and let it run, dance, or fly, and still the mind will stay with it in a stable way without being disturbed. When this experience is firmly established, the mind will be constantly calm and clear. The image of the deity will be present whether or not we meditate. This is the third of the five meditational experiences that will occur during the development of *shiné*. It is called the "experience of familiarization," which is analogous to a calm river slowly flowing through a plain.

5. Mixing the Mind with the Deity

> "This is the essential point: the deity that is meditated upon and the mind of the meditator are not separated or seen as two different things. They are one, and you should rest evenly within this oneness. When in the course of this practice you are no longer separate from the clear and distinct appearance of the deity's form and have become at one with it in every respect, this is called 'the experience of stability, which is like a mountain.' This is a sign that extraordinary steadfastness or stability in practice is achieved. At this time there will be the four signs of clarity and the four signs

of stability. Clarity is brilliant, sharp, vivid, and total. Stability is unmoving, nonfluctuating, truly nonfluctuating, and flexible."

When the exercise of stability in movement is fully accomplished, there will be the experience of actual stability, the fourth of the five experiences of the development of *shiné*, which is likened to a high mountain. A mountain is there all the time. It is not shaken no matter what happens. It stays the same whether the wind blows, snow falls, or storms come. At this stage, the deity to be meditated upon and the mind of the meditator are no longer separate; they have become one. There is no longer a distinction between times of meditation and times of nonmeditation. The mind abides continuously in a meditative state. When this is achieved, there are four signs of clarity and four signs of stability. Clarity is described by means of four terms, which are called *sal lé, sing ngé, lhag gé,* and *lhang ngé* in Tibetan. These are very difficult to translate. *Sal lé* stands for a great brightness and lucidity, the absence of any darkness, a very clear light that illuminates everything. *Sing ngé* means that nothing is blurred or hazy. Everything is very distinct and stands out on its own. When looking at someone's hair, for instance, every single strand will be seen clearly and separately. *Lhag gé* means that everything is seen fully and completely in all its aspects, not just in a two-dimensional way, but from all sides and angles at the same time. *Lhang ngé* means that everything is seen continuously and to the same degree. Whether or not we look at something intensely, everything is seen clearly all the time.

The four signs of stability are called "unmoving," "nonfluctuating," "truly nonfluctuating," and "flexible" or "malleable." With these, the mind is totally undistracted and stable and will in no way change by itself. Wherever it is put it will stay, but at the same time it is completely malleable. It can be changed into anything deliberately. One can do with it whatever one wants.

Altogether, these are called the "eight signs of clarity and stability." They constitute the goal to be achieved by the practice of the five preliminaries of the creation stage.

> "When you meditate while the eight signs of clarity and stability are immediately manifest, whatever appears will definitely shine forth as the deity's form. This is the experience of final accomplishment, called 'appearance is the mandala of the deity.' It is the sign that total stability is achieved.

"These are the five preliminaries, which are the means of training, familiarization, and stabilization. In this way, the experiences
of movement, attainment, familiarization, stability, and final
accomplishment will gradually appear."

The level of final accomplishment on which the eight signs of clarity and
stability manifest continuously is the fifth of the five experiences of the
development of *shiné*. It constitutes the highest stage of *shiné* meditation,
which is achieved through the five preliminaries that precede the actual
practice of creation stage, which is described in the sixth part.

In the course of the actual practice of creation, any duality between a meditator and an object to be meditated upon is transcended. To facilitate this,
the visualization is changed. During the five preliminary practices the deity,
the embodiment of wisdom and compassion, or of the enlightened state, is
visualized in front of oneself, and thus remains somewhat different or separate. This is called "the symbolic deity." The true deity is our own mind in
terms of its true nature. The true nature of mind being the union of wisdom
and compassion, the practitioner is not different from the deity. This is not
easy to understand and experience, so the preliminary stages are necessary.

In the course of the actual practice itself one visualizes oneself as the deity,
thereby fully identifying with the enlightened principle. The goal is to
achieve enlightenment by actualizing ultimate bodhichitta in seeing the
true deity, called "Mahamudra," and to be able to carry out enlightened
activity for the sake of all sentient beings, such as peaceful, enriching, powerful, and wrathful actions. Thus, the perfection of the creation stage of meditation mainly serves to bring forth the full ability to help any sentient being,
whereas the completion stage of meditation will lead to deepening the first
initial vision of the truth into its full extent.

As mentioned above, the actual practice of creation has four stages, called
"the four nails," equivalent to four steps, namely the "approach" practice, the
"close approach" practice, the "accomplishment" practice, and the "great
accomplishment" practice. The old yogi describes them as follows:

6. *Actualizing the Deity*

"This has four parts. When you have reached the period of mantra
recitation, first you practice the 'approach,' which is called the

'nail of *samadhi*.' Until then, the deity has been visualized as being in front of yourself. At this stage you meditate visualizing yourself as the deity. If it does not appear in full clarity, you should look at an image or a statue, and then meditate not wavering for even an instant.

"The second is the 'close approach' practice, which is called the 'nail of mantra.' Assume the pride of the deity and rest in *samadhi* until the eight signs of clarity and stability occur. Within these you should train reciting the mantra. This can be done by number, such as reciting each syllable a hundred thousand times; by time, such as setting four periods of recitation; or by sign. The latter means that you recite the mantra until the actual experience is there and you see its signs in dreams and so on.

"The third is the 'accomplishment' practice, also called the 'nail of irreversible understanding.' At a certain point you will see that the deity to be meditated upon, the mantra to be recited, and so on, are just concepts, mere contributions of the mind. Apart from mind, there is nothing to accomplish. Thus, all hopes are cut from within."

The sixth point describes the integration of the deity that was visualized throughout the five preliminary stages into the actual practice itself. This is called "deity yoga." Deity yoga practice consists of four parts, of which the first is the "nail of *samadhi*," or the stage translated as the "approach" in English. The Tibetan term is *nyen pa*, which means "mantra recitation." This name should not be understood in the literal sense, though, as the mantra is not actually recited at this point. The first part is a preparation toward the recitation of the mantra.

In the course of the preceding five stages, the deity has been visualized as something slightly different from ourselves, as something appearing in front of us and being looked at. At this point we transform into the deity. We become identical with it and meditate upon being the deity. When the image is not clear in our mind, we make it clear, and the moment it has become clear we meditate on it unwaveringly. This is the practice of *nyen pa*. Although it is called "mantra recitation," it is the period in which we try to stabilize the mind on the meditation.

The second part is the "close approach" practice, which in Tibetan is called *nye nyen.* The word *nye* means literally "near," and *nyen* means "recitation," but this does not convey the actual meaning. During this period the practice of *nyen pa* is intensified and strengthened. We reach nearer to actual realization. This is the part of the practice in which the mantra is actually recited. It is therefore called the "nail of mantra." We visualize ourselves as the deity, assume what is called the "pride of the deity," and make this as stable as possible. We try to give rise to the eight signs of clarity and stability. Then the mantra is recited within this state of mind.

Mantra represents—as does the visualized form of a deity—the expression of enlightenment, of our true nature. It is recited in the recognition of our own true nature being the inseparable union of wisdom and compassion, or of emptiness and bliss. The Vajrayana makes use of the working materials at hand, of form, sound, and so on. It teaches us to employ our ordinary senses in order to feel and experience what we truly are. In light of this recognition of our own true nature we assume what is called the "pride of the deity," or "vajra pride."

Since this phrase may easily arouse false assumptions, it may be useful to explain it a bit further. When speaking of "assuming the pride of the deity," this should not be understood in the literal sense. In the beginning, we usually have the concept that we should view ourselves as the deity. In actual fact we should not think of ourselves at all. We should just think of the deity. It does not mean that we should develop pride by imagining, "I am this deity." It is very important to understand this properly. Everything is the deity, and our consciousness is the deity. We do not aim at strengthening our continuous impulse toward asserting our self. We should let go of any identification. We should just have the awareness of the deity and of this deity being not different from ourselves. Our usual concept of ourselves should not be present. Instead of that, there should be the awareness of only the deity and nothing else.

There are many different ways of doing mantra recitation. It can be done by number, by time, or until the signs are achieved. The first means that a fixed number of mantras are set, such as reciting the mantra one hundred times and so forth. A very frequent form of this recitation practice is to recite the mantra one hundred thousand times during however many meditation sessions may be needed to do so. The second way of recitation means that a fixed period of time is set, such as resolving to recite the mantra for one month, three months, one year, three years, and so forth. The last way is the most important: a firm resolution is made to recite the mantra until the signs of achievement appear and the practice is actualized.

The third part is the "accomplishment" practice, which in Tibetan is called *drub pa*. Literally, this term means "practice," though again this does not indicate exactly what is involved at this level. Perhaps the meaning is better conveyed through its other name, the "nail of irreversible understanding." After meditating for as long as intended, here it is seen that the deity being visualized, the mantra being recited, and so forth are nothing but concepts, mere creations of our mind. One realizes that, apart from this, there is no deity to be meditated upon. There is the clear and firm understanding, "This is it." There is no separate thing to be gained or accomplished. The old yogi describes this insight further as follows:

> "The Dharma to be practiced becomes lost. The practitioner vanishes on his own. The rope of fixating mindfulness is cut. The deliberate effort of applying an antidote shatters. Expectation and apprehension are freed from within. The inconceivable isness of everything—peace, openness, and relaxation inexpressible—reveals itself directly as the great primordial wisdom beyond thoughts. This is called 'Mahamudra,' the supreme *siddhi*. The exalted and true deity's countenance is seen immediately."

Dharmata, the true state of all phenomena, cannot be accessed by any concept or idea. There is no means to conceive of or express it. When felt it is totally boundless, open, and spacious, free from any narrowness or suffocation. It is the great primordial wisdom, completely beyond all mental constructions, and at this point it is unveiled, becoming apparent and clear. This is the ultimate *siddhi*, or accomplishment.

In the context of the Vajrayana, two kinds of *siddhi* are described, called "common" and "ultimate." The common *siddhis* are different types of extraordinary faculties, such as clairvoyance and so forth. The ultimate *siddhi* is Mahamudra, *chag gya chen po* in Tibetan. This can be translated as "the Great Seal," "the Great Gesture," or "the Great Symbol." At this point, the actual face of the deity is seen, or as it is sometimes described, there is the vision of the deity. This does not mean that a face appears in front of our eyes. The realization of Mahamudra is seeing the true deity. This is not the symbolic one that was visualized. The real aim and purpose of visualization is to demonstrate how to see our own face, or our own true nature, which is Mahamudra.

> "The fourth is the 'great accomplishment' practice, also called the 'nail of manifestation and absorption.' By visualizing one supreme deity, you engage in profound activity, such as pacifying, enriching, powerful, and wrathful actions, and so on. Thus you only need to know how to emanate this one deity.
>   "These are called the 'divisions of the actual practice itself.' Therefore, they are very important points."

The fourth part is the "great" practice, or the "great accomplishment" practice, which in Tibetan is *drub chen*. This is called the "nail of manifestation and absorption," and consists of the different types of enlightened activity, such as peaceful, enriching, powerful, and wrathful actions. Peaceful action has the purpose of purification and pacification. It comprises the four kinds of healing and is associated with the color white. Enriching activity is associated with the color yellow and engenders prosperity and the expansion of everything that is positive. Powerful activity is associated with the color red. It entails force and energy, the ability to accomplish whatever needs to be done. Wrathful activity is a forceful way of accomplishment and vanquishes everything that is negative. It is associated with the color blue. Beside these, there are innumerable other ways in which a buddha or a realized bodhisattva will act in order to help all sentient beings. When the capacity to fully perform all these different activities has been achieved through the practice of a particular deity, the great practice, or the great accomplishment practice, has been mastered.

The four nails described above represent the entirety of the actual practice of the creation phase. In this context, it is very important to understand that the visualization described here represents the final goal, the perfect practice of the creation phase. As beginners, we cannot expect to be able to visualize in this perfect way. This capacity needs to be developed and built up gradually, and it may take a lifetime or even many lifetimes until it is achieved. A person with this ability is a very highly developed and realized practitioner. Therefore, we should not give rise to false expectations and thus ask too much of ourselves.

7. Carrying Everyday Experience onto the Path

Now we come to the seventh aspect of the creation stage, which describes how to carry our practice of the deity into our daily lives. It has two parts, the first of which teaches the correct understanding, or view. The second part teaches us how to practice on the basis of this view during daytime, during sleep, and during dreams. The purpose of these exercises is to enable us to turn the processes of dying, of being in the intermediate state between death and rebirth, and of being reborn into a path that will allow us to reach liberation within one of the three *kayas* during either of these processes. The three *kayas* are the dharmakaya, sambhogakaya, and nirmanakaya. They represent the state of enlightenment, or buddhahood, and will be explained in more detail in the section on Mahamudra.

The old yogi describes the seventh aspect as follows:

> "This has two parts. The first is what needs to be understood. It consists of the 'three domains' of the mandala of the peaceful and wrathful deities. The domain of the five male and five female tathagatas is the pure aspects of the five skandhas and five elements, respectively. The domain of the eight male and eight female bodhisattvas is the pure aspects of the four sense organs, the four sense consciousnesses, the four sense objects, and the four times. The domain of the four male and four female wrathful deities is the pure aspects of the body consciousness, its sense organ and sense objects, as well as the pure aspects of an eternalistic view, a nihilistic view, a view holding the belief in an existing self, and a view that sees things in terms of their characteristics.
>
> "From the very beginning, what needs to be purified has been primordially pure. The fruit of purification has always been present. It is the way everything is. Knowing this is the special feature of the activity of us yogis, yet people who understand it are rare. However, if you do not understand this, calling food and drink a 'ritual feast' might perhaps turn into a lie."

The correct understanding is the vision of utter purity. The five skandhas, or aggregates, are viewed as the five male buddhas, the five elements as the five female buddhas, and so forth. Everything experienced and related to is

seen as a deity, though this should not be understood in the literal sense. It
does not mean that things are suddenly seen differently, as a blue deity holding a flower and so forth. It means that everything is seen in its pure aspect.
We see the pure side of all phenomena. We understand that the five aggregates, for instance, are not something negative. They are not to be disliked
and abandoned. In truth, they are utterly good and pure. When the inherent
purity of the five skandhas and elements is seen, they are known to be the
display of the five buddhas and their consorts. There is real union. There is
nothing that is not joyful. That is what needs to be understood from the
viewpoint of the creation stage. In light of the completion stage, we have to
understand that our mind is buddha, the dharmakaya. This understanding
is not easily gained. It has to be developed gradually in the course of practice
and cannot be just intellectual. It has to arise from genuine experience.

> "The second part is called 'carrying everything onto the path.'
> This has three aspects, which are: (1) carrying birth onto the path
> of nirmanakaya, (2) carrying death onto the path of dharmakaya,
> and (3) carrying the intermediate state onto the path of samb-
> hogakaya.

> "(1) During the whole time from early morning until night, do not
> be separate from the clear appearance shining forth as the perfect
> play of the supreme deity. This is the utter purity of the vessel and
> its content, or the mandala of the peaceful and wrathful deities
> with its three domains. Maintaining this inseparability is called
> 'carrying birth onto the path of nirmanakaya.'

> "(2) Secondly, while going to sleep, dissolve the aspect of appear-
> ance of the creation stage into the appearance-free sphere of the
> completion stage. Then rest evenly, free from reference point.
> Merging sleep with clear light is called 'carrying death onto the
> path of dharmakaya.'

> "(3) Thirdly, when at night you reach the city of dreams, recognize
> what happens as being a dream. Make the creation and comple-
> tion you carry out in daytime and the dream appearances coemer-
> gent and thus transform them into your path. This is called
> 'carrying the intermediate state onto the path of sambhogakaya.'

"These are called the 'division of meditating by carrying everything onto the path in postmeditation.' It is necessary to turn the three aspects of birth, death, and intermediate state into our path by transforming them into the three *kayas*. Through accomplishing the transformation of death into the path of dharmakaya, we will be liberated in the same instant our breathing stops. Through accomplishing the transformation of the intermediate state into sambhogakaya, we will attain the *kaya* of joint manifestation within the self-appearing bardo of *dharmata*, although we did not manage to reach liberation at the moment of death. Through accomplishing a sound familiarity with the transformation of birth into nirmanakaya, at least we will have the certainty of traveling into the self-appearing pure fields of Ogmin, Khachö, and so forth, during the bardo of becoming. This is the particular quality of the unsurpassable lineage of the secret Mantrayana."

The description of how to practice in our daily lives has three parts. It teaches how to practice during daytime, during sleep, and during dreams. This relates to the time while we are living, while we are dying, and while we are in the bardo, the intermediate state between death and birth.

The way to practice during daytime is called "carrying birth onto the path of nirmanakaya." From the moment we get up until we go to sleep, we try to remind ourselves to see the pure side of ourselves and everything that is around us. We do not have to visualize anything during our waking hours. We just try to stay in the state of mind that was present during our sessions of meditation on the creation stage. We take the impact of our visualization, its force and environment, into our daily lives and try to maintain the joyful, pure, clear, and stable experience that was gained from it. We try to see everything as the utterly pure manifestation of the Buddha.

The second part describes the way to practice during sleep. It is called "carrying death onto the path of dharmakaya." When we go to sleep, the aspect of appearance, the creation stage, is allowed to dissolve into *dzog rim*, the completion stage, and we let our mind rest in its natural state. When one is really able to do that, sleep dissolves in clear light. The aim is to go to sleep in the meditative state of the first of the three *samadhis* and to wake up in that same state. When this happens, it shows that we have been able to mix meditation with sleep and to transform sleep into clear light.

The third part teaches the way to practice during dreams. This is called "carrying the intermediate state onto the path of sambhogakaya." It means that while dreaming we try to recognize that we are dreaming. When this recognition is present, we integrate the practices of creation and completion, which are carried out during daytime, into the dream appearances. We visualize the deity while dreaming and then dissolve it into the completion stage. What is meant here is the completion stage at its ideal level that will be explained further in the next section and especially in the section on Mahamudra. When we are able to do so, we can actually turn into the deity. In dreams everything is possible. There are no limits, and we can do whatever we like. For this reason, our practice will become very effective once we can recognize our dreams for what they are and use them as a means.

The reason why we should try to identify the aspects of birth, death, and the intermediate state with the three *kayas* and thus carry them onto the path of practice during our lifetime is as follows. Truly mastering the practice of transforming sleep into clear light, we will be liberated within the dharmakaya the moment our breathing stops at the time of dying. There will be spontaneous liberation at the very instant of death. The teachings on the bardo speak of "mother and child luminosity." When the mother luminosity arises at the moment of death, we will understand and recognize it. As soon as this happens, we will be liberated within that state. The mother and child luminosities merge, and we become aware of the true state of our primordial nature. At this point, there is instantaneous liberation.

If we fail to reach enlightenment in the above way, but are able to carry our practice into the bardo during dreams, we can do so in the intermediate state as well and will be instantaneously liberated within it. When the bardo of the *dharmata* arises, we become enlightened in the *kaya* of union. Understanding that everything that arises and happens is not separate from ourselves, we lose our fear. Not being afraid, we see everything as our own manifestation and become liberated in that state.

Then, if we are not liberated at that point, but are soundly familiarized with taking our practice into daily life, this will be of great benefit when reaching the fourth stage of the bardo, during which rebirth is taken. Though we have not managed to attain enlightenment in death or the bardo, we will be reborn in a very conducive existence, in one of the pure realms such as Akanishtha. This is the reason why it is said that through the practice of the Vajrayana we can be liberated in one lifetime. When training thoroughly throughout our lives, we can attain complete enlightenment in the three stages of death, bardo, and rebirth. This is the uniqueness of the Vajrayana.

"Up to here, this was a very short and abbreviated rendering of the creation stage as practiced by us yogis."

The Completion Stage

As was said earlier, during the practice of creation and completion we train in being born and dying. The training in being born is represented by the creation stage, while the completion stage relates to the process of death. In the course of this process our consciousness leaves the body and is left nakedly to itself. Accordingly, the visualization that was carried out during the creation phase is dissolved, and the mind is left to itself in its natural state. The true nature of mind is totally beyond concepts and thus inexpressible. Being able to meditate in this state is the ideal practice of the completion stage, which the old yogi describes below. As beginners, though, we cannot hope to meditate in this perfect way. We will therefore employ means that are individually suited to our level of spiritual progress and which will make us understand the nature of our mind gradually. These means might be the different stages of the meditation on emptiness as taught by the Svatantrika and Prasangika systems, or similar methods presented on the Sutrayana level of teaching.

The purpose of all creation stage practices is to dissolve our attachment to the solidity and independent existence of ourselves and the phenomenal world around us. We create the image of a deity in our mind that stands out clearly in all its features, and yet is neither solid nor real. It comes into the mind like a rainbow and is not graspable in any way. At the same time it radiates all goodness and any perfect quality, thus being an image of the true nature of mind. Nevertheless, it is still an image, a further creation of our mind, and we may easily develop an attachment to this pure and radiant manifestation that we have created. This is a more subtle attachment, but still an attachment.

The purpose of the completion stage is to cut this attachment as well. We come back to the state of mind from which the first creation of the deity arose, to the *samadhi* of suchness. Thus the wheel comes full circle: the mind is left in complete emptiness. From this emptiness the pure and vivid manifestation of the deity arises, which while present is not different from emptiness, and which then dies—dissolving back into emptiness. In the context of the Vajrayana, emptiness is to be understood as "emptiness endowed with all perfect aspects." This refers to the fact that the nature of mind—when realized—proves to be not just empty. It has radiance and displays appearance, manifesting in unceasing play. Thus it is the inseparable union of emptiness and appearance, or of emptiness and clear light.

The stage of completion practice that the old yogi points out refers to this understanding and therefore requires a very high level of insight into the true nature of mind. It is presented here to give an impression, and an inspiration to aspire to the final goal. Completion stage practice, when carried out in this light, has a more elaborate and a totally unelaborate aspect, the first involving a focus and the second being without focus. The former consists of different practices commonly called "yogas," such as the "six yogas of Naropa." They are usually practiced in a retreat situation and involve working with the subtle aspects of the psycho-physical body, which are the channels, chakras, bindus, and winds. Although these methods involve a great amount of technique, such as very detailed visualizations and so forth, they are considered as completion stage practices.

The completion stage practice without focus means resting in the true nature of mind itself. This is called "Mahamudra" in the Kagyü tradition and "Maha Ati" in the Nyingma tradition. The latter is what the old yogi describes. It will not be explained further in this book. From the description of the tantras given by the old yogi the reader will clearly see how tantric practices relate to whatever the Buddha taught in the preceding vehicles. As for the final completion stage, it is described here in the following section on Mahamudra..

For further information on the creation and completion stages I would recommend, for instance, the text by Jamgön Kongtrül, as translated, annotated, and introduced by Sarah Harding (*Creation and Completion* from Wisdom Publications).

The old yogi describes the completion stage as follows:

> "Now, the third is the completion stage. This again has two
> aspects, which are with focus and without focus. There are many
> different ways of completion stage with focus. When summa-

rized, they are contained in six profound dharmas. The root is inner heat. The ground is illusory body. The essence is clear light. The evaluation is dream. The escort is bardo, and the measure of mental strength is the transference of consciousness. You should meditate, becoming intimately accustomed with these."

As for the completion stage involving a focus, there are many ways of practice, which are summarized by the six yogas. The root of these is the practice of inner heat, or *tum mo*. The basic ground is the practice of illusory body, or *gyu lü*, which can be said to be the completion of the creation stage. The real essence of the six yogas is the practice of clear light, or *ö sal*. The evaluation (or the measure of attainment) is the yoga of dreams, or *mi lam*. The fifth is the practice of the teachings on the bardo, which is the preparation (or guide), and the sixth yoga is the practice of the transference of consciousness, called *pho wa*.

"The second is the completion stage without focus. When presented as the practice of us followers of the old translations, it is called the 'Secret Oral Instructions of the Great Perfection,' and was translated into Tibetan due to the kindness of the Indian Pandita Vimalamitra. If you understand it in the morning, you will meet with the Buddha's intention in the morning. If you understand it in the evening, you will meet with his intention in the evening. There is one particular teaching for achieving this ability. As a basis, establish the view of *threg chö*, then take the four appearances of *thö gal* as your path. They are inexpressible and free from thought. The method is to practice within these."

The completion stage that is free from focus is called "Maha Ati," or the "Great Perfection," in the Nyingma tradition. In the Kagyü tradition it is called "Mahamudra," or the "Great Symbol." In the Sakya and Gelug systems it is called the "Fruit of the Path" and "Madhyamaka" (or the "Great Middle Way"), respectively. Though there are different names, the main practice is the same. It is the practice of ultimate bodhichitta. We are introduced to and gain the direct and experiential understanding of our own true nature. That is completion stage practice in the actual sense, which will be discussed in more detail in the next section of this book.

Now we come to the fourth of the Four Great Streams of Transmission that form the content of the old yogi's explanation.

THE EXPLANATION OF THE TANTRAS

"Then, you may wonder what the fourth point mentioned before, the explanation of the tantras, is about. It has ten sections, called the 'ten subject matters of the tantras.' These are: (1) empowerment, (2) *samaya*, (3) mandala, (4) mantra recitation and mudra, (5) practice, (6) offering, (7) activity, (8) view, (9) meditation, and (10) conduct."

Though the way of explanation varies, as does the terminology used, these ten points are the main subjects taught in any tantra. The old yogi continues:

"Concerning each, you must know its nature, definition, synonyms, categories, concise and detailed explanations, and essential meaning. Furthermore, you should understand the necessity of knowing these points, and why not knowing them is a shortcoming. You should know the benefit that will arise from properly understanding them, and their results. Toward that end, you need to take the path of thorough examination through scripture and logic, and gain experience in accordance with the words. Thereupon, you need to internalize them and comprehend them fully. Nevertheless, please be lenient with me. Being not so bright, I, an old yogi, could not practice them all."

At this point the monk is seized by a new and unexpected devotion for the old yogi, and says respectfully, "Thank you very much for your great kindness. We monks usually think that you yogis are just old folks in the village. We never imagine that you hold oral instructions like these. Now I, a monk, ask you old yogi, 'Could you find it in your mind to grant me a tiny instruction, no more than fits on a piece of paper, that will benefit me at the time of my death?'"

The old yogi agrees and says, "What you need, monk, is the three trainings, and especially the actual nature of the three types of discipline. Though everything depends upon that, there are few nowadays who practice these exactly as the Buddha taught. Even if you succeed in practicing some, you will surely know that the path to reach enlightenment in one lifetime is only shown in the Anuttarayoga tantras. It is not contained in the other sutras and tantras. So, you must know how the three trainings the Buddha taught can be practiced in the context of the Mantrayana.

"How is it done? From the time you have received the preparation for empowerment, you take the Vinaya, bodhisattva, and tantric vows. Observing these three vows is the essential meaning of the training in discipline, as it is contained in the sutras. The actual ground of practice is the two aspects of creation and completion. Of these, the creation stage contains the actual meaning of the training in *samadhi*, and the completion stage contains the essential meaning of the training in discriminative wisdom.

"Furthermore, unifying the two aspects of creation and completion, you practice the three types of discipline. During the creation stage, vessel and content (the outer world and its inhabitants) fully manifest as the outer support of the deity and the deity dwelling therein. This is discipline in terms of the vow to refrain from negative conduct. The creation stage is the accumulation of merit, and the completion stage is the accumulation of primordial wisdom. Meditating both in union is the discipline of gathering all virtuous qualities. Focusing on the four kinds of activity, radiating, absorbing, and so forth, is the discipline of accomplishing the benefit or seed of all sentient beings. Once you know that the meaning of all the essential points of training contained in the sutras is fully included in the Mantrayana, and you practice accordingly, it is said that you travel toward liberation in one single lifetime."

In this way, all three trainings are practiced in the course of one *sadhana*. Moreover, combining the two aspects of creation and completion stage and practicing them in union constitutes the best way of exerting discipline. There are three different types of discipline, or ethical conduct. These are refraining from negative conduct, engaging in all virtuous and positive actions, and accomplishing the benefit of all sentient beings. When the creation stage is practiced through acting with the clear understanding and vision that all outer and inner phenomena are the mandala of the deity, this is discipline in terms of the vow to refrain from negative conduct. If everything is seen as a mandala, as being pure and perfect, we will not fall into negative actions. Practicing the two stages of meditation, we simultaneously cultivate the two accumulations, the creation stage representing the accumulation of merit and the completion stage representing the accumulation of wisdom. This is the discipline in terms of engaging in all virtuous and positive actions. When motivated by the wish to help all our fellow beings, we engage in the four kinds of activity, such as radiating, absorbing, and so forth, as they are carried out during the practices of *drub pa* and *drub chen*; this is the discipline in terms of accomplishing the benefit of all sentient beings. Thus, all the main points of training as taught in the sutras are fully contained in the purpose of the Mantrayana teachings. If we can practice in light of this understanding, we are traveling toward being released in this very lifetime.

> Here, the monk's faith becomes even deeper, and he addresses the old yogi with utter respect, "Yes, indeed. The meaning of everything you said entered my mind quite easily, and I do understand it. Nevertheless, there is one doubt not yet eliminated. Whoever you ask these days will say that you gradually reach buddhahood by chanting and performing pujas. Now, when I hear that meditation will lead to full awakening, I am not sure whether or not this is true. So, I humbly ask you to eliminate this doubt."
>
> The old yogi replies, "You are right, monk. Once you have realized the hidden secret of the view and meditation from within, there is no need for your conduct to be very restricted. This is the secret of us yogis. Yet, these days this essential point is not understood. People give too much emphasis to trivialities of conduct and overestimate the importance of merely doing pujas. Unwittingly applying fragmentary means and not leaving aside the unnecessary, they do not have the slightest understanding that the two aspects of creation and completion are what needs to be done. For this reason, most yogis, though they are called by that name, have in truth become more careless than worldly householders. Whatever you explain, they do not understand. They just sit there stubbornly, persisting in foolishness. But the

method to reach buddhahood in our near lifetimes is not just doing pujas or reciting mantras. Just practicing meditative stability is also not enough. Careful persistence in creation and completion is the only thing needed. Furthermore, the main point is mixing yourself with the ultimate completion stage. Just abide evenly in the inexpressible true nature and experience everything as it really is."

Then the monk says with a voice trembling with utter devotion, "From the bottom of my heart, thank you for your great kindness. Though a yogi like you abides in an ordinary body, you hold the oral instructions that ripen the mind into dharmakaya. There are 'hidden buddhas,' and you must be one of them. Now, please grant me one single instruction that contains a hundred words in one and will quickly lead me to attain buddhahood. If I, as a monk, could also just practice meditation, this would be my heartfelt wish."

To this the old yogi agrees and says, "The intention of all buddhas is showing the *dharmata*, which is inconceivable. It is perception of nowness, the true nature of everything, free from any mental construction. That is it. Whether or not you have realized this marks the very difference between a buddha and an ordinary being. All the eighty-four thousand teachings of the Buddha, all the countless tantric teachings and the commentaries on the sutras and tantras represent two aspects: the means and the direct pointing out instructions to realize this point. You should not think too much or just follow the words. Be a master in establishing the meaning. Closely grasp the way it is, the true nature of yourself and everything else, which has existed since beginningless time and is free from any conceptual elaboration.

"At this time, you may have an experience of bliss, from which you feel you cannot bear to be parted. Do not cling to it. There may be an experience of clarity. Do not hold onto it, getting the conceited idea, 'This is the flow of my innermost nature, which is clear and distinct.' You may be in total absence of thought, resembling all remembrance and scheming being cut. Do not get attached to this either. Within the notion, 'This is freedom from conceptual mind,' remain beyond. You should turn toward the one who perceives and creates all these things. Get to the top of that itself and settle right there. Then you will remain in meditative equipoise with nothing to settle upon. The nature of everything is apparent. There is no reason for thought or conceptual grasping. When you are meditating, there is no inner onlooker present. When you are not meditating, the cause of distraction is lost. Mindfulness being self-liberated, the knot of hope and apprehension is untied within the sphere of openness and relaxation. The chains of doubt are severed. There is ever-present purity, beyond bondage and liberation. This is primordial wisdom, freed from the need of applying an antidote. It is *dharmata*, in which everything to be abandoned is exhausted. From this alone we realize our nature, the mind of the primordial protector."

Through this pointing out the monk was instantaneously liberated and equaled the mind of the spiritual master. At that time he offered this song to expose the shortcomings of himself and others:

> To eyes that see in conventional fashion you appear in ordinary
>   form.
> In truth, you are the deity of all deities of the three domains,
> A practitioner of secret Mantrayana whose title and meaning do
>   not contradict.
> May you, the old yogi, my father Kyémé Dorjé, always protect me.
> Since childhood I practiced artificially what seemed to be Dharma,
> And there is hardly any reason to consider my idea of renuncia-
>   tion.
> I wasted this human existence like a newcomer among young
>   monks.
> Foolishly ignorant of the three trainings, I did not know what to
>   adopt and abandon.
> Alas for these degenerate times!
> Applying the teachings of the Buddha for show, in terms of only
>   the outer signs,
> There is many a monk who is just a feeble imitation of what he
>   should be.
> Pure conduct is rarer than a star in daytime.

There are also some monks and lamas who proudly claim to be
    followers of the tantras,
But do not train in the supreme practices of study, reflection, and
    meditation,
And do not study the scriptures of the path of creation and com-
    pletion.
They are just distractedly eyeing each other, ranking view and con-
    duct "high" or "low."
Here in this place called "Golden Valley of Misty Ravines"
Are some who boastfully assume the title of "yogi."
But being deluded, they do not know the practice that is the pur-
    pose of life.
This is not the fault of the disciples alone.
There is only one in this land of Do Kham
Who fuses the intent of all sutras and tantras into one
And is able to explain how to achieve ultimate perfection
Of all the paths and levels in one single lifetime.
This is the Protector and King of Dharma Dodrubchen.
In this land of the mountains of snow some claim to be learned,
But cannot distinguish the systems of the old and new translations.
They are biased and divide the Muni's teaching into their own side
    and that of others.
This is a sign that the teachings in word and realization are
    degenerating.
When I think about this again and again, the wind in my heart
    gets agitated.
Those of understanding should inspect their minds.
We do not know where this human life is going.
If we died this very instant, what would we do?
When the guru who shows us the path is mistaken,
What is the use of being named "Vajra So-and-So"?
If we do not realize the profound meaning of creation and
    completion,
What is the benefit of enumerating the seven aspects of deep
    teaching?
If we seek for liberation in one lifetime,
Why not preserve our true nature, free from ideation?

To say, "I preserve this" is just words.
If there is something to preserve, this is neither the view nor the
  meditation.
If, while looking everywhere, nothing is fit to be seen,
This opens the view, but the term, again, is just a lie.
If there is no one to preserve the meditation either,
Claiming meditation experience is the talk of a fool.
Adopting and abandoning certain ways of conduct is also our own
  projection.
Once we discern the fundamental root of our mind, all doubts are
  exhausted.
The full maturation of the view, meditation, and conduct
Is the instantaneous awareness of the nature of everything.
This I realized by the kindness of my master Kyémé Dorjé.
May, by the virtue arising from this realization and from express-
  ing it in this song,
All sentient beings in every realm who, blinded by ignorance,
Have not gained realization attain the *kaya* of the primordial pro-
  tector, the state of my father.

Having sung this, he instantaneously went into Akanishtha,
the sphere of the inner truth.

The author then explains the reason why he wrote this text:

My teacher who instructed me in the art of painting, the master of
realization Jamyang Gyatso, and others, as well as many yogis
endowed with faith, have repeatedly requested me, "Please write
something that by means of examples explains the creation and
completion stages along with their fruit, the way view and meditation are to be practiced in our yogic tradition." I thought that if
I wrote a long explanation it would not be understood or appreciated. Therefore I kept it very short and put it into colloquial language, so that my writing here is almost a joke. May it nevertheless
help some of those who have newly entered the path of the yogis
to attain the eye of true intelligence.

This was written by Dzogchenpa Shönnu Yeshé Dorjé. May it be virtuous.

SECTION TWO
MAHAMUDRA
THE *Dorjé Chang Tungma*

To explain the subject of Mahamudra I thought we could look at a short text that plays a very important role in the Karma Kagyü tradition, the *Dorjé Chang Tungma* by Bengar Jampal Zangpo. It is used as a lineage prayer at the beginning of almost any practice, especially in the context of Mahamudra meditation. It is condensed and at the same time complex, containing everything that needs to be understood and practiced.

As well as being used as a prayer, it became traditional to use the *Dorjé Chang Tungma* when a disciple was initiated into Mahamudra. I received the Mahamudra introduction from my great-aunt, a nun who lived until her late nineties. She was an exquisite storyteller, so as time permitted, I tried to see her as much as I could.

She was married as a very young girl, so as is the custom she had to follow her husband and live in his home. After a year or two she decided that she did not like this too much, so one day she just ran away. Eventually she reached a place where a great khenpo was staying and became his student. This was Khenchen Tashi Özer, a direct disciple of the first Jamgön Kongtrül Rinpoché, Lodrö Thayé, whom she also met and received teachings from. After meeting these teachers, my great-aunt did not go back to her husband, but became a nun. She said that whenever Jamgön Kongtrül the Great gave Mahamudra teachings, he began by explaining the *Dorjé Chang Tungma*. Khenchen Tashi Özer did likewise, and even His Holiness the Sixteenth Karmapa would use this prayer as a basis when giving an initial introduction to Mahamudra. Thus it is a very blessed and traditional text, as well as a very important and concise one.

So, I thought we might use this prayer and go through it slowly, without too much rush. It starts with a supplication of the lineage, which reads as follows:

To the great Vajradhara, Tilo, Naro, Marpa, Mila,
To the Dharma Lord Gampopa, and the Karmapa
Who sees all fields of reality throughout the three times,
To the holders of the four great and eight smaller lineages
Who have fully discovered the profound path of Mahamudra,
Glorious Drugpa, Drikung, Taglung, Tsalpa, and others,
Dagpo Kagyü, unrivaled guardians of all sentient beings,
I supplicate from the depth of my heart.
Please behold me with kindness and grant your blessing.
Glorious Kagyü lamas, may I follow your footsteps
And uphold the lineage of the oral transmission.

The introductory part of the prayer describes the Kagyü lineage. Throughout Buddhism the lineage of transmission has been of utmost importance, especially so in the Tibetan tradition. This is because the Dharma is not just information. It is an experience that has to be transmitted by someone. It cannot be derived from books or tapes, as books are not equivalent to the personal experience felt and expressed by an individual.

Since trying to practice is trying to gain experience, we have to share the experience of someone who similarly relied on an authentic master and achieved genuine realization. The lineage of experience can only emerge from person to person and from heart to heart. Therefore, it is very important for a disciple to receive personal guidance and instruction from a living teacher. Otherwise, someone might write something and pass it on to ten different people, who might then interpret it in ten different ways. Once a writing is published it is subject to all kinds of interpretation. There is a Tibetan saying: "Like well-tanned deerskin, a quotation can be stretched in any direction." Written teachings are very helpful, but they should not constitute our main source of learning.

The transmission and exchange of experience between master and disciple is not a single event; it is a slow, ongoing process of refinement. The disciple repeatedly expresses his or her findings, and the teacher corrects or confirms them. This goes on until all misunderstandings and doubts are clarified and the disciple's insight has reached the level of the teacher's. This is not achieved in a weekend; it might take quite a while. We must learn directly from a living example and gain our own genuine experience through the genuine experience of someone else.

For this reason, the lineage is of crucial importance. A reliable ground is needed to evaluate the genuineness of a teacher and see whether an instruction is right or wrong. Anyone can turn up and claim, "I am truly great! I know everything!" But if we have connected with an authentic lineage, we will not fall into traps. Knowing where an instruction comes from enables us to judge its validity. Once we make a decision to pursue serious practice, we will not want to accept everything that comes our way and waste our time on fantasies. Instead, we will look for quality, for something that is pure and authentic and sustained by genuine realization.

In modern terms we might say that a teacher should have a good reputation and proper references, so that we are able to trace the origin of his or her teaching. When a pure and authentic lineage is present, we will find instructions that stem from a truly experienced great master who has received them from an equally accomplished teacher, and so forth. Then, we can have justified confidence that we are practicing the right kind of teaching. Confidence is essential since doubts can arise anytime. Doubt is a very common phenomenon—everybody has doubts. In the course of our Dharma practice, we will fall into doubts again and again until we reach the first *bhumi*, or level of enlightenment. This is the point at which the truth of cessation is seen directly to a certain extent—no longer in terms of a passing experience but in terms of stable realization.

There are different ways in which this level of direct insight is presented. In the Shravakayana system someone who has reached this stage is called a stream-enterer. This system names four levels of spiritual growth: stream-enterer, once-returner, non-returner, and arhat. The first level describes someone who has gained an actual glimpse of the truth, someone with a certain amount of real understanding. Once this is achieved, the practitioner is on the path and there is not much doubt anymore. From then onward one passes through the different stages of realization until one becomes an arhat.

In the Mahayana system, spiritual progress is described through five paths: the paths of accumulation, junction, seeing, meditation, and no more learning. The first two paths describe phases of development that have to be mastered before the first *bhumi* is reached. The path of accumulation refers to the period of practice when the main focus is on accumulating whatever is meaningful and beneficial. One tries to improve in every possible way—through studying, acquiring understanding and wisdom, and doing beneficial deeds.

When an initial definitive knowing has arisen, one arrives at the second level, the path of junction. Of the five paths, the path of junction is the one where there is the very strong feeling that truth is right there to be seen, when one can almost sense it, but cannot see it yet. If, for instance, there is a fire behind a wall, by touching the wall we will feel the heat and know that there is a fire, but we will not be able to see it directly. The term "junction" is used because this phase leads to and joins us with the path of seeing.

The path of seeing refers to the moment when truth is seen as it is and experienced directly. Through this seeing one reaches the first *bhumi*, which in the context of the Mahayana is the first of the ten bodhisattva levels. The path of meditation then refers to the stage of traveling through the remaining nine levels. The initial direct vision of the truth gained on the path of seeing is deepened and expanded until one reaches the final stage, the state of buddhahood, called "the path of no more learning."

The Vajrayana system does not use these terms, but it describes the same process of the development of insight. Until the first genuine experience has dawned, doubts can arise any time. But if the teaching we practice stems from a lineage that is strong, unbroken, and pure, and therefore trustworthy, we will know that nothing is fundamentally amiss. Then, even when our practice is not going so well, we will have a sense of basic doubtlessness, a wholesome and well-grounded confidence. We will know that the disturbances we undergo are passing episodes and that the methods we apply are valid and will prove effective over time.

In my view this basic confidence is very important. Doubts and problems will arise again and again in anyone's practice. If in such situations we have confidence and trust in the lineage, we will be well equipped. This opens far greater opportunities to deal with our problems in a constructive way. Having first tried to understand them from our own point of view, we can clarify and deepen our understanding through asking questions and seeking advice. Once our doubts are cleared away, we will be back on the path.

As a general guideline for practitioners to take to heart, it is traditionally recommended to rely on four principles rather than upon four alternatives. This advice says:

> *Rather than relying on words, rely on the true meaning.*
> *Rather than relying on personalities, rely on the Dharma.*
> *Rather than relying on the relative, rely on the ultimate truth.*

Rather than relying on the provisional, rely on the definitive meaning.

The final line refers to the two ways in which the Buddha taught. The first is the "provisional meaning" (*neyartha* in Sanskrit). It is also called the "meaning requiring interpretation" and refers to teachings that the Buddha gave for a specific purpose, and which are not identical to truth itself. These teachings are meant to lead us gradually to the understanding of the actual truth. However, this does not mean that these teachings are false; they are simply not totally true. They are valid to a certain extent and on the relative level. The Buddha has described these teachings by means of the following example. Suppose there is a house with children inside and the house is filled with all kinds of beautiful toys and attractive things. Then, suddenly you see that the house has caught fire and is about to go up in flames. You call to the children, "Come out quickly! The house is burning!" But being immersed in their toys and pleasures, they do not listen. Their playthings are far too exciting to be left behind, and the children are not aware of the danger. So, to attract their attention you say, "There are so many wonderful toys out here, much more and far nicer ones than those in the house! You should come outside and have a look!" Hearing this, the children become curious and run from the house. In fact, there may not be any toys outside, but the children have been saved from the fire.

This illustrates what is to be understood as "provisional meaning." In a way, it is not telling the truth, but this is done for a purpose that otherwise would not be achieved. Then again, it cannot be said to be totally untrue. There may not have been any toys right outside, but it would have been possible to find and provide some later. If the children had died, they would not have had a further chance to enjoy any toys. A statement that was not totally true saved their lives and provided a future opportunity. For this reason it is called a provisional truth. All the teachings expressing the relative level are contained in this aspect.

The second way of teaching is called the "definitive meaning" (*nitartha* in Sanskrit). This refers to teachings that directly express the ultimate level of truth, or the way everything really is.

The lineage to which this prayer is directed is called the Kagyü lineage, and it consists of the masters who have gained the immediate realization of Mahamudra, which is the most definitive and direct teaching of Vajrayana

Buddhism. As explained in the previous section, Vajrayana practice consists of the creation and completion stages of meditation. Of these, the completion stage has a more elaborate and a totally unelaborate aspect. The first is the practice of the six yogas. Mahamudra is the unelaborate aspect, meaning that it is far subtler and completely free from all complications. Therefore, it constitutes the deepest and most final instruction. Once it is understood and experienced, nothing else is needed.

All the other teachings of the Buddha, starting from refuge and bodhichitta up to the visualizations and methods of the Vajrayana, are only meant to lead to and facilitate nonconceptual understanding. This is the understanding of Mahamudra, the culmination of the Buddha's teachings and the realization into which they merge. It represents the final stage. For this reason it is said, "When one understands Mahamudra and is able to practice it, all other practices are included therein." Since Mahamudra is the highest teaching of the Buddha, representing the definitive meaning, the lineage of the Mahamudra masters is the ultimate and most accomplished lineage.

The first master of this lineage was Tilopa. Although he received a vast amount of instruction from many teachers, he mainly assimilated and unified the teachings of four lineages. This is how the name "Kagyü," or the "oral tradition," came about. "Kagyü" is short for *ka shi gyü denpa*, which means "holding the lineage of the four oral transmissions." Tilopa received the transmissions of the six yogas from four great masters: Sharyapa, Nagarjuna, Lavapa, and Sukhasiddhi. Sharyapa was a great *siddha* and saint who granted Tilopa the teachings on *tum mo*, or inner heat. From Nagarjuna he received the instructions on the illusory body and clear light, and from Lavapa those on dream yoga. The dakini Sukhasiddhi, a great female teacher, gave him the teachings on *bar do*, or the intermediate state, and on *pho wa*, the transference of consciousness.

Yet, according to Tilopa himself, these four teachers were not the source of his final realization. He said, "I, Tilopa, do not have a guru in human form. My guru is Vajradhara, the primordial Buddha." Tilopa's statement means that he did not gain his realization of Mahamudra from an outer source. He received it from within, from the primordial Buddha Vajradhara, or Dorjé Chang in Tibetan. When Buddha Shakyamuni gave the Vajrayana teachings, he often transformed his outer appearance into Vajradhara and taught in this form, so we can say that the Buddha is Vajradhara.

Further than that, Vajradhara signifies the fact that the understanding of buddhahood is present in the consciousness of all sentient beings, and thus always there to be realized. This is slightly difficult to understand. On the Vajrayana level it is said, "Reaching enlightenment, one awakens as the primordial Buddha." When buddhahood is attained, we become the original Buddha. This means that enlightenment is the realization that one has never been anything else than a buddha—one has been enlightened all the time. Through connecting with this inner source, Tilopa received the realization of Mahamudra. Here the term "received" should not be understood in the usual dualistic sense of getting something from someone or somewhere else. Tilopa "received" enlightenment by discovering the true primordial Buddha within. For this reason, the *Dorjé Chang Tungma* mentions Vajradhara first, as the source of the lineage.

Tilopa's main student was Naropa. While Naropa was a great scholar at Nalanda University, he was instantly filled with intent longing upon hearing Tilopa's name and immediately went in search of him. He found Tilopa sitting by the banks of the Ganges River, catching fish with his bare hands and eating them raw. Although Tilopa's behavior was unconventional, Naropa did not have the slightest doubt and followed him everywhere. Tilopa never bestowed a single word of teaching, but gave Naropa an extremely hard time, heaping trouble upon trouble upon him. On at least thirteen occasions Naropa neared the brink of death. Then, one day, Tilopa became seemingly angry and took off his sandal and threw it at Naropa. When it hit him, Naropa fainted, and when he regained consciousness he knew everything that Tilopa knew. He experienced realization from mind to mind.

Naropa's foremost student was Marpa, the first Tibetan to receive the Mahamudra teachings. As a child Marpa was totally wild; he became angry for the slightest reason and fought with anyone who came his way. His behavior worried his parents deeply and they said to each other, "This boy is running headlong into ruin. Sooner or later he will plunge us into real disaster, either by killing someone or getting killed himself. Something needs to be done as soon as possible. He must learn some discipline before it is too late." So they gave him provisions and sent him away to study under the great translator Drugmi Lotsawa.

During his studies, Marpa's interest in the Dharma grew increasingly, and he developed a strong wish to receive the teachings directly from their Indian sources. At that time there were large gold deposits in Tibet, so Marpa first traveled to the western region to collect gold. Then, he went to

Milarepa

India three times, where he spent sixteen years and seven months with Naropa. During this time Naropa granted him all his teachings and sent him to other teachers as well, particularly to Maitripa, who gave him the Mahamudra instructions.

After his final return to Tibet, Marpa translated all the instructions he had received, and then started to teach. Of his many students, four were especially outstanding: Tsurtön Wang-ngé, Ngogtön Chödor, Metön Tsönpo, and Milarepa. Marpa's foremost disciple was Milarepa, who became the main holder of the lineage.

You will have heard of Milarepa, the greatest poet and saint of Tibet. Like Marpa he also had a very strong personality. After the death of his father, Milarepa and his family were subjected to appalling ill-treatment at the hands of malevolent and greedy relatives. His mother sought revenge and urged Milarepa to study black magic. Following his mother's wish, he gained enormous power, like the ability to launch hailstorms, and thus destroyed the tormentors of his family. Afterwards, he repented of his evil deeds and went to seek the Dharma.

Finally, he met someone who spoke of Marpa, and the instant Milarepa heard his name, he was so moved that the hairs on his body stood on end and tears welled up in his eyes. He immediately knew Marpa to be his teacher, and from that moment onward never had the slightest doubt about him. Milarepa went in search of Marpa, and after he had found him, for a long time Marpa exposed him to the most severe hardships, until Milarepa had purified most of his former negative acts.

Eventually, he received all the teachings from Marpa and went into solitude to practice. He worked so hard that it is almost inconceivable. Seeing the caves in which Milarepa meditated, most people would think, "He must have been a madman!" Milarepa chose the most barren and isolated places, where it was very difficult even to get water, let alone any other necessity of life or companionship. One of the caves he used for retreat was about three miles away from any source of water, and there was no firewood or anything else. Yet, since Milarepa employed meditation techniques such as the practice of inner heat, he did not need clothes to keep himself warm. He wore a sheet of white cotton cloth, and this is how he received his name. The Tibetan term for "cotton" is *re*, and *repa* means "one who wears cotton cloth."

Having realized the very core of the Buddhist teachings from his own direct experience, Milarepa became a great master and had countless stu-

dents from all over Tibet. His two main disciples were Rechungpa and Gampopa. Rechungpa was a yogi like Milarepa and, being his junior by many
years, he was given the name of "Little Repa," or Rechungpa. Gampopa was
a monk from central Tibet who gained such profound realization that he
became Milarepa's successor in holding the Mahamudra lineage.

Originally, Gampopa lived an ordinary worldly life with his large family.
He was a wealthy and very skilled physician, but also learned in the Dharma.
Then his wife and all his children fell sick and died; for all his proficiency, he
could not help them. The sudden death of his family aroused a heartbreak-
ing feeling of renunciation. From the core of his being Gampopa sensed the
futility of samsaric existence and developed a strong desire to practice the
Dharma as earnestly as possible. He sought the guidance of many Kadampa
lamas and received numerous profound instructions from them.

Eventually, Gampopa heard of Milarepa. At that point he had reached a
stage of considerable spiritual growth and was able to remain in meditation
for seven days without interruption. One day he dreamed of a yogi with
bluish skin coming toward him. The yogi blessed him, and then walked on.
When the dream recurred many times, Gampopa related it to his teacher
and asked for its meaning. His teacher thought it might be the indication of
an obstacle and advised him to withdraw into retreat. Gampopa followed
the advice and went into retreat near a monastery where he went for walks
in the evening.

One evening three beggars were sitting by the wall of the monastery talking together. There was famine in the area at that time, and Gampopa overheard one of them wishing that the following day a rich benefactor should
come along and distribute hot soup to everybody. The beggar imagined
drinking a delicious soup made with lots of meat, fat, and *tsampa*, and how
satisfying it would be. However, this did not appeal to the second beggar,
who accused him of being small-minded. Instead, the second beggar suggested that he should wish for something far better, like becoming the king
of Tibet, and not for just a bowl of soup.

The third beggar, who was the eldest among them, shook his head and
told his companions that they should be ashamed of themselves for such
foolishness. He said that their wishes were petty and worthless, and that if
the retreatant who usually went for a walk at that time heard them talking
like that, he would laugh at them. He told his friends that instead they should
wish for something that was truly worthwhile, such as becoming like Mila-

repa, who had completely freed himself from all samsaric suffering. He said that Milarepa needed neither clothes nor food, and feared nothing, not even dying. He had reached total liberation and could benefit all sentient beings. He told them that Milarepa could even lead people to the realization he had attained himself and that they should wish to become like him, a buddha in person.

Gampopa overheard their conversation, and the moment Milarepa's name was mentioned, he experienced the same type of overwhelming devotion that Milarepa had felt when he first heard of Marpa. Gampopa went back to his retreat place and was so inspired that he was unable to sleep that night. He prepared a rich and nourishing soup, just like the first beggar had imagined, and as soon as it was light he invited the three beggars to his home. After offering them the soup, he asked, "Do you know anything about Milarepa?" They must have been rather shocked. The eldest replied, "Yes, I have seen him and heard many things about him. At present he is somewhere in Yannam, which is quite far from here." Gampopa asked if he could lead him there, and offered an ample reward. The old beggar agreed to be his guide.

When Gampopa was a few days away, Milarepa said to his disciples, "A great being who has been a bodhisattva for many lifetimes is coming here. Whoever is the first to introduce him to me will be liberated without any further effort." Upon his arrival Gampopa met a lady who asked his name and the purpose of his visit. Realizing that he must be the person Milarepa had spoken of, she invited him to stay at her house, and said her daughter would take him to Milarepa the following day. Having learned what Milarepa had said of him, Gampopa thought to himself, "My teacher knew of my coming even before I arrived and said such wonderful things about me. I must be a very special person!" The next morning the daughter went to Milarepa and announced Gampopa's arrival, but Milarepa said, "I do not want to see him." He repeated his refusal for about fifteen days, by which time Gampopa's pride was quite deflated. At that point Milarepa agreed to see him.

After that, Gampopa received all Milarepa's teachings and gained the corresponding experiences. Finally, Milarepa sent him away to meditate. As words of farewell he said, "The right time for you to teach will be when you realize that I, your old father, am a buddha." Gampopa left and practiced for many years until finally he realized that Milarepa was none other than a buddha in person. At that point he started to teach.

This shows that trust and devotion are not acquired artificially. They can be developed to a certain extent, but the unwavering feeling of devotion is born from deep experiential understanding. When we have practiced the Dharma and gained authentic inner experience, our trust in the lineage and devotion to the teacher will become deeper and deeper. Finally, there will be the recognition, "This is really the truth. There is nothing beyond this, nothing further." Once truth is felt, the person who has initiated this experience will be seen as a buddha, a fully enlightened being.

When Gampopa had gained this vision, he began to teach and had thousands of students. His three main disciples came from Kham, a large area in eastern Tibet, so they were known as "the three men from Kham." The three men from Kham were the first Karmapa, Düsum Khyenpa, Saltong Shogom, and Phagmo Drupa.

One day Gampopa gave each of them a piece of fine cloth and told them to make a hat from the cloth and bring it to him after seven days. Phagmo Drupa was a very obedient and hardworking person. So, he took up his task immediately and made a very elaborate hat, adorning it with beautiful embroidery and silken tassels hanging down here and there. The Karmapa had a slightly different mentality. He paid attention to Gampopa, but did not think about the hat until the day before it was to be delivered. At that point there was not much time left, so he took the cloth and just folded it, but did so in a rather intricate manner. Saltong Shogom did not care at all and almost forgot about the whole thing. When the day came and the students met, the other two asked, "Where is your hat? We are supposed to give our hats to the guru today." Saltong Shogom exclaimed, "Oh, the hat!" He hurriedly took the cloth and turned it into something that only bore a faint resemblance to the item required.

Then, they went to Gampopa and offered their hats. Gampopa first took the one Phagmo Drupa had made. He was very pleased and said, "This is done in a very elaborate and beautiful manner. It shows that you will have a vast number of disciples and your lineage will become great and divide into many branches." Next, he looked at the Karmapa's hat and said, "You have also done very well. Your hat is quite plain and unadorned. It is only one piece, but at the same time it is very compact and durable. This means that you will have only one lineage. This lineage, however, will be very strong, and become stronger and stronger in the future." Finally, he took Saltong Shogom's product and told him, "You were too careless. You will not have any lineage at all."

In Tibetan, this kind of correspondence or link, as it is to be seen from these three predictions, is called *ten drel*, which is a term difficult to translate. It could be said to mean "connection" or "meeting with a basis," in the sense that everything comes about through causes and conditions, and a small cause may yield a considerable effect.

The four great and eight smaller Kagyü lineages mentioned in the *Dorjé Chang Tungma* all originate from Gampopa's disciples. The four great lineages are the Karma Kamtsang, Baram, Tsalpa, and Phagdru Kagyü. The first Karmapa initiated the Karma Kagyü lineage. Two lineages, the Baram and Tsalpa, trace back to Gampopa's nephew, Tsultrim Nyingpo. Phagmo Drupa originated the Phagdru Kagyü lineage, which later divided into eight branches: Drugpa, Drikung, Taglung, Trophu, Martsang, Yelpa, Yangsang, and Shugsep. The *Dorjé Chang Tungma* mentions only some of the names of the four great and eight smaller lineages: "Glorious Drugpa, Drikung, Taglung, Tsalpa, and others." Of the eight smaller lineages the Drugpa Kagyü tradition became particularly large. As their history shows, all lineages, great or small, go back to one origin and contain the same instruction. They are simply various lines of transmission, but as far as the teachings are concerned, there is no difference between them.

At the beginning of the *Dorjé Chang Tungma* we turn to the holders of all these lineages. We pray to all the great masters who have gained the direct experience of Mahamudra and actualized the enlightened state of their mind. Nowadays the term "enlightenment" bears a somewhat cheap connotation, being often used too hastily and thoughtlessly. As opposed to that, a person who has realized Mahamudra is a truly enlightened being and equals either a buddha, or a bodhisattva who dwells on the *bhumis*. Such beings are actually able to give us blessing, inspiration, and guidance. They can give us the transmission of their own understanding. So, we pray to the masters of the lineage that we may come to an authentic understanding of Mahamudra and gain a direct and immediate experience that cannot be lost.

From the Buddhist point of view, praying is very important. The reason for this is expressed in two lines: "All phenomena are cause and effect, so everything depends on firm aspiration." Everything is interdependent. Whatever occurs is an effect that arose from causes and conditions. At the same time, it constitutes a new cause which gives rise to another effect. Due to interrelatedness, anything can happen once the right conditions are there, no matter how small they may be.

Praying works on this basis. When we develop a strong intention and make a vast and genuine wish, a sincere and heartfelt prayer, this can snowball and eventually result in something that is truly meaningful and great. Our frame of mind and our intention precede and dominate every action we take. Everything depends on the way we direct our mind; everything we experience depends on our motivation. When our mind moves in the right direction, it can totally reform our lives. Since a prayer is the expression of a very deep and strong intention, it can radically change our course of action. This is the reason that this introduction to Mahamudra is in the form of a prayer. At the beginning we pray to all the masters of the lineage who have gained the realization of Mahamudra; we ask for their blessing that we may follow their example and become able to uphold the lineage as well.

What is to be understood by "upholding the lineage" can be illustrated by an example Dzogchen Pönlop Rinpoché has used when teaching this prayer. He says that holding the lineage is not like preserving old bread. It is not that the lineage is made at one point and then kept in cold storage to prevent it from getting stale. Trying to preserve the lineage in this manner would be useless; it would not be alive. Preserving the lineage is like learning how to make the bread. There is no need to use the same materials as were used two thousand years ago; we do not have to use flour which is that old. We can use the ingredients and the oven that are available wherever we live now. We just need to know how to do it exactly. Then, we can make fresh bread that is just as tasty and nutritious as the loaves made in the past.

The next stanza of the *Dorjé Chang Tungma* says:

> Renunciation is taught to be the feet of meditation.
> Please bless me to cut the fetters of this life.
> May I be free from craving for food and wealth
> And meditate without desire for gain and honor.

The contents of this prayer are closely connected to one of the most fundamental Buddhist teachings, called "the four thoughts that turn the mind from samsara." These four thoughts are contemplations on the preciousness of human life, impermanence and death, the natural law of karma, and the shortcomings of samsara. These are basic teachings that we might receive many times, so there is the danger that after a while we may think we understand them fully. Having heard something many times we might easily think, "Oh, I know that. I have been taught it again and again." This is not the best approach—as with any teaching, we should always check to see if it is being internalized in terms of an actual understanding.

Knowing many things by heart can sometimes become a hindrance. We may say, "I learned this fifteen years ago." We may even have learned something twenty or forty years back, yet when we actually look at ourselves, we often find that we have not learned anything: the teachings we received have not turned into actual genuine insight. Instead, there is just a shallow intellectual knowledge. This process can go quite unnoticed. We are often not aware that we have only an idea in our head and lack any true understanding. When this attitude is not recognized, it can turn into a great obstacle.

For this reason, the very basic teachings of the Buddha, such as the four thoughts that turn the mind from samsara, the teachings on refuge, bodhichitta, and so forth, are emphasized and repeated again and again. According to the Tibetan Buddhist tradition, bodhichitta in particular is brought to mind at the beginning of every Dharma teaching. Almost invariably a teacher starts with the words, "May we become able to help all sentient beings, our mothers whose numbers are as vast as space, to attain the precious state of buddhahood." This is repeated to make us reflect again and again, and eventually assimilate this understanding.

The four contemplations that turn the mind from samsara are meant to engender weariness and renunciation of cyclic existence. Samsara is not the world around us that we see and feel. Samsara is a state of mind. In this state of mind we face continual difficulties. There is constant suffering due to not understanding the law of karma, due to our wrong way of identifying things, and our wrong way of reacting to them. As long as we are caught in the samsaric frame of mind, as long as we are subject to craving, we will have problems no matter what we do.

The prayer uses the example of wealth. Being poor is a problem familiar to everybody. We can try to attain some wealth, but the effort involved constitutes a further problem. Finally we achieve our goal, and then we find that the possession of wealth is also a problem. Recently a friend told me about an extremely rich American friend who owns several banks but, despite his wealth, his friend is always anxious. He lives in constant fear of his child being kidnapped and employs many bodyguards for protection. Worrying day and night, he cannot find any rest. This shows the way it is.

We may not be subject to the same anxieties as this banker, but as soon as we acquire some wealth, fears arise as to whether it will increase or even be lost. When we encounter its loss, we have a new problem, the biggest problem of all. In this way, there are always problems, from beginning to end. When we are rich we have problems, when we are not rich we have problems, when we exert ourselves to become rich we have problems, and when we lose our riches we have problems as well. These problems do not lie in the presence or absence of wealth; they lie in our mental attitude.

As long as we believe that wealth is the solution to our problems, we are subject to a fundamental misconception. Deep down inside we know this, more or less, yet at times we do not want to accept that wealth cannot be our refuge. Possessing some wealth is good, but it does not mean that everything will be all right, that we will be fully satisfied and not need anything else. Once we have gained a deep understanding of that, we will have developed a certain amount of renunciation, and will grow weary of chasing after money or other equally futile pursuits. We will understand that these things are not sufficient, and cannot give us real satisfaction and peace. They cannot help us to gain liberation and final freedom from any bondage.

There is something else we need much more. Once we understand the nature of the samsaric state of mind and its functioning very clearly, we will become weary of it. We will not give in to it all the time and just follow its compulsory urging. With a clear recognition of the nature of samsara we will know things for what they are, and be able to distinguish what causes further and deeper difficulties from things that do not cause any problems at all. From the Buddhist point of view, when this weariness of samsara has arisen, it is equivalent to renunciation.

This is frequently misunderstood, and sometimes people say that Buddhism teaches escapism when it advocates renunciation. However, renunciation and trying to escape from the world are totally opposite. We can easily become frustrated and even paranoid about the world around us, about our life situations and relationships with others. When this happens we may look for a way out and think, "This is unbearable! Something has to be done. I have to get out of here as fast as possible. There must be a place that is not so hostile, where I will not have to see all these horrible people anymore. Maybe I could go to an island, perhaps Holy Island, the retreat place near the coast of Scotland. Or I could go to the Himalayas, somewhere where these people and things are simply no longer around."

But—and this is a very big BUT—wherever we go we take ourselves with us. The way we react will be the same. If we fought with the people where we lived before, we will fight with the people we meet next. As long as we do not change our attitude, we can go anywhere and it will be the same. We could even go to Holy Island, but we would fight with the people there, or we might hate the wind and the sound of the sea, or detest the ponies that graze in its meadows. As long as we are in a fighting mood, anything will serve our purpose. We can leave behind the things that seemingly cause our problems, but in truth we cannot escape from anything. Our behavioral patterns, our ways of saying and doing things, and our state of mind remain the same. They are here with us and we cannot avoid them.

So, running away is not what is meant when Buddhism speaks of renouncing the world. We could even decide to live in a monastery or in a Buddhist meditation center, but this will not make any real difference either. There are many misconceptions about this point and in my view it is important to clarify them. Someone might think, "Ah, a Buddhist center! Buddhism talks about loving-kindness, compassion, joy, and equanimity, so the people there must be very gentle. They must be really warmhearted, truly compassionate, and open. If only I could stay in such a place, all my problems would be solved." Then you pay a visit and what do you find? Well, perhaps I had better not go into detail.

The people who live in Buddhist centers are the same as people everywhere else. This is quite naturally so. Most likely they came to these centers for similar reasons: they wanted to find the wonderful qualities that are emphasized so strongly in the Buddhist teachings. And doubtless all of them would like to develop these qualities, but sometimes it is not so easy. Good qualities do not pop up just like that. They have to be cultivated gradually in an ongoing process of refinement and maturation. Thus, not everyone who lives in a Buddhist center will be the living image of all Buddhist virtues. This should not be viewed as being negative, though, and does not mean that such places are useless. For people who have a congenial wish to improve and become good human beings, a center can be very conducive. It opens the opportunity for people to work together and help each other in pursuing this aim. When everybody is willing to learn, improvement is far more likely to happen. So, living in a Buddhist center can be helpful to a certain extent, but it is not enough to solve our problems. The same is true of living in a monastery.

In order to arrive at the real solution, we have to understand samsara.

Once we deeply feel what the nature of cyclic existence is like, we will become weary of it and wish to do something about it. This is the starting point of the path of meditation, of Dharma practice in its actual sense. When we have developed the feeling of weariness from the depth of our heart, true renunciation will be born within us. It will be apparent that there is no alternative—we have to change our state of mind, the way we see ourselves and react to the world. Otherwise, there is no solution to any of our problems. The pain we feel will go on forever.

When this understanding has dawned and is deeply rooted in us, we are moving toward meditation, toward the actual practice of Dharma. So, weariness of samsara and renunciation are said to be the "feet of meditation." One may wonder why the prayer uses this term. Without feet we cannot walk, and once we are on our feet, we are ready to go. Likewise, without the feeling of renunciation we are not ready to follow the path. We may say and do many virtuous things, but these are not enough to truly practice the Dharma.

Meditation is the means to reach enlightenment and free ourselves from all suffering, but such practice is not possible without renunciation. The purpose of all practices preliminary to the actual practice of Mahamudra is to engender renunciation. Once a deep and genuine sense of renunciation has dawned, the preliminary practice, or ngöndro, is done. Having carried out the four traditional ngöndro exercises, such as the four practices of prostration, Vajrasattva mantra, mandala offering, and guru yoga, is no guarantee that we are really prepared. They are just recommended as suitable means. Their aim is achieved when the nature of samsara is understood and true renunciation has dawned. Then, the actual ngöndro will have been completed.

Genuine renunciation is not easy. We may understand that our samsaric state of mind, filled with attachment and fear about all kinds of things—wealth, gain, fame, and so forth—cannot give us true satisfaction and peace. Even when we see that our continuous strife cannot lead us to liberation, it is not that easy to just let go and no longer care for all these things. We are so used to running after or away from things, and are totally conditioned to act through attachment and fear. Over time, these have turned into deep-rooted habits, all-pervasive underlying patterns. They will not be overcome by mere intellectual understanding. This would be practically impossible.

The development of renunciation is extremely important and will have a very strong impact on any Dharma practice we carry out. Even the practice of Mahamudra in terms of view, meditation, and action is driven by this foundation. Renunciation constitutes the strongest impulse and basis. We all have the intention to practice the Dharma, to be kind and compassionate, and to do whatever is good for ourselves and others. Yet, as soon as the first problem arises, we become defensive and fall back into our usual ways. However, when this happens we should not feel guilty about it. We have followed this habit for such a long time; it is so deeply ingrained and rooted in us that it is not easily overcome.

For this reason we pray. We turn to the lamas of the lineage and ask for their blessing that we may be able to free ourselves from attachment. When the prayer speaks of desire for gain and honor, it implicitly includes apprehension and fear. The attachment to things we want and the fear of things we do not want are just two sides of the same coin. So we pray, "May I realize the futility of my samsaric pursuits. May I actualize true solitude in being away from all these endeavors." This requires a firm recognition on our own part, an active acceptance. We should not foster the mistaken idea that once we understand, it will happen. Understanding is not enough. Fear and attachment are far stronger within us.

The importance of acceptance is strongly emphasized in the Buddhist teachings. In this context, acceptance means clearly recognizing the truth, seeing the way things are and what needs to be done. Yet, it is sometimes misunderstood as the thought, "Yes, all right. Samsara is like that. What can I do? I just have to accept whatever happens." Leaving it at that is not what is meant. Acceptance should lead us into activity. Once we clearly perceive the reality of our lives and know our problems for what they are, we gain the ability to do something about them. But then, we actually have to do it.

Acceptance is the recognition, "This is the problem. I must work on it. I am not going to continue my usual ways and let myself be overpowered by my difficulties all the time." As long as we are just overwhelmed by our problems there is no room to accept anything. Acceptance means seeing precisely what the problem is and knowing the possibility of solving it. This is not easy, but it can be done in a gradual way, once we exert the necessary effort.

So, we pray that we may gain the strength to detach ourselves from our worldly pursuits, that we may see how unnecessary it is to run after or away from things all the time, and that we will transform our samsaric state of mind. We are aware that it will not be easy and, therefore, we pray. Through praying we take a first step in the right direction.

The next stanza says:

> Devotion and respect are taught to be the head of meditation.
> May I meditate, while continuously praying to the precious guru,
> Who opens the door to the treasury of the oral instructions.
> Please bless me so that uncontrived faith may be born in my heart.

Just as renunciation is the feet of meditation, devotion is taught to be its head, meaning that it is of central importance. The head is the starting point of all our actions; without it we have no life and cannot function. In my experience, although it is so fundamental, devotion is one of the most difficult subjects to discuss in the West. It is often said that Westerners do not find devotion easy, since they are so strongly rational, "all head and no heart." I do not think this is utterly true. There are many people in the West who are "all heart and no head." In my view the main problem is having a split between head and heart. Some people totally follow their instincts, whereas others totally follow their intellect. Of course, this is not true of everybody, but the point is that without a combination of head and heart we cannot develop devotion.

Devotion can only arise when intuition and intellect go together. Real devotion is not based upon mere feelings; if it were, it would be blind. I know many people in the West who solely rely on their intuition. This is good to an extent, but not entirely so. Each of us has a certain amount of intuition, some a bit more and some a bit less. Sometimes we will be right but sometimes also wrong. Given that, we may run into trouble by just following our intuition. On the other hand, when we solely follow our head, we cannot find anything to really trust, and will doubt everything. If we constantly evaluate everything that might occur and always take the worst into account, we can find fault in anything. We can easily imagine all kinds of things and project our doubts onto any person or thing. For this reason it is important not to fall into either extreme, but to bring our heads and hearts together.

From the Buddhist point of view devotion is based on trust, and trust is based on understanding. It is foolish to trust something that we do not understand. Devotion arises from trust and trust arises from understanding. Understanding, therefore, is crucial. In the Tibetan Buddhist tradition many scriptures start with an instruction on how to test the qualification of the guru, the lineage, and the teaching. This initial part is very important. Even the Buddha said, "Do not accept my words merely out of respect. Accept them after you have examined them as you would test the purity of gold by rubbing, cutting, and burning it." The Buddha did not mean to say that his words were faulty. He was pointing out that if we accept something without examining it closely, we have no real understanding of it.

Without a basis of understanding, our trust will be blind, lacking a real foundation. Since understanding is the actual basis of Buddhism, study is viewed as being very important. According to the Buddhist tradition we need to develop three types of wisdom: the wisdoms of listening, reflecting, and meditating. Both listening and reflecting are part of study. We first listen to the teachings and acquire knowledge. Then we reflect upon what we have heard and try to understand its meaning. We try to find out whether the teachings are right or wrong and in consequence reliable or not. In this way we gradually develop genuine understanding. As our understanding grows stronger and deeper, we gain more trust. As our trust grows stronger and deeper, our devotion comes to light and deepens.

The Buddhist method for verifying whether something is valid is called *tse ma* in Tibetan, which means "logic" or "valid cognition." There are three types of valid cognition: direct perception, inference, and valid cognition based upon reliable words. The first form of valid cognition refers to direct, immediate experience. When something is experienced directly and seen exactly as it is, there is no further question about it. One simply must believe it. The second kind, inference, is traditionally described through the example of fire and smoke. When we see smoke rising in the distance, we know that there must be a fire. There is no smoke without fire. The third kind of valid cognition is an understanding based upon the expression of another person's direct experience. This refers to the words of the Buddha or of other highly enlightened beings.

All three of these ways of finding out whether something is true are grounded in experience. First we study and reflect upon what we have learned, thereby developing understanding through reasoning and the direct experiences related by others. Then we meditate and try to turn that understanding into our own direct personal experience. Once everything is understood directly and exactly as it is through our own realization, we will not have the slightest doubt since we will have experienced it ourselves.

For this reason Milarepa said to Gampopa at their parting, "The time for you to teach will be when you see me, your old father, as a buddha." This meant that through the practice of meditation Gampopa would come to recognize by his own experience the validity of all the instructions and transmissions he had received from Milarepa. The same is true for us. When we see everything as it is in all its detail, we will have total trust, since truth will be right there in front of our eyes. When this unshakable trust has arisen, we will feel deep devotion to the person who has proved so trustworthy, who imparted to us the direct experience of the truth. At that point we will see our teacher as a buddha, the highest among all beings. So, from the Buddhist point of view, understanding is the basis of everything, and is therefore considered as the most important asset in the practice of Dharma.

Genuine devotion based upon trust and understanding is a very important medium in meditation. In a devotional state of mind we are free from negative emotions; there is no jealousy or anger, and not much attachment either. At the same time, devotion is very strong. It is an extremely intense, clean, and pure emotion. It is very distinct and has an almost nonconceptual quality. When real devotion arises, we feel so uplifted that the hair on our body may stand on end and tears may well up in our eyes. In this state negative feelings do not have an opportunity to surface, so there is no delusion and no dullness either. It is an undiluted experience, very clear and precise. Devotion is not conceptual and does not involve any judgment. It is therefore the ideal state of mind in which to meditate. This is especially true of Mahamudra meditation, which develops strongly in a state of devotion.

There is a story about a lama and a famous yogi who both lived in Kham, eastern Tibet. The lama eventually reached a high level of attainment and later in his life became very renowned. When he was young, however, he was somewhat taken in by the strong experiences that arose from his practice, and at that time he thought that he must have attained real accomplishment. The yogi, in contrast, was a truly great master. He stayed in a cave in the mountains and never kept any belongings whatsoever. Whenever he was offered a gift, he immediately let it roll down the slope beneath his cave to be picked up by the beggars who knew of his ways. He hardly ever spoke; he just sat in his cave, and whoever approached him would receive his blessing and then go away.

One day the lama decided to see this yogi and thought to himself, "Today I will show him how good I am!" He sat down in front of the yogi and immersed himself in the deepest meditation he could perform. After some time he looked up, but the yogi did not seem to be pleased. He was obviously not impressed at all. Realizing this, the lama felt slightly hurt that his outstanding capacities were not appreciated. In his grief he remembered his guru and spontaneous devotion arose in him. Then, he became totally immersed in his devotion and sat there for quite a while, not doing anything. When the lama became conscious of the world again, the yogi was very pleased and showed him by a sign that this time he had done very well. He had been in real meditation whereas before he was just displaying his pride. This story shows the significance and value of devotion.

Like renunciation, devotion does not arise easily. It requires a firm basis of understanding and experience. Unless we practice the Dharma, and thus gain authentic personal experience, we cannot feel true and unconditioned devotion. How could we, not knowing what to be devoted to? The more our experience grows, the more our devotion will deepen. The first step is to try to understand and find a reliable teaching or teacher, something that fully justifies our trust. Of these two, the right teaching is more important, but it has to be received from a teacher.

So, our teacher, being the source of our meditation experience, will be the object of our deepest devotion. Of course, it is more difficult nowadays to find a teacher on whom we can fully rely, who is totally enlightened and without any fault. Yet, we should look for someone who is nearing these qualities. Then, the more we understand his or her teachings and the more we practice them and gain experience, the more our trust and devotion will grow.

Praying for this growth means accepting that total trust and devotion will not arise easily, no matter how much we wish they would. At the same time, they form the strongest basis, the most effective medium to engender the experience of Mahamudra. Therefore, we ask for help and try to develop these qualities. We pray to the lamas of the lineage for complete trust and devotion to be born in us.

The next two stanzas describe the actual Mahamudra meditation, the first stanza dealing with calm abiding and the second with special insight. They read as follows:

Being undistracted is taught to be the actual ground of meditation.
Whatever thought arises, may I meditate resting naturally at ease

In its very essence itself, which is not artificial and is ever fresh.
Please bless my mind to be free from anything to meditate upon.

The essence of thought is taught to be the dharmakaya.
It is nothing at all and yet arises as everything.
May I meditate while it unfolds in unceasing play.
Please bless me to realize the unity of samsara and nirvana

The first stanza describes calm abiding, or *shiné*, meditation as it is to be understood in light of Mahamudra. This is said to be equivalent to nondistraction. Mahamudra meditation takes place when the mind is neither distracted nor sleepy. The last two lines explain how this is carried out: whatever comes to mind, whatever thoughts and emotions arise, one should simply rest in their very essence, in the state of mind which is uncontrived. This is as easy to say as it is difficult to do. We need to understand that the mind itself is uncreated, and gain the ability to rest in that uncreated nature. This is the most fundamental point of meditation.

Mental creations are the source of our delusion. We constantly make up all kinds of things. As it is sometimes said in the context of the Mahamudra teachings, we never act but always react. Whatever we see, hear, sense, or feel, we do not leave it at that. Instead we create images in our mind to which we attach names that we then evaluate as good or bad, positive or negative, and so on.

Here, we need to see clearly who is doing this. We are the ones who are making these judgments; the labeling is our contribution. There is nothing stuck on the object of perception itself that says "good" or "bad." Our labeling everything in those terms gives rise to desire, hatred, and so forth. The constant process of contriving something, of artificially imposing names and evaluations that have nothing to do with the object perceived, is the first and major source of the entire samsaric state of our mind.

Therefore, what we try to do in meditation, and especially in Mahamudra meditation, is to go back to our completely simple and natural form of being, to the most original and primordial state of our mind. We try to find our true being as it is, before we make up all these additional things that we constantly patch together and then believe to be our world.

Looking closely, we find that the whole world can be said to exist in our mind. We have created a self-contained system of so many thoughts and emotions. On this basis we relate to each other and bring forth an elaborate world. There is an image of the world that we have created in our mind, and we cannot get rid of this image because it is our own creation. This is the philosophy behind Mahamudra meditation.

As for practice, we try to remain in our most natural state. Being not artificial means not reacting, not making a contribution to what is there. It means just being in the original and primordial state of our mind. In this state we can experience the newness and freshness of the essence of every thought. When a thought comes up and we do not take it as a basis for further conceptualizing, it is very fresh and new. It is simply the present moment's thought, which does not bind us in any way. We can rest in its nowness.

The moment we become fascinated and involved with a thought, we grasp onto it and add it to our patchwork of memories, thus making it part of our imagined world. In this way, we become ever more deeply embedded in the structure of aversion and attachment in which we revolve constantly. When we are able to refrain from that impulse, we can be completely fresh and clear in our mind—we will no longer be carried away by the waves of grasping and clinging. Once we can let our mind be in that state, then we will be meditating, we will be within the core of our being and at one with the subtlest expression of our mind.

There is no need for even the notion that we are meditating. As long as distinctions are made, we are just doing the same thing we normally do all day long. We think things like, "Now I am meditating and a good experience is arising. I am so great!" or, "I am not really meditating. This shouldn't happen; I am too distracted." Either we become attracted to something and run after it, or we become afraid of something else and run away. This is not meditation, but just the same old pattern clad in a meditative style. Actual meditation means being in the state of mind in which there is no artificiality and no contriving. This is something we have to learn slowly and gradually by trying again and again. To be told how to do it and to gain an intellectual understanding is not enough. In fact, it is not even close to being enough. Meditation needs to be learned through doing, otherwise we just develop another image in our mind, another contrived idea or dogma.

This is illustrated by a story from the Christian tradition. One day the devil was sitting on a cloud surrounded by his retinue. Looking down on the earth they saw a man walking back and forth, again and again, intensely searching for something. Suddenly a brilliant light surrounded him, so clear and magnificent a light that he had obviously discovered something truly significant. "What happened?," the devil's followers said. "He found the truth," the devil replied. Hearing that, they became very nervous and said, "He found the truth? This is terrible; it will be the end of us. Aren't you worried?" The devil said he wasn't, and when they asked him why, he said, "So, he found the truth. But as soon as he talks to someone else, they will turn it into a dogma. Why should I worry? There is no problem at all."

This is what usually happens. As far as truth is concerned, in meditation or in anything else, we have to find it ourselves through direct experience. What we usually relate to is the image of truth we have created in our mind. This image is not enough. We need to arrive at the direct and immediate vision of the truth, which is uncontrived and free from any artificial additions. This is the main meditation, the most crucial point. It is not very different from calm abiding, but constitutes another way of practicing this technique that is strongly supported by *lhakthong*, special insight. In Mahamudra practice the two aspects of meditation—calm abiding and special or vivid insight—are not separate. As soon as the mind has reached a state of nondistraction, vivid insight, the means of seeing the truth, will be present.

Mahamudra meditation means nothing other than just being there, being within the simplest state of ourselves. Most of you will have heard of the meditation technique in which one does not heed any thoughts of the past or future. One neither dwells upon memories nor speculates about future plans. One just rests in complete nowness. This is what is meant here. When we do not follow thoughts of the past and do not anticipate future events, but are just here, in tune with the present moment, we are in a state of newness and freshness. The text describes this as the essence of whatever thought arises being ever new.

This means that we let things arise and do not stop or manipulate them. We just sit there totally open and unblocked, completely fresh and alert. We hear things, see things, sense and feel things, but do not react in anyway. We just are in the precision and newness of the very moment itself. This is the uncontrived state of being in which we are completely natural and fresh, totally uninvolved, not speculating or manipulating or making up images. We are just then and there, conscious, alert, and clear.

If we are able to remain in that state and look at our present mind, completely leaving what is there at this moment, without interfering with anything, just relaxing and being in that very moment, this is the meditation of Mahamudra beyond preparatory stages. Being in the present moment does not mean being stuck there. It means being in the stream of passing moments, leaving ourselves to the flux. Whatever arises, let it arise. Do not label it, just let it be. Let it arise and arise, and do not react no matter how good or bad it may seem. Do not fall to evaluations and concepts about it. When we are able to do that, we will be in a state that is free from contrivance. In this state there is no distraction, as one does not follow or react to anything.

Being distracted means pursuing a thought that comes up. For instance, when we hear the sound of a car passing by, this in itself is not a distraction. But the moment we think, "There is a car," we have labeled what we heard as being the sound of a car. Then, we build up a chain reaction: "This place is noisy. I shouldn't be distracted, but now I am. There are too many cars in this city." In this way we become more and more angry, thinking, "This is terrible! I am disturbed. I cannot meditate in this place." This is distraction. When a car passes by, let it pass by. Then, it is finished, it is all right; there is nothing wrong with it. The problem is not the sound of the car, but our reaction to it.

There is a story of two Japanese monks who were traveling together and arrived at a river where they met a beautiful girl who could not cross the river on her own. So the elder monk took her on his back and carried her across. When they had reached the far bank, he put her down and they went on their way. The younger monk did not say anything. But he strongly felt that the elder monk had not behaved properly. After some time he asked, "Do you remember the young woman we met at the river? Was it proper for a monk to carry her across? She was a beautiful lady." The elder monk turned to him and said, "I left her by the bank of the river. Are you still carrying her?"

This shows how we usually become distracted. Distraction has nothing to do with our sense perceptions as such. Our senses are always open. We cannot shut them even if we wanted to, so there is no need to try to close them. Our pattern of making up things in our mind and creating so many images is the source of all our problems. This is the way the samsaric state of mind is produced. We need to abandon that state, and the only way to get out of it is to go back to the pure and original state of our mind, which is free from contrivance. This is the meditation we try to do.

Student: I have heard that analytic meditation is also very important, or even more important than calm abiding.

RTR: Analytic meditation is a part of the path to special insight. It is a means to understand, to see the way things are, and to an extent it is important. But no matter how good the analytic meditation is, it is still conceptual, a mentally fabricated image, and cannot substitute for actual experience. We may arrive at a certain level of intellectual understanding, but even if this is very profound, it is not equivalent to complete realization.

However, as human beings we are very intellectual, and having an intellectual understanding as a working basis is very helpful in coming to genuine experience. Through analysis we try to gain a correct understanding in our head, and then slowly try to bring it to our heart. That is a long journey— the longest journey of all.

Shiné meditation is a straight experience and has nothing to do with the head. It means just being ourselves and experiencing how we are in the most fundamental way. There is nothing to do; we cannot cheat or manipulate anything. All we can do is to be totally honest, exposing ourselves to our own experience. *Shiné* meditation is of great significance, since it deals directly with our mind, trying to make it calm and clear.

The level of meditation described in this stanza, however, is not just calm abiding. It is the means to combine *shiné* and *lhakthong*, being a meditation in which the mind is seen as nakedly as possible. We try to see our true consciousness completely uncovered in its uncontrived state. Once we are able to do that, we will be very near to actual realization. We start seeing our true nature, not by way of analysis but in a direct, experiential way. This meditation is therefore extremely important.

As far as analytic meditation goes, there are many different methods and traditions. In Tibet this practice would be conveyed very individually from person to person, with varied emphasis according to the teacher's tradition and the student's specific capacities. For someone who is very intellectual, this type of meditation might play an important role, whereas for someone who is not too intellectual it might not, since such a person could not do much analysis anyway. Generally speaking, both discerning and resting meditation complement each other and are used together in most traditions. Nobody would say, though, that analytic meditation is enough on its own. Meditation has to lead to genuine realization.

Student: When I just watch my thoughts without following them, is that meditation as it is meant here?

RTR: What I was trying to say is that you do not watch your thoughts. You just are, and let your thoughts come and go. Can you understand that?

Student: It is very difficult.

RTR: No, it is not difficult at all. The difficulty lies in saying, "It is very difficult." Once that thought is there, then it is difficult. Meditation means just being, and this does not involve any strain. Thinking, "This is very difficult," constitutes one of the main impediments.

Student: I sometimes wonder whether I am doing it right or wrong.

RTR: Yes, but there is no need for that. The moment we wonder whether we are doing it right or wrong, we are distracted. In the context of Mahamudra practice we do not ask ourselves whether it is good or bad meditation. We do not evaluate it; we just are, we are not even meditating in a way. When it says in the prayer, "Please bless my mind to be free from anything to meditate upon," this also means, "Please grant your blessing that I may be free from the idea that I am meditating."

It should not be too difficult to simply be, to not do anything, to just have a vacation and rest. This is what this meditation is about. We just try to let ourselves be totally within the simplest and most naked state of our being. We are not even trying, we just are. That is all there is. When we think, "This isn't meditation. I shouldn't be doing this," or "Now I'm meditating, I should be doing that," this is a contribution from our side. We are contriving something and manipulating what is there.

Instead, we should refrain from any manipulation and just be completely at rest. All the things that we believe we have to do are part of our usual habitual patterns. Whenever we fall into these patterns, whenever we start doing something, we should simply be aware that we have been naughty and then bring ourselves back to rest. That much we have to do, since otherwise, we cannot rest. We should not even think that we are meditating. We should not actually watch our thoughts. We just let them be. Trying to watch our thoughts would be doing too much.

Student: Sometimes it is said that one should observe one's thoughts.

RTR: That is another way of saying that we should just be aware and let our thoughts come and go. It does not mean watching. If we start watching our thoughts, it becomes too much, and we label our thoughts, saying, "Oh, this thought is there, that thought is there." Labeling is no issue in Mahamudra meditation. In the beginning we can do that as part of calm abiding practice. But according to this stanza we should not watch our thoughts.

The second stanza explained here describes the practice of *lhakthong*, vivid insight, and can be said to represent the heart of the Mahamudra understanding. When it says, "The essence of thought is taught to be the dharmakaya," I am not exactly sure whether one should say "the essence of thought" or "the nature of mind." What difference do you see between thought and mind? Is there something called "mind" besides all our thoughts?

Student: Mind is more spacious, it is where thoughts and emotions take place.

RTR: An emotion is not a thought?

Student: It is different from a labeling thought.

RTR: So the first thing that arises is a thought, and next there is an emotion? Is there a mind beside the thought and the emotion?

Student: There is awareness.

RTR: What is awareness?

Student: It is experience.

RTR: Experience is not a thought?

Student: No.

RTR: Well, what is experience?

Student: There may be information that makes us react very quickly, but behind layers and layers there is perhaps an experience that is not a thought, but a state of being.

RTR: A state of being. Is experience a state of being? What is a thought? Is it not a state of being? Do we have any moment in which there is absolutely no thought?

Student: This question is not fair. Sometimes in the last moment of thought there is something like a gap for some time.

RTR: Where is that?

Student: That is inexpressible. It is just the absolute.

RTR: But are you aware of it or not?

Student: That is the problem.

RTR: You are aware of it and that is a thought. So where is the gap? Between one thought and another there is a gap. But how do you know there is a gap?

Student: Because I am thinking.

RTR: If there is your thinking, there is no gap. There is a thought.

Student: Before the thought there was a gap.

RTR: Who knows that?

Student: I know that. I think as long as we have a sense of self there must be thoughts.

RTR: But what is the self? Is it different from thought or is it the same as thought? There seem to be four different things: thought, emotion, experience, and mind. You say experience is not a thought. But is thought an experience?

Student: Thought is an experience but experience is not a thought.

RTR: Are you sure?

Student: There are more experiences than only thoughts.

RTR: How do you experience? Do you experience anything without a thought?

Student: Yes, for instance, when I am just looking at colors.

RTR: But do you know that this is a color?

Student: Maybe not.

RTR: Maybe not? Well, how can you say that you are are looking at colors?

Student: Maybe I don't even know that I am looking at colors.

RTR: Then you are not looking at colors. When you say you are looking at colors, you have to be aware that you are looking at colors. You have to have that concept, even if you are not looking at colors at all.

Student: But what about pain?

RTR: How do you experience pain? When you have a pain, how do you know it is a pain?

Student: I feel it.

RTR: Yes, you experience pain, and then you say, "This is painful." Is the awareness of pain not a thought?

Student: Well, once I say, "This is painful," that is a thought.

RTR: But you cannot experience pain without being aware of it, can you?

Student: It is not a thought. It is just uncontrived. It just comes ever so quickly.

RTR: Why do you say that it is uncontrived?

Student: Because one does not think that it hurts. It just hurts and one feels that it hurts at the same time. There is no time to build up a concept thinking, "This is painful."

RTR: Are you sure?

Student: Maybe it is more unconscious.

RTR: Give an example. What causes you pain?

Student: A shock, for instance, an electric shock.

RTR: So, you feel the electric shock, and the more you feel it, the more you are aware of there being an electric shock. Then you say, "This is an electric shock." Do you or not? Is that a thought? And when you have that sensation, do you think, "This is unpleasant?"

Student: Yes, but this happens ever so quickly.

RTR: That is true. But sometimes we do something ever so quickly and then believe it to be spontaneous, though it is not necessarily spontaneous at all. It just happens so fast that it goes unnoticed. One of the main difficulties in dealing with matters such as these is the fact that we have so many assumptions and preconceived ideas. We constantly say, "Of course, this is such-and-such." This makes us unable to talk about things as they are described here. When we are told that our thoughts are dharmakaya, or our mind is dharmakaya, we do not understand what that means at all. In this part of the teaching it is very important to look carefully at our assumptions and to see them for what they are. This is the analytic meditation that was mentioned earlier. Analysis plays an eminent preparatory role, as we first have to see to what extent we create what we believe to be true. It provides the understanding necessary to any meditation practice.

What we are trying to do in the whole process of Buddhist practice, and especially in the context of Mahamudra meditation, is to go back to our basic true nature and to find out what it is in a direct way, without creating any kind of image. It is very important to learn how to see more directly through our own experience. We have so many names in our mind, and because there is a name, we say, "This is so-and-so." We constantly create an image, as for instance, saying, "Thought comes from mind," as if our mind were a big bucket from which our thoughts are poured. When looking more carefully, this image does not prove to be correct. What is left, when we take out our thoughts, emotions, and experience? And what is experience? What is thought? What is emotion? These are our own classifications and products that we mentally contrive. They are our own contributions and we categorize them into "this kind of thought," "that kind of experience," and so on.

Constantly saying, "this and that," we separate things and divide them into categories so that they are easy to put into all kinds of conceptual boxes. When looking at our actual experience, though, it may not be exactly like that. When we say, "There is a mind, and from this mind come experiences, thoughts, and emotions," we already assume that there is a mind that is something apart from thoughts, emotions, and experience. But is there a mind behind these, or from which all these things originate?

This kind of subject cannot be taught or understood intellectually. It is not as if the teacher just comes and says, "Thought is dharmakaya," and we realize it. Even if the Buddha appeared and said this, it would not help us very much. We might say, "Oh, yes, thought is dharmakaya. Very nice. That's all right. Dharmakaya sounds very profound." But what is dharmakaya? It could be something great and wonderful that buddhas have, or it could be something else, I'm not sure. Definitely it must be something really great. It sounds very special. DHARMAKAYA!

So, this does not work. For this reason it is said that Mahamudra teaching and practice is very individual and personal. All Buddhist practice is individual, but this is especially true of the approach where we look at ourselves in a totally honest way. We try to endure ourselves and see everything as it is without any preconceived ideas. This is why too much study can sometimes become a hindrance. Apart from receiving the reading transmission of the texts, teachings on Mahamudra were traditionally not given in public, but were transmitted from person to person.

These teachings have to be dealt with individually through our own experience, and are given step-by-step according to our respective capacities and progress. In this context most of the talking is done by the student and not by the teacher, since it is the student's experience that matters. The teacher just gives a certain amount of guidance and tries to separate the intellectual understanding from actual experience. This is the real task of a Mahamudra teacher, since it is very difficult to tell these apart.

The teacher will try to find out whether the student has gained some genuine insight and will do so by asking questions, by poking into the spot where it hurts, extracting the experience little by little and separating it from all the things that are just ideas and intellectual understanding. This is an experiential learning process, and as such is often much more difficult for someone who is very learned than for someone who is quite simpleminded. It does not depend too much on how many teachings we have received or how much time we can spend with our teacher.

In a way it is very strange. Milarepa, for instance, had thousands of disciples, many of whom followed him for their entire lives. Some of them became great masters, whereas others made no real progress at all. Then, there were disciples who could not spend a long time with him but still attained great accomplishment. Gampopa stayed with Milarepa for only a year or so. And there are seven famous disciples, known as "the three male and four female students," who did not stay with Milarepa very long, and yet all reached the attainment of the rainbow body.

This shows that experience does not depend upon the length of time we are able to spend with our teacher. It does not depend upon our external behavior or life situations, either. I was told of a lama who lived in my monastery in earlier days. He was a student of Jamgön Kongtrül of Shechen, and he seemed to be perfect in every respect. He dedicated his whole life to doing retreat, gave away everything he had, and never drew any personal benefit from his position. He was almost like Milarepa. But whenever he related his experiences to his teacher, Jamgön Kongtrül of Shechen was not pleased. Sometimes he became so annoyed that he actually beat him, because this lama did not manage to get beyond certain ideas. I do not know what they were.

Then, there was another student of Jamgön Kongtrül of Shechen, a man named Damgön, who was crippled from an accident and could hardly move. He just sat in the monastery and did not do much retreat or formal practice, except that he sometimes performed a small offering puja. Yet, whenever Shechen Kongtrül visited the monastery, he would go see this student and talk with him about his experiences. I did not witness this personally, but I was told that each time he saw him, Shechen Kongtrül became excited and very pleased. He used to say, "This is not Damgön, this is Drogön!" *Drogön* means the "protector of beings" and is an epithet of Avalokiteshvara. So, this student's experience must have been extremely good.

What I am trying to say is that the only thing that matters is the disciple's own experience, and the precision and depth to which he or she understands. Mahamudra is said to be very simple. Mahamudra teachers usually say that the reason why we do not understand Mahamudra, Dzogchen, or similar teachings is that they are too simple. Being so complicated ourselves, we find them very difficult. We have such intricate ways of speaking that we are unable to express something that simple. So, it is also quite difficult for the teacher to find out whether the student has some genuine recognition. I myself do not have too much experience, but when I speak with people about this subject, I sometimes feel, "Here it is, truth is coming up." Later, I often discover that the student has been talking about something totally different.

I remember one incident that I found quite shocking at the time. One of my students went on a pilgrimage to Bodhgaya and other holy places. Afterwards, she came to see me and told me about it, relating all kinds of feelings and experiences. At first I was very pleased and thought that she was arriving at some understanding. Yet, over the time there was one thing which did not seem right—she was feeling very sad and out of place. Eventually, I understood that this was not a dawning understanding of the truth, but rather a certain psychological problem. If we really understand Mahamudra, be it only to a tiny extent, we become very joyful and happy, we can feel our burden being lifted. In my view this is a very good criterion and sign of true understanding.

It is often said that in the course of Dharma practice our inner negativity will surface and we will have a lot of problems. I do not understand this and personally think it is not true. When this happens, something is wrong. Once we really practice the Dharma and gain a certain amount of experiential understanding, nothing negative comes up. All negativity dissolves and we become much freer and more joyful.

This can be seen from the name of the first *bhumi*, the "supremely joyful," which is the stage when one has the first direct, irreversible glimpse of the truth. It is said that the joy felt at this point is far greater than any joy ever felt before, since it stems from realizing that there will be no suffering anymore. One deeply feels and definitively knows that all unhappiness and pain have ended. So, real understanding of Dharma is accompanied by joy. Of course, we will not reach the first *bhumi* too quickly; but even on the way there should be a certain feeling of this.

When we talk about looking at our mind, this often seems to me to constitute a problem. According to the Mahamudra teachings, first we must find out what our mind actually is and then look at that. This is not what we usually do. When we try to look at our mind, where is our mind? We try to look at our mind as a whole. When we say we are looking at our mind, we are mostly looking at an image we have created and called "mind." Actually, we are not looking at our mind at all, we are just looking at something we have contrived, thus missing the point without being able to do much about it. Whatever we discover about that contrived mind is not a direct experience. It is derived from ideas and concepts we have formed and continue to form all the time.

When we want to look at our mind, it is of utmost importance to find out first, "What is it that I am supposed to look at? What is my mind?" This is because when we try to bring this down to insight, awareness, or consciousness—whatever we prefer to say—we find that we can only be aware of something that we experience, something that comes to our senses. We see something and that is a consciousness; we hear something and that is a consciousness; we smell, taste, or feel something, and that is a respective consciousness. Through our five senses we make contact with whatever is there, and this contact results in a concordant consciousness or awareness. We make contact with something we see, hear, taste, smell, touch, or feel, and then are aware of that.

But we do not leave it at this awareness or first moment of mental perception. The information is then processed conceptually by what we call our mind. Whenever we smell something, we think, "My mind is smelling it," or we see something and have the notion, "My mind is seeing something," and so on. We are under the impression that the mind is behind all our sense consciousnesses. This is not what we are trying to look at. We should look at the actual contact, at the sense experience itself. The moment we see something and the mental perception or awareness of seeing arises, we can look at that very moment of seeing.

We can look at this particular awareness directly, in an experiential way. This moment is very precise. For instance, if I feel an acupuncture needle being pricked into me, and I think, "That is painful," or "Not so painful," this is my mind. Of course, there are many things coming to my senses all the time of which I am conscious. I am conscious most of the time, and when I put all these things together, then that is my consciousness or mind as I normally experience it. In fact, though, there is a specific consciousness of each sense impression, one by one and instant by instant. If we can look at our consciousness as it is present at each of these moments, we have immediate vision, looking directly at our mind. If I see the stupa in the garden and think, "Oh, a stupa," there is the consciousness of seeing a stupa and that moment of consciousness is my experience. When the Mahamudra teachings say, "Look at your mind," they are referring to that very consciousness, to the first moment of being aware of a sense impression before it is elaborated further.

Once we can do that, we will see directly, in a nonconceptual way. Of course, this is not easy since sense impressions fluctuate and change so rapidly—one instant it is a stupa, the next instant it is the sun, a flower, the sky, or the sea, all kinds of things. They come so quickly that I may sometimes feel that I am thinking of them all simultaneously. For example, I smell the incense on the shrine, I hear the car passing by outside, I see the flower in front of me, and I am under the impression that I perceive all these things simultaneously. This would only be possible, though, if our senses were always open and functioning at the same time, which is not the case. The moment our mind takes care of a particular sense perception, the other gates of consciousness are shut. So I smell, then I hear, and then I see. These may arise extremely quickly, but nevertheless they happen one after another.

What we should try to look at is the first perception of whatever comes to our mind or, as it is literally called, "of whatever arises." This is something that we have to experience ourselves. It cannot be transmitted through words in books or lectures, although to a certain extent these are helpful. So, maybe I should say a few words from the viewpoint of Buddhist psychology, even at the risk that they will be turned into another concept. I might as well try. There is nothing wrong with it. We have so many concepts already that one or two more would not make any difference.

In Buddhist psychology it is said that the first contact we make is through our five senses, which are nonconceptual. For example, I see all of you with my eyes. Your images are reflected in my eyes, with all your different hair colors, dresses, and so forth. It is almost like looking at a picture. Yet, the moment this reflection comes to my mind, a selection takes place and I perceive only fragments. I may only remember one or two people. I have a problem, for instance, of not consciously perceiving the color of hair. Someone may say, "You know, the blond lady who was sitting in front of you." Blond lady? I cannot remember a blond lady. Normally I remember faces or other things, but I do not recall people's hair color. Nowadays, I try to be more careful about that! Still, even if I do not recall something, that does not mean that my eyes did not see it. My eyes saw everything. But I do not remember because I did not look at it when the visual consciousness came into my mind.

From the complete picture that is reflected in our eyes we select fragments. For many different reasons we single out certain things and neglect the rest. We see the bits we have chosen and say afterwards, "I saw this or that." We have actually seen many things, but we only know the aspects that stood out at the time due to various conditionings and patterns built up in the past. That is the part conceptualization plays in the process of perception. That is our usual mind. Our mind is the one that comes after the actual seeing and is therefore almost a memory. Our mind does not actually see the object. It only sees its image.

For this reason, our mind has ample opportunity to contrive a great variety of things. Everything can be made ever so beautiful or ugly. There is only an image in our mind, and being a mere image it can be shaped in any way. Direct perception is nonconceptual, but as soon as our mind or conceptual understanding takes over, we define whatever we perceive, adding many things and omitting many others.

The very first moment of "I have seen the stupa" or "I have seen a flower," once arisen in the mind, is a thought and thereby a mental creation. The same is true of feelings like, "This is nice," or "This tastes sour," or "This tastes bitter." These days I am taking a Chinese medicine that is made from ten, twenty, or even fifty ingredients, I do not know exactly. When I drink it I think, "This is quite bitter." But it is not just bitter—there are sweet things in it, sour things, bitter things, all different kinds of tastes. My tongue tastes all of these flavors but in my mind I say, "It is bitter." And then it is bitter, because I single out the bitter taste and just pick up on that. Maybe if I am in a very good mood, I may say, "It is sweet."

All of these things are concepts, the activity of mind. The basis of all these thoughts and emotions, the basis of all our experience, is direct, nonconceptual perception, the contact of our sense organs. But what we actually experience comes from thinking, "I am tasting something bitter. It is unpleasant." Then I wish I did not have to drink it again. The emotions arise from concepts such as, "I do not like it," or "This is good," or "This is bad." In this way everything is created by thoughts which are based on something that is nonconceptual.

Once we become used to reacting so quickly and frequently in this manner to everything we perceive, after some time we forget and the whole process goes unnoticed. It happens so quickly and we react immediately. The moment I see this medicine, there is a feeling of dislike. After some time I may even just see the thermos in which it usually comes, and say, "That? Oh, no!" I have not even tasted the contents yet. If I did, I might find that this time there was something sweet and delicious in it. But because of my preconceived ideas, when I see the thermos, immediately my mind concludes that it contains this bitter medicine that I do not like. So I do not like the flask either. It can seem very ugly at times. It could actually be a very nice flask, but this experience would not occur to me.

With this example I am just trying to convey an impression of how much our mind is making things up and does not see reality. It happens to such an extent that our whole experience is just a creation of our mind. We are usually not aware that the way we deal with our sense perceptions, the way we pick out fragments that we name and react to with judgments, brings about the entire samsaric system. As long as we are immersed in selecting our sense perceptions and making images of them that we impose on everything else, we are in the samsaric state.

Then where does the dharmakaya part come in? It says here, "The essence of thought is taught to be the dharmakaya." If we can see our momentary thoughts one by one, and look at them directly, there is no need to fall into this chain reaction. It is not inevitable. Once we can make immediate contact with our consciousness and thoughts, we do not have to create this built-up thing. The first contact of our senses is nonconceptual. It is difficult to talk about this, but it is said that if we look directly at one moment of thought, it does not have any tangible substance, it is not a solid thing. If we do not elaborate it and make it complicated by following our usual pattern, but just rest in each present moment's thought, without adding or subtracting anything, we can actually be in the subtlest form of our mind. We can experience the simple state of our consciousness, which is called the dharmakaya.

The dharmakaya is nothing other than the most basic, naked, natural, clear, and direct awareness of whatever arises. If we can just look at whatever arises without any artifice, we experience the dharmakaya. This is said in the teachings on Mahamudra, but the understanding they describe is not an intellectual one. We need to understand through experience. To arrive at that experience we use the technique of just letting ourselves be, as it is described in this prayer. It is therefore vital for us to be able to apply this technique.

Student: You said that the first contact of the senses is not conceptual. Does the reference to or the connection with the first moment of perception produce thoughts, emotions, and everything?

RTR: Yes, I think so. For instance, direct visual perception comes from the eye and the object that is seen. From their contact the eye consciousness arises. Our mind identifies the seen object. The very first moment of mental perception is also nonconceptual. In the immediately following moment, nonconceptual mental perception becomes the object of conceptualization. On top of that we add our memories and other experiences. That is our delusion, our conceptual elaboration, the artificial part we contribute. This is why we sometimes see something and immediately do not like it, although we may not know why we react with instant dislike. Maybe we had a bad experience once, long ago in the past. In the same way, we may see something and immediately like it. All of this is due to our habit of bringing in everything from the past, of imposing our memories on every new sense perception. But if we do not do that and look at whatever arises in our mind directly, leaving it as it is and just being in it, we can be free from that moment onward. This is the potential we have.

A great meditator can experience everything and view all the impressions of the senses without getting involved and entangled, without making anything up. The point is how we deal with and react to appearances. This is clearly expressed in *dohas* by Saraha and other great Mahamudra masters. For example, Shri Singha said, "Whatever arises does not bind you. So let arise and arise whatever arises, and do not bind it either." And Tilopa said to

Naropa, "My son, appearance does not bind you; it is your grasping that binds you."

The essential point in Mahamudra practice is to let go of grasping. If we are able to do that, we can be truly liberated from any kind of problem. Letting go of grasping does not mean that we would not remember anything. Of course we would remember, but the experience would not be contrived. We would neither make something up nor try not to make something up.

This is *lhakthong* in the actual sense that comes almost naturally once a firm foundation of *shiné* is developed. For this reason the practice of *shiné* is used so much in the Mahamudra context as a gradual path toward that experience. When we have developed a strong, unwavering *shiné* meditation, our mind becomes calm and clear. If we are able to look then, within this state of calmness and clarity, we can truly experience being aware of and at one with everything around us. We can experience everything as it is without elaborating and thereby distorting it. We do not become stuck in the patterns of aversion and attachment. This is liberation. Our true nature is seen nakedly as it is.

When we can look while we let our mind rest in the Mahamudra way, and see our thoughts manifest in a continuous display—free from thought—at which we do not grasp, then the very moment we do not grasp, we are not trapped in the web of clinging. Then, naturally the ego is no longer there because the ego functions upon concepts. It is the strongest concept of all, but no matter how strong and powerful it is, it is no more than a concept. Within nonconceptual, direct experience there is no ego, so we do not have the feeling of a separate self. This is quite subtle and profound. Thus, this way of seeing is not something that we can reach just like that, but it is also said to be very easy, too.

When we can be without concepts, we can be completely free and enjoy the whole thing without any thought or ego. Once free from that, we will have the experience of the enlightened state. This is not something that we gain from outside. It comes from freedom from entanglement. The samsaric state of mind is viewed as a net that we have woven around ourselves. We are like a caterpillar who produces something from its own body that totally binds it. It is imprisoned for some time, and then suddenly it eats a hole in its cocoon and comes out and flies away as a butterfly. That is exactly what is supposed to happen. When we break the shell we have created around ourselves, we can be completely free and in tune with the qualities of enlightenment.

Student: Is our sense of self the entirety of our accumulated experience?

RTR: Yes, this is exactly what I said. The self, or ego, is the strongest concept since it constitutes the point on which all our other concepts and experiences are built. Therefore, it will not vanish by itself. If we are able, though, to meditate as it is described here and reach the point where we see that we can do without it, we will have what is called nondual or nonconceptual experience. When this experience is stable, there will be no need to work with the self because this concept is simply no longer there. It has dissolved effortlessly and naturally. This does not mean that a person who has reached this stage does not have any senses. When enlightenment is described as a state in which there is no ego, no dualistic view, and no concept, this is frequently misunderstood as being something really terrible, like having fallen into a coma. This is a wrong idea. It is said to be the total opposite, as has already been discussed.

In explaining "The essence of thought is taught to be the dharmakaya," I have tried to approach it from the experiential point of view, to relate it to our actual experience of finding the dharmakaya in our present thought or perception. This means that buddhahood, or the dharmakaya, is not somewhere else or something different from what we already have. It is not something that we need to generate or develop. It is here in this very consciousness at this very moment.

This does not mean that the experience of realization would be the same as our normal experience. When we see the truth, we will have a completely different experience. But the dharmakaya is nowhere else. It is not something that we get from somewhere else, as if something completely different happened and transported a totally different experience into us. At the point where we meet our own being, precisely what we actually are, we discover the dharmakaya. The only difference is whether or not we have this understanding and way of looking.

When we see our true nature as it is, now at this moment, all our fabrications and deluded ways of seeing dissolve in that very instant of immediate vision. Samsara is a state of mind, it is our way of seeing things. When we see ourselves as we truly are, the samsaric way of seeing dissolves, and our way of seeing completely changes. This is the experience of the enlightened state, which is described in the line, "It is nothing at all and yet arises as everything." The nature of thought or the nature of mind is not something that one can pinpoint saying, "It is like this," or "Here it is," but at the same time it is clear and radiant, and manifests unceasingly in every possible way. Thus the nature of our mind has three aspects—it is empty, clear, and unceasing in appearance. These three aspects are totally inseparable from each other and can be understood as three *kayas*, which are the dharmakaya, sambhogakaya, and nirmanakaya. The enlightened state is described in terms of these three *kayas*.

The aspect of emptiness is to be understood first. When we try to definitively identify our mind, we look at any thought that comes up and ask, "Where does it come from? Where does it go? What is its nature?" At that point we cannot really find where the thought comes from. It is just there. It just pops up, and it does not go anywhere, either. It just dissolves. Even while it is there, one cannot find a particular place where it abides. It is not a thing. One cannot really identify and see it. There is no way to capture it. Its nature is so fluid, so ungraspable and unidentifiable, it changes so quickly, that we can say it is something like emptiness. This totally empty, unfindable, and intangible quality is the essence of thought or mind. This is called the dharmakaya.

At the same time, we cannot say that our mind is nothing at all or that nothing is there. Although it is unidentifiable, there is something arising that is clear and luminous. This aspect of clarity is the nature of mind and is called the sambhogakaya. This nature proves to be unceasing. Thoughts manifest all the time, one after another. Everything arises unceasingly. There is total unimpededness of appearance. This uninterrupted continuity, the fact that thoughts are continuously manifesting, is called the nirmanakaya.

Every moment of thought is these three *kayas*. And so we pray, "May I meditate while it unfolds in unceasing play." Thought appears, its nature is nothing whatsoever, yet it manifests as anything whatsoever, in unhindered and unceasing play. It comes and goes, comes and goes.

Someone who is skilled in actual meditation, who is able to see the nature of thought, will not be trapped in the web of contrivance and by the cunning tricks of the ego. For such a person there is total freedom. Anything that might come to mind manifests, anything is visible and vivid and nothing is blocked, but at the same time there is no bondage to anything. There is no burden and no struggle of running after or away from anything. Everything is all right. This is the actual experience of someone who truly masters meditation.

This experience is described in the last line of the stanza on *lhakthong*, which in my view is very important. We pray, "Please bless me to realize the unity of samsara and nirvana." The indivisibility of samsara and nirvana is what is experienced when we really see the true nature of our mind. In our present mental state we make a distinction between these. We view samsara as something disagreeable that we need to give up, and we view nirvana as something desirable that we need to acquire. We think we have to get out of samsara and into nirvana. This view is exactly the samsaric state of mind, marked by aversion and attachment. We are afraid of something, so we try to run away in order to get out of it; and we desire something else, so we try to run after it in order to obtain it.

As long as this dual reaction is there, there will not be the slightest way to get out of samsara, because our mind will be trapped in this structure. This very same structure binds our meditation experience. If a disciple who is trying to practice Mahamudra has a good meditation experience and tells his or her teacher, "I had such a fabulous experience," most likely the teacher will say, "It is neither good nor bad." And if the disciple says, "I had such a terrible experience," probably the answer will also be, "It is neither good nor bad."

At first I could not understand this. Why should a meditation experience be neither good nor bad? Something is happening, so it must be either good or bad. Looking more deeply, though, one will understand that. Even if we have the best possible experience, it is still an experience, not realization. Experiences will not last. Moreover, once we say, "This is a good experience," we will not leave it at that. We will want it again and desire it to be even more exciting. Once the longing for good experiences is present, there is also the fear that bad experiences might come next. This apprehension is already contained in the good experience itself.

Being an experience and not realization, it has to end. So, there is always the possibility of it going away. And when it ends, we will feel the frustration of losing it, wanting it to return, and being scared that a bad experience might follow. So now we are back in our usual state of mind. The real and final purpose of meditation, therefore, is not just to attain good experiences, but to go beyond fascination and apprehension, and be able to bear all experience at the same level. We have to reach the point where one experience is as good as another. When we undergo a nasty experience and it does not matter at all, we will not be afraid of bad experiences anymore. Similarly, we will not have a particular longing for good experiences, either.

At that point we will be free and all experiences will be good. There will be no bad experiences because we will have transcended the dualism of good and bad. Once that stage is reached, there is nothing to be disparaged as "samsara" anymore, nothing that we have to get out of. Samsaric experiences are not something to be afraid of. There is nothing bad, nothing to be thrown away. Then, there is nothing to attain either, and that is actually nirvana. We can find nirvana within our samsaric experience; it is not something separate. Even our worst experience would be the same as the best we could possibly dream of. So, there is no division between samsara and nirvana. There is nothing famed as nirvana that we need to go after, and nothing blamed as samsara that we need to escape from. This is the real and final stage of meditation.

If we can get an understanding of that, be it only a tiny glimpse, we will have a certain amount of confidence, a certain openness. When I said earlier that as we practice the Dharma we should become more joyful, I did not mean the excited and elated feeling that we usually call "joy" nowadays. What is meant here is a kind of deep understanding that whatever happens does not really matter, an attitude of saying, "It is all right. Everything is not too bad." With this attitude we will not be overwhelmed and will not despair. Even when we are exposed to severe difficulties, we will not feel utterly sad and forlorn.

The last stanza says:

> May I be inseparable from the sacred guru
> In all my future lives, enjoying the glory of Dharma.
> May I perfect every quality of the paths and levels
> And swiftly attain the state of Vajradhara.

This verse emphasizes the overriding significance of an authentic and highly qualified teacher. Although weariness of samsara and devotion are very important in being able to practice Mahamudra teachings, we also need the right guidance. This is the crucial point, because even devotion is not enough on its own. It has to be guided in the right direction. Otherwise, we might be completely mistaken. A truly genuine master is most important for our spiritual progress. So, we pray that we may meet this right guidance in all our future lives. We also pray that once we have met it, we may not waste our time.

Since early childhood it has been very easy for me to meet the great teachers of all Buddhist traditions, many of whom are profoundly enlightened. But in this kind of environment it is very difficult to see how great these masters really are, and I feel I have wasted much time. Now that they have passed away, I am slowly coming to realize this. Such teachers are great, not only because of the extent of their attainment, their compassion and wisdom, but their willingness to teach anybody, their embodiment of complete selflessness.

I had the great fortune and opportunity, for instance, to meet Dilgo Khyentse Rinpoché. He was, as you may know, the most learned lama of Tibet. He was a teacher of His Holiness the Dalai Lama, as well as the guru of the king of Bhutan, and many others. Nevertheless, whenever I went to see him and asked for teachings, he would agree to give them. He did not have any extra time, since he started his daily schedule at 5:00 in the morning, or even at 3:30 on days when he was giving a big initiation, and then he continued throughout the day until 9:30 in the evening. But he never said, "I have no time." He might choose odd hours and say, "Come tomorrow around 4:30 a.m." He did that to me at times. At that hour of day it is not so easy to get up. I would get there at 4:30 a.m., and he would already be doing his pujas. Then, he would stop everything and give the teaching for fifteen minutes or maybe half an hour. In the same way he might say, "Come tomorrow in the evening at around 9:30 or 10:00." He did that not only for me; he did it for everybody. What can one say? I had nothing to offer, nothing whatsoever.

If we can find this kind of genuineness, not only in what these masters have to teach, but in their total generosity, the way in which they dedicate their whole lives to others and keep nothing back for themselves, it is impossible not to have devotion. There is no need to develop it; it is just there. But if we do not meet people with these qualities and personality, how should devotion arise? It does not come from nowhere. Contact with great masters is the greatest good fortune we can have, and it is possible for this kind of teacher to be found still, although they are getting fewer these days.

Therefore, we pray that we may meet authentic lamas in this life and in all our lifetimes to come, and be able to practice the Dharma with them. When this connection is made and we have come into close contact with such people, we have made it in a way. We have been really lucky, we are very fortunate and have fulfilled the purpose of our lives. This connection is therefore extremely important.

And yet, it is not enough by itself. Once we have met a great master and received his or her teachings, we have to practice them ourselves. Knowing how to practice is not sufficient. There are lots of people who know how to practice; this is especially true of us Tibetans. I, for instance, have been studying all my life, so I more or less know how to practice. But as long as I do not do it, my knowledge is not enough. I like to eliminate procrastination by writing a statement to that effect on my wall, but since I will start "from tomorrow," it is of no use.

So first, it is important to learn how to practice, and second, it is even more important to do it. Otherwise our knowledge remains only knowledge, and after a while we become hardened. Tibetans have a good analogy for this: to preserve and transport butter in Tibet, it was packed very tightly into leather bags. This leather would become totally impregnated with butter and was thus very tough and hard. It is called *mar ko*, which means "butter leather." Normally, when leather is too tough, it is moistened and rubbed with butter to soften it. But butter leather cannot be treated this way: no matter how much butter is rubbed into it, it will not become any softer because it is already saturated.

Similarly, if we have heard many Dharma teachings and have many ideas about how to practice them, but do not do it, we become like this butter leather. The teachings cannot do anything to us; we have become immune to Dharma. This is a great danger. If we have studied extensively and know almost everything, but do not practice the teachings we received, they will not go deep inside and transform us. They will sound too familiar to really inspire us anymore. So, we will remain where we are, unable to progress. The only way to reach the levels at which realization takes place is by practicing what we have understood from the teachings we received.

So, we pray to be able to practice to the same extent that we learn how to do it, until we experience the state of Vajradhara, the primordial Buddha. Vajradhara is the state of an enlightened being, and when we become an enlightened being, we will see our true nature. We will see and understand, "I have been like this all the time. This is not something new; it has always been this way." Within this vision we become the first Buddha, or Vajradhara.

That is the end of the prayer. It is very short, but at the same time very important and significant. It contains the true meaning of all Dharma and is usually recited before every session of meditation, not only when practicing Mahamudra.

DEDICATION

May any merit achieved from creating and reading this text result in utmost benefit for all sentient beings. May they reach temporary and ultimate peace and happiness.